MW00804899

Hou Hsiao-hsien

Edited by Richard I. Suchenski

Österreichisches Filmmuseum
SYNEMA – Gesellschaft für Film und Medien

A book by SYNEMA ☰ Publikationen
Hou Hsiao-hsien
Volume 23 of FilmmuseumSynemaPublikationen

This book is jointly published with the Center for Moving Image Arts at Bard College,
with the support of the Ministry of Culture of the Republic of China (Taiwan).

© Vienna 2014
SYNEMA – Gesellschaft für Film und Medien
Neubaugasse 36/1/1/1, A-1070 Wien

Design and layout: Gabi Adébisi-Schuster, Wien
Copy editors: Alexander Horwath, Regina Schlagnitweit
Cover photo: © Yao Hung-i
Printed by: REMAprint
Printed and published in Vienna, Austria.
Printed on paper certified in accordance with the rules of the Forest Stewardship Council.

ISBN 978-3-901644-58-0

Österreichisches Filmmuseum (Austrian Film Museum) and SYNEMA – Gesellschaft für Film & Medien
are supported by Bundeskanzleramt Österreich / Kunst - Abt. (II/3) Film and by Kulturabteilung der Stadt Wien.

Table of Contents

Foreword

The Taiwanese film director Mr. Hou Hsiao-hsien is certainly the all-time Poet Laureate in the film industry for his audience and his country.

The stylish cinematic aesthetics and humanistic compassion spilled through his camera lens have not only inspired the cinemas of the world, they have also mapped Taiwan onto the best-lit spot in the global film community.

Awarded prizes from many prestigious international film festivals like the Venice Film Festival, Berlin Film Festival, and Tokyo Film Festival – and nominated six times by the Cannes Film Festival for the Palme d'Or – Hou has successfully transcended geographical and language boundaries with his provocative messages to the world.

As a veteran filmmaker of more than forty years, Hou continues presenting new works and at the same time endeavors to help young talents and promote the development of our film industry. His achievements and devotion to Taiwan's cinema have been recognized by the 32nd National Cultural Award in 2013, the top honor in the field given by the government.

I feel very grateful to Professor Richard Suchenski for his extraordinary efforts on this book, the first English-language anthology on Hou's films. With this publication, the expansion of international cultural exchanges with Taiwan, on and beyond film art, is surely commencing.

Lung Ying-tai
Minister, Ministry of Culture, Republic of China
(Taiwan)

Hou Hsiao-hsien shooting *Flight of the Red Balloon*, 2007

Richard I. Suchenski

"Also like Life"

The Films of Hou Hsiao-hsien

The decision to make Hou Hsiao-hsien the subject of the first joint book and retrospective project coordinated under the auspices of the Center for Moving Image Arts at Bard College was an easy one. For younger critics and audiences, Taiwanese cinema has a special status, comparable to that of Italian Neorealism or the French New Wave for earlier generations, a cinema that was and is in the midst of introducing an innovative sensibility and a fresh perspective. Hou is the most important Taiwanese filmmaker and his sensuous, richly nuanced work is at the heart of everything that is vigorous and genuine in contemporary film culture. An heir to the great modernist legacy – with its use of elegantly staged long takes, the performance of many non-actors, and a radically, even vertiginously, elliptical mode of storytelling – Hou's cinema does place unusual demands on the viewer, but its sophistication is understated and its formal innovations are irreducibly bound up with the sympathetic observation of everyday experience. By combining multiple forms of tradition with a unique approach to space and time, Hou has created a body of work that, through its stylistic originality and histori-

cal gravity, opens up new possibilities for the medium, redefining the relationship between realism and modernism. The texts that follow, almost all produced expressly for this volume, help elucidate the methods, significance, and global impact of these extraordinary films.

One would be hard-pressed to find a filmmaker working today with deeper compassion for the vicissitudes and foibles of ordinary human lives or greater respect for the intelligence of his audience. Hou's films are accessible to anyone willing to meet them halfway, but his unwillingness to pander to commercial expectations has resulted in an entirely undeserved gap between reception and distribution in North America and, since the mid-1990s, in an increasingly Hollywood-dominated Taiwan. By contrast, the films have long been celebrated in Japan and Europe – especially in France, where *Flowers of Shanghai* (1998) played continuously for months – and they have been a staple of the film festival circuit since 1984. As Jean-Michel Frodon and James Udden elaborate, several of Hou's early features played a key role in the growing international recognition of Taiwanese cinema, culminating in the Golden Lion for *A City of Sadness* (1989) at Venice and the Jury Prize for *The Puppetmaster* (1993) at Cannes.[1] Enthusiastically

1) At the time, the award for *A City of Sadness* was the most prestigious award given to any Chinese-language film.

championed by such critical doyens as Frodon, Hasumi Shigehiko, J. Hoberman, Kent Jones, James Quandt, and Jonathan Rosenbaum, Hou has also been an inspiration for filmmakers in many parts of the world – from Olivier Assayas in France to Jia Zhang-ke in China and Koreeda Hirokazu in Japan. Each of these filmmakers has contributed a text informed by their individual circumstances, from Jia's post-Maoist youth to Koreeda's background as the son of a man born in colonial Taiwan. These suitably multifaceted pieces are complemented by Taiwanese director Chung Mong-hong's "What I Know about Hou Hsiao-hsien," which provides insight into the effect of Hou's many efforts to encourage local production and mentor younger filmmakers.

Since the late 1980s, Hou has himself become an increasingly international figure. The lifting of travel restrictions with the end of Martial Law in 1987 made it possible for him to act as executive producer on Zhang Yimou's *Raise the Red Lantern* (1991) and to shoot scenes of *The Puppetmaster* in China. The three features (*Good Men, Good Women*, 1995; *Goodbye South, Goodbye*, 1996; and *Flowers of Shanghai*) that followed were facilitated by producer Ichiyama Shōzō of Shochiku, which later commissioned the Ozu Yasujirō centenary tribute film *Café Lumière*

(2003). Hou has also received support from French organizations and he made *Flight of the Red Balloon* (2007) as part of a series initiated by the Musée d'Orsay. Nevertheless, Hou, born in 1947 to a Hakka family that migrated from Guangdong the following year, remains a distinctively Taiwanese filmmaker profoundly invested in the landscape and history of his adopted home. Asked whether he saw himself as a Chinese or a Taiwanese director, he tellingly responded, "Culturally, you can't deny that you are a Chinese. But with the political reality, together with the [cross-Strait standoff], you can't deny that you are a Taiwanese."[2] Hou maps out that political reality neither through abstruse theoretical posturing nor through the ultimately passive framework of "'Third World"

2) *HHH: A Portrait of Hou Hsiao-hsien* (Olivier Assayas, 1997)

3) See "Remapping Taipei" in Frederic Jameson, *The Geopolitical Aesthetic: Cinema and Space in the World System* (Bloomington, IN: Indiana University Press, 1992), 114–157. Jameson's widely quoted comments about the novel apply equally to his approach to that consummately Western "machinery of representation," the cinema: "All third-world texts are necessarily, I want to argue, allegorical, and in a very specific way: they are to be read as what I will call national allegories, even when, or perhaps I should say, particularly when their forms develop out of predominantly Western machineries of representation" (Frederic Jameson, "Third-World Literature in the Era of Multinational Capitalism," *Social Text*, Number 15, Autumn 1986, 69).

Flowers of Shanghai, 1998
The Puppetmaster, 1993
A City of Sadness, 1989
Goodbye South, Goodbye, 1996
[Images 1–4]

allegory that Frederic Jameson famously applied to Edward Yang's *The Terrorizers* (1986), but through the delineation of quotidian life.[3] In addition to the most overt examples – the prominence accorded to eating in almost every film [Images 1–4]; the many scenes in which translation between languages and dialects causes confusion (in films ranging from *Cheerful Wind*, 1981, to *A City of Sadness* and *Good Men, Good Women*); the grandmother who asks Hou surrogate Ah-hsiao to walk back to mainland China with her in *A Time to Live and a Time to Die* (1985) – there are also suggestive markers unobtrusively incorporated into conversation, letters, and intertitles. The casual discussion of the differences between local and mainland tea in *Goodbye South, Goodbye* or of family naming practices in *Dust in the Wind* (1986) and *The Puppetmaster* reveal more about the warp and woof of Taiwanese society at different junctures than a more didactic method ever could.

Many of Hou's films are set in the past – even the contemporary drama *Millennium Mambo* (2001) is narrated retrospectively from 2011 – and they are all shaped by the complex history of an island that has until very recently been the subject of various imperial powers. "For me, retrieving history basically has to be as objective as possible," Hou has argued, and

he achieves this by concentrating intently on its ground-level manifestations.[4] In film after film, a holistic impression of the cultural layering and vital energies of a period gradually emerges from the accumulation of seemingly anecdotal minutiae. Hou's carefully orchestrated (but never fastidious or studied) *mise-en-scène* reflects this through its overall form as well as through elements of set design and decor. In *A City of Sadness*, for example, both Japanese *ukiyo-e* prints and Chinese paintings can be seen on the walls [Images 5–6]. Much like the calligraphic patterns analyzed by Abé Mar Nornes, these objects are plausibly integrated with the surrounding architecture, quietly underscoring the hybrid nature of Taiwanese identity during the transition from Japanese to Kuomintang rule. Here, as elsewhere, concrete details are interrelated with the abstract developments that help determine their meaning.

Hou's narratives are dense and oblique, dependent upon the attentive engagement engendered by visual textures and by rhythms that are both hypnotically immersive and contemplatively detached. The correlative to this is a fusion of intimacy and distance created by a treatment of the camera that is consistent enough to be immediately recognizable and flexible enough to accommodate differences from film to film (and three cinematographers: Chen Kun-hou, Mark Lee, and Chen Huai-en). Hou has eschewed conventional close-ups since his earliest days as a director of commercial entertainments, instead situating characters within environments whose contours are so clearly defined that repetition and variation become as expressive as gestures or speech [Images 7–12]. This penchant for medium and long shot framings, often with doorways or partitions used to amplify the sense of spatial remove, enables both group interactions and intensely personal activities to be displayed with maximum precision [Images 13–14].

4) Chen Kuan-hsing and Wei Ti, "Political Participation in 2004: An Interview with Hou Hsiao-hsien," *Inter-Asia Cultural Studies*, Volume 9, Number 2 (2008), 329. As Hou put it in another interview, "A precise action seems to me more representative [of an era] than a linear narrative" (Michel Ciment and Yann Tobin, "Entretien avec Hou Hsiao-hsien," *Positif*, Number 537, November 2005, 18).

A Time to Live and a Time to Die, 1985 [7–10]

Good Men, Good Women, 1995 [11–12]

Dust in the Wind, 1986 [13], *Café Lumière*, 2003 [14]

Although the combination of lengthy shots and, in the early work, a relatively static camera has given Hou an exaggerated reputation as a minimalist, his is above all a cinema of movement. All of his films include scenes in which motion occurs in multiple zones, with characters and modes of transport moving into and out of the frame, sometimes obstructing important figures [Images 15–18].[5] The camera roves so actively in the more recent films – most noticeably in *Flowers of Shanghai* (subject of a penetrating essay by Hasumi) – that highly confined spaces seem porous, with the frame acting as a mobile window onto a fluid social world. This aspect of Hou's style invites comparison with earlier long take masters like Mizoguchi Kenji, but where the supple and dance-like sequence shots in Mizoguchi's films are organized around the turn towards stasis after dramatic action, Hou's are oriented around spatial dynamics and shifting viewpoints.[6]

Hou's work is also fixated on movement between places, especially on the mixture of excitement and unease created by the relocation to an unfamiliar environment – from a village in the Penghu Islands to Kaohsiung (*The Boys from Fengkuei*, 1983), the small town of Houtong to Taipei (*Dust in the Wind*), Taipei to Tongluo (*A Summer at Grandpa's*, 1984), Taiwan to Japan (*Millennium Mambo*), or even from Taiwan to China (*Good Men, Good Women*). In *Goodbye South, Goodbye* and *Three Times* (2005), special emphasis is placed on location names and the changing perceptions of geographic boundaries. "What's the difference between Tokyo and Kyoto," Kao [Gao] – who hopes he will have more success in Shanghai and is encouraged by his girlfriend to travel with her to America – asks the man who can identify the style of his tattoo in *Goodbye South, Goodbye* ("Big difference," the man replies). *Three Times* addresses Taiwan's ambiguous position not only through the tripartite temporal structure thoughtfully examined by James Quandt, but also through a sort of South to North mapping from Kaohsiung to Chiayi ("Chia as in Chiayi," Kao says on his cell phone) to Huwei in "A Time for Love," to the historic port of Tataocheng [Dadaocheng] in "A Time for Free-

5) David Bordwell thoroughly analyzes Hou's framing and blocking strategies in *Figures Traced in Light: On Cinematic Staging* (Berkeley, CA: University of California Press, 2005), 186–237.

6) Hou told Emmanuel Burdeau that, although producer Ichiyama Shōzō did lend Hou videos of several Mizoguchi films, his use of long takes in films like *Flowers of Shanghai* "has nothing to do with Mizoguchi" (Emmanuel Burdeau, "Rencontre avec Hou Hsiao-hsien" in Jean-Michel Frodon, ed., *Hou Hsiao-hsien*, Second Edition, Paris: Éditions Cahiers du cinéma, 2005, 107).

The Boys from Fengkuei, 1983 [15], *Dust in the Wind* [16], *A City of Sadness* [17]

The Puppetmaster [18]

dom," and finally to a Taipei highway near the Tanshui [Danshui / Tamsui] river, which empties out into the Taiwan Strait, in "A Time for Youth" [Images 19–21].[7] Not coincidentally, both films were made around decisive moments in the modern political history of Taiwan: the first direct presidential election in 1996 and the highly contentious election of 2004, in which incumbent, independence-leaning President Chen Shui-bian narrowly won after a failed assassination attempt.[8] The Chinese title for *Goodbye South, Goodbye* (南國再見‚南國) alludes to these concerns through its repetition of 南國, a reference to the Southern regions visited by the characters in the film and also to Taiwan's status as "the South" from the vantage point of China and Japan.[9]

Hou grew up in the southwest of Taiwan, and his breakthrough film, *The Boys from Fengkuei*, extends its consideration of "Southernness" by excerpting Luchino Visconti's landmark *Rocco and His Brothers* (1960). One of Hou's most compelling reflections on film viewing, the sequence shows protagonist Ching-tzu sneaking into the theater as Milanese locals speak pejoratively of the central Sicilian family from "way down South." Hou draws attention to the specific material conditions of regional exhibition by having Ching-tzu watch a worn, Mandarin-subtitled print of an English-dubbed version of Visconti's film. Ching-tzu's interest in the film is piqued when actress Annie Girardot looks enticingly at the camera, and the simulated shot-countershot between them captures the strange, quasi-erotic, reverie of cinema while also summoning up the traumatic memory inserted in between [Images 22–24]. In recent years, Hou has increasingly emphasized the precariousness of the type of art cinema epitomized by Visconti's films (and his own), most poignantly through the Road of Cinema section at the end of *Millennium Mambo* and the empty theater screening *Mouchette* (Robert Bresson, 1967) in *The Electric Princess Picture House* (2007) [Images 25–26].[10] These anx-

7) Tataocheng was called Daitotei in Japanese during the period depicted in "A Time for Love." Tamsui is the Taiwanese Hokkien romanization for the river more commonly known as the Tanshui or the Danshui.

8) Hou advocated a neutral position as part of the Alliance for Ethnic Equality (see Hou Hsiao-hsien, Chu Tien-hsin, Tang Nuo, Hsia Chu-joe, "Tensions in Taiwan," *New Left Review*, Number 28, July-August 2004, 18–42).

9) Hou elaborated on this point in his interview with Burdeau, arguing that Taiwan's self-definition has "always been more or less stolen from outside" (Burdeau, 105).

10) As Edward Yang pointed out, Bresson's films were commercially distributed in Taiwan (Duncan Campbell, "Edward Yang: Take Two," *The Guardian*, April 2, 2001, available online at www.theguardian.com/ culture/2001/apr/03/artsfeatures).

Three Times, 2005 [19–21]

The Boys from Fengkuei [22–24]

Millennium Mambo, 2001 [25]

The Electric Princess Picture House, 2007 [26]

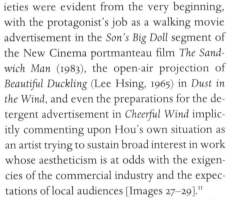

Son's Big Doll segment of The Sandwich Man, 1983 [27],
Dust in the Wind [28]

Cheerful Wind, 1981 [29], The Boys from Fengkuei [30]

ieties were evident from the very beginning, with the protagonist's job as a walking movie advertisement in the Son's Big Doll segment of the New Cinema portmanteau film The Sandwich Man (1983), the open-air projection of Beautiful Duckling (Lee Hsing, 1965) in Dust in the Wind, and even the preparations for the detergent advertisement in Cheerful Wind implicitly commenting upon Hou's own situation as an artist trying to sustain broad interest in work whose aestheticism is at odds with the exigencies of the commercial industry and the expectations of local audiences [Images 27–29].[11]

Similar questions are raised in The Boys from Fengkuei when Ching-tzu and his friends are cajoled into buying tickets to a "big screen, color" film. What they find in lieu of a theater is a dilapidated apartment containing a gigantic window out onto the city that has a "widescreen"

aspect ratio [Image 30]. The look onto Kaohsiung from this apartment window evokes the famous gaze out onto the streets of Berlin in Roberto Rossellini's Germany Year Zero (1948) and, seen in conjunction with the reference to Rocco and His Brothers, it puts Hou's film in dialogue with Italian Neorealism [Images 31–32]. In the early 1980s, Hou bristled at suggestions that he was simply imitating European practices, and it is clear even from these two sections of The Boys from Fengkuei that he viewed Neorealism as a model to be worked through rather than emulated.[12] His style never presumes, or aspires to, unmediated transparency, owing less to the tendentious social consciousness espoused by Cesare Zavattini than to the more exploratory outlook of Rossellini or the reflexive post-Neorealism of early Godard. The "free-style structure" of Breathless (Jean-Luc

The Boys from Fengkuei [31], *Germany Year Zero,* Roberto Rossellini, 1948 [32]

Godard, 1960) was a formative influence that helped Hou overcome creative blocks when making *The Boys from Fengkuei* and, later, *Goodbye South, Goodbye*.[13] He made equally intelligent use of *Oedipus Rex* (Pier Paolo Pasolini, 1967) while he was working on *A Summer at Grandpa's*, not by trying to adapt "free indirect discourse" – "the immersion of the filmmaker in the mind of his character and then the adoption on the part of the filmmaker not only of the psychology of his character, but also of his language" – but by treating Pasolini's ideas as a foil for his own reimagining of cinematic point of view.[14] As Hou explains in the interview for this book, he always tries to work within limits, whether that means not looking at rushes (*The Puppetmaster*), editing a two-hour film from many hours of largely improvised material (*Goodbye South, Goodbye*), constructing a feature out of fewer than forty shots in a closed environment (*Flowers of Shanghai*),[15] or trying to work with a Bolex (*The Assassin*, 2015). What Hou gleaned from his predecessors was the confidence to continually reinvent the parameters of realism, discovering a film's form in the process of making it.

11) *Beautiful Duckling* is one of the classic examples of the Central Motion Picture Corporation (CMPC)'s "Healthy Realism," location-based melodramas that promoted Confucian values by offering positive portrayals of family and community life. The fact that the print used for the open-air screening in the CMPC-produced *Dust in the Wind* has a faded, reddish tint is a slight historical anachronism (since the period depicted is the 1970s), but it strengthens the impression of geographic remoteness. Director Lee Hsing was one of Hou's first cinematic mentors (Hou wrote the script for Lee's *Good Morning, Taipei*, 1979).

12) Paul Shackman, "Evergreen's Hou Sparks Realist Film Trend," *Free China Review*, Volume 35, Number 4 (April 1985), 32–34

13) To give one example, Hou told Peggy Chiao: "Ellipses and other indirect narrative methods are, ironically, more clear-cut and to the point. It all depends on how you master these methods. In this, I have been influenced by Godard's *Breathless*, by his free-style structure and methods. If you get your surroundings right and check the tension, you can jump about as freely as on a trampoline. You don't have to be restrained by the perspective of traditional drama" (Peggy Chiao, "Great Changes in a Vast Ocean: Neither Tragedy nor Joy," *Performing Arts Journal*, Volume 17, Number 2/3, May–Sept 1995, 48). Hou describes his experiences watching the film while editing *The Boys from Fengkuei* and *Goodbye South, Goodbye* in Burdeau, 86–87 and 102.

14) Pier Paolo Pasolini, *Heretical Empiricism* (Washington, DC: New Academia Publishing, 2005), 175

15) Hou has stated that there "are only thirty-nine shots in the entire film. It basically comes down to one shot per scene" (Michael Berry, *Speaking in Images: Interviews with Contemporary Chinese Filmmakers*, New York: Columbia University Press, 2005, 250). Most detailed analyses of the circulating version of the film include only thirty-seven shots.

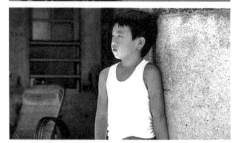

The Boys from Fengkuei [33–36]

The fruitfulness of Hou's inclinations is amply demonstrated by the increasingly original form of editing developed with long-term associate Liao Ching-sung (their decades-long collaboration is matched in modern cinema only by Martin Scorsese and Thelma Schoonmaker). *The Green, Green Grass of Home* (1982), Hou's last studio assignment and final anamorphic film, includes a wedding ceremony whose fantasy status is indicated, conventionally enough, by a zoom and a dissolve. One year later, the sepia-tinged interlude in the early New Cinema film *Growing Up* (1983) – co-written by Hou, edited by Liao, and directed by Hou's first cinematographer Chen Kun-hou – is framed by an image of a train.[16] Flashbacks are similarly bracketed by shots of the protagonist's face in *Son's Big Doll*. With *The Boys from Fengkuei*, however, Hou's approach changes; reinflecting the strategies of the earlier films, he commingles past and present, layering space and time by introducing the protagonist's reminiscence of his dead father within a continuous panning movement and closing it with a countershot from the present [Images 33–36]. Comparable in affect to the time-shifting long takes of Andrei Tarkovsky's *Mirror* (1975), this section of *The Boys from Fengkuei* sets the stage for increasingly innovative experiments in the films that follow,

from the switches into and out of a character's subjectivity in *A Summer at Grandpa's* and *Goodbye South, Goodbye* [Image 37] to the elastic temporality of *The Puppetmaster*.

Even when they are explicitly designated by techniques such as desaturation, Hou's memory sequences have an equivocal relationship to the main body of the films they appear in. In *Dust in the Wind*, a television program on mining provokes a cascade of fragments – including a mining accident involving the protagonist Wan's father, a religious ritual, and a conversation between Wan's father and grandfather that was conducted when he was a sick, four-year-old child [Images 38–44]. The first-person shot of the ritual seems to be associated, in Wan's mind, with a priest seen on a beach several minutes earlier and it can be retrospec-

tively contextualized only after his grandfather mentions an exorcism in a "remembered" exchange held together by shots from an angle Wan could not have adopted. Hou pushes this unusual form of sound/image montage even further in *A City of Sadness* by using the Japanese song "Red Dragonfly" to bridge a series of memories, thereby connecting the perspectives of (Taiwanese) Hinomi, her brother Hinoe, and their Japanese friend Shizuko [Images 45–48]. At another point in the film, during an exchange of letters between Hinomi and deaf-mute Wen-ching, a recording of the German folk song "Lorelei" leads Wen-ching to recall a Chinese opera performance from his childhood [Images 49–50]. Beautifully encapsulating the shared mental space of romance, these two sequences also suggest that every point of view shot has an array of counterparts and that the historical experience of individuals and nations is constituted by, and can only be understood through, the interaction of these partial views.

Liao, who has described Hou as a Taoist on several occasions, has argued that "the poetic spirit of Chinese literature is contained in [his long takes]."[17] Hou has long maintained that

16) The image of a train is linked to the sound of a train, initiating a series of memories interwoven in the manner perfected by the baseball bat montage in Kurosawa Akira's *Ikiru* (1952). For an overview of the New Cinema movement in Taiwan, see Emilie Yueh-yu Yeh and Darrell William Davis, *Taiwan Film Directors: A Treasure Island* (New York: Columbia University Press, 2005).

17) Liao discusses both subjects in the interview included in this book. He also addresses the influence of Taoism in the documentary *Métro Lumière: Hou Hsiao-hsien à la rencontre de Ozu Yasujirō* (Harold Manning, 2004). The comments about Hou's long takes are in *The Taiwan New Cinema* (Chou De-yung, 1998).

Dust in the Wind [38–44]

A City of Sadness [45–48]

Chinese tradition is important to his thinking. After making *The Puppetmaster*, he told Peggy Chiao, "I am increasingly aware that what I am searching for is an attitude or a certain lifestyle of a Chinese, and I am greatly moved by this."[18] In the same interview, he explained that by tradition, he means "the value system of Chinese philosophy that has evolved from the three pillars of Chinese thinking – Confucianism, Taoism, and Buddhism... I feel that Chinese tradition encompasses a beauty which I have always wanted to explore – something spiritual and dreamlike."[19] Hou has sustained this interest through his most recent film, *The Assassin*, an adaptation of a story from the Tang dynasty.

He has been trying to make a film in this period since the late 1980s and he once predicted that making a *wuxia* (martial arts) film would be critical for his career, giving him the chance to talk about "Taoism," of people who "are like nature."[20] In different, but complementary, ways, the essays by Chiao, Frodon, and Ni Zhen consider Hou's evolving interest in Chinese aesthetics. Chiao and Ni help to explicate Hou's debt to the Chinese classics he studied in his youth, while Frodon's arguments – explicitly influenced by the work of French Sinologist François Jullien – relate his work to developments in postwar international cinema as well as premodern Chinese culture.[21]

18) Chiao, 46

19) Ibid, 43–44. In the pressbook for *The Puppetmaster*, Hou made similar comments: "By 'the past,' I mean re-evaluating my own origins of growth, the concept of 'Chineseness' and the Chinese idea of the family. My films have by-and-large been about people and family and I tend to shoot what is familiar to me and within my experience. In the case of *The Puppetmaster*, I wanted to use Li Tien-lu's life to re-examine the concept of the Chinese family and its power to constrain and restrict... Through the three strands of the film, I want the audience to feel something about the Chinese people, about the traditional family and traditional morality. I hope it will illuminate a bit about Chineseness. And I hope it will produce many different emotions."

20) Tony Rayns, "*Beiqing Chengshi* (A *City of Sadness*)," *Monthly Film Bulletin*, Volume 57, Number 677 (June 1990), 155; Burdeau, 130

21) In an interview about *Flowers of Shanghai*, Hou makes a distinction between the idea of "China" and the contemporary People's Republic of China: "It is a China that, as a Taiwanese and due to the education that I received, is very familiar. I know it through books and through traditional theater. I am immersed in it and it is my cultural background. One must not forget that Taiwan was created by a government brought over from outside, but it is the same civilization. This ancient Chinese culture... is very close to me" (Michel Ciment and Yann Tobin, "Entretien Hou Hsiao-hsien," *Positif*, November 1998, Number 453, 8). Similar comments are quoted in Chu Tien-wen, *The Complete Record of* Flowers of Shanghai (Taipei: Yuan-liou Publishing Company, 1998), 25.

Discussions of "Chineseness" invariably risk essentialism and Orientalism.[22] Hou has deftly circumvented these vexing issues through his sensitivity to geopolitical nuance and the pressures that complicate the transmission of established paradigms. Despite his "very strong desire" to "make something on Confucius," he observed that "one can no longer find the ideal manner and method to explain the system of ancient Chinese thought. It is as if a break was made."[23] These invocations of "ancient Chinese thought" need to be understood not as the ahistorical endorsement of unchanging values, but as part of a continually developing artist's probing investigation of practices and mindsets rooted in vanished eras, from across an insurmountable divide. Much of the poignance of Hou's work stems from the way that rupture, an effect as well as an agent of the cultural transformations addressed in the films, is presented. In this respect, the under-rated *Good Men, Good Women* is the hinge, a film that regards both the leftist idealism of the 1940s and the materialist narcissism of the 1990s with equanimity, using formal devices (camera position and movement, alternations between black-and-white and color) to set up distinctions that are blurred by the mirroring structure of the narrative.

Realism is Hou's overarching artistic framework and he remarks in the interview included here that his appreciation of Chinese landscape painting grew when he realized (after going to China) that "the mountains, the highlands, the fogs, and the trees… are very realistic, not impressionistic." Hou's understanding is not the result of assiduous study, but he is in effect recapitulating the dominant arguments from the great age of illusionistic painting in China during the Tang and Song dynasties.[24] The praise of eleventh century critic Liu Daoshun for the great Northern Song landscape painter Fan Kuan is representative: "He lived amid mountains and forests, and often sat on high for a

22) Rey Chow reads several Fifth Generation Chinese films in this way in *Primitive Passions: Visuality, Sexuality, Ethnography, and Contemporary Chinese Cinema* (New York: Columbia University Press, 1995).

23) Thierry Jousse, "Entretien avec Hou Hsiao Hsien," *Cahiers du cinéma*, Number 474 (December 1993), 45

24) Richard Barnhart has recently argued that this type of representational art was most prominent from approximately 900 to 1250 CE. Barnhart identifies tenth century artist Jing Hao – who claimed in ca. 900 that "After sketching ten thousand trees… my drawings came to look like real trees" – as an early proponent of these methods (Richard M. Barnhart, "The Song Experiment with Mimesis" in Jerome Silbergeld, Dora C. Y. Ching, Judith G. Smith, and Alfreda Murck, eds., *Bridges to Heaven: Essays in Honor of Professor Wen Fong*, Volume 1, Princeton, NJ: Princeton University Press, 2011, 115–119).

北宋范中
立谿山行旅
圖

Travelers among Mountains and Streams
Fan Kuan, 990–1020, The Collection of the
National Palace Museum [51], with detail [52]

A City of Sadness [53]

whole day, letting his eyes gaze in all directions... He created his own ideas confronting the scenery and did not choose to ornament abundantly but sketched the very bones of the mountains, forming his own style."[25] Fan's *Travelers among Mountains and Streams* (990–1020), one of the treasures of the National Palace Museum in Taipei, is exemplary in its balance of the precise and the suggestive and in the varied tonalities used to produce three spatial planes, corresponding fairly closely to the "three distances" later theorized by Guo Xi [Kuo Hsi] [Image 51].[26] The human figures wind their way across near the bottom, dwarfed by what Wen Fong has described as a "leaping

scale [that] exponentially heightens the impression of size and distance, [with] blank areas... [serving] as perceptual respites, inviting the viewer to roam freely through a space that is infinite because it is unmeasured and unmeasurable" [Image 52].[27]

Films like *A City of Sadness* include extreme contrasts between the mountainous landscape and moving figures seen in long shot, but the affinities to landscape paintings like Fan's are less a product of composition than of viewing method [Image 53]. Hou strives for an active realism that mentally involves the audience in the construction of spatiotemporal coherence by employing "a concept from Chinese painting –

---

25) Susan Bush and Hsio-yen Shih, eds., *Early Chinese Texts on Painting* (Cambridge, MA: Harvard University Press, 1985), 116. This contrasts strikingly with the conceptual approximation advocated by earlier writers like Zong Bing (Tsung Ping, 375–443 CE): "...the [Kunlun] mountains are immense and the eyes' pupils small. If the former come within inches of the viewer, their total form will not be seen... a vertical stroke of three inches will equal a height of thousands of feet, and a horizontal stretch of several feet will form a distance of a hundred miles. That is why those who look at paintings are only troubled by awkwardness in the likeness and do not consider that diminution detracts from verisimilitude. This is a natural condition. In this way, the lofty elegance of the Sun and Hua mountains as well as the soul of deep valleys can all be included in one picture" (Ibid, 37).

26) In "The Lofty Record of Forests and Streams," Guo Xi (1020–1090) explicated: "Mountains have three types of distance. Looking up to the mountain's peak from its foot is called the high distance. From in front of the mountain looking past it to beyond is called deep distance. Looking from a nearby mountain at those more distant is called the level distance. High distance appears clear and bright; deep distance becomes steadily more obscure; level distance combines both qualities. The appearance of high distance is of lofty grandness. The idea of deep distance is of repeated layering. The idea of level distance is of spreading forth to merge into mistiness and indistinctness" (Ibid, 168–169).

27) Wen Fong, *Beyond Representation: Chinese Painting and Calligraphy, 8th–14th Century* (New Haven, CT: Yale University Press, 1992), 86

liu bai (literally, 'to leave a whiteness'), which means that even after a character has left the frame, or even when you have an unexplained space outside the frame… the audience must join together with me to complete the shot."[28] The presence of multiple doorways in interior shots and diagonal pathways in exterior shots helps to unite the space contained in the frame and the imagined space outside with which it continually interacts [Images 54–57]. Sound/image relations are handled in a similar way, with the sound of one scene regularly continuing into another, linking actions that would otherwise be temporally and spatially discrete. In one of the most remarkable sections of *The Puppetmaster*, Hou compresses pivotal events into a small series of shots, over the course of which Li Tien-lu becomes separated from his parents, engaged, married, a father, reconciled with his own father, and head of his own puppeteering troupe [Images 58–64]. The jumps in time are seamless and the shots are subtly connected by audiovisual rhymes (footsteps, fireworks, the placement of chairs), but their im-

plications become clear only when the entire sequence is completed. Without offering any voiceover explanation, Hou condenses a span of several years into a few minutes of screen time and leaves it to the viewer to put the pieces together.[29]

Hou's treatment of objects is equally evocative, both playful and profound [Images 65–66]. The distinctiveness of his approach is most apparent in the use of the vase that appears peripherally in a number of scenes in *A City of Sadness* and becomes prominent in the extended final shot [Images 67–68]. In their "still life" shots, Fei Mu's *Spring in a Small Town* (1948) and Ozu's *Late Spring* (1949) – two of the greatest films from the 1945–1949 period depicted in *A City of Sadness* – provide apposite reference points.[30] Orchestrated paratactically, the most enigmatic scene in *Spring in a Small Town* begins with shots of the moon in the heavens, blowing wind, and moving feet; the forbidden feelings of the couple are symbolized after they enter the house by a brief shot of an orchid, which covers over the gap separating the

28) Chiao, 51

29) Interestingly, this sequence includes the only comparatively normal example of shot/countershot editing in the film, when the young Li discusses his marriage plans with his father.

30) *A City of Sadness* begins with Emperor Hirohito's famous surrender broadcast on August 15, 1945 and ends with a superimposed title announcing the Nationalist (Kuomintang) retreat to Taiwan in December 1949.

A City of Sadness [54], *A Summer at Grandpa's*, 1984 [55], *Three Times* [56]

The Puppetmaster [57]

The Puppetmaster [58–64]

Flowers of Shanghai [65], *Three Times* [66]

A City of Sadness [67–68]

Spring in a Small Town, Fei Mu, 1948 [69–70]

woman lighting a cigarette and the man lifting her up [Images 69–70]. Fei's orchid is as contextually grounded as Hou's vase (it is brought into the room in an earlier scene), but its status as a self-consciously poetic cutaway gives it a very different charge.[31] The empty moonlit

vase in Ozu's *Late Spring* is instead inserted within a network of shots and countershots between a father and his daughter. Despite the repeated cuts from the vase to the daughter's face, however, it does not actually "match" the direction of her glance. Rather than functioning as a point of view shot, the vase (unseen, but presumably present in the alcove, for the rest of the scene) acts as a mental interruption, what director Yoshida Kijū has called "an image of

31) These techniques are supplemented by an expressionist use of sound: there is silence from the moment the door closes behind the characters until the woman tries to break through the window at its center with her arm.

purification and redemption" blocking potentially uncomfortable emotions [Images 71–73].[32] Reinforcing this interpretation, the rigorously composed shot, with shades of darkness redolent of the traditional Japanese aesthetics embraced by Tanizaki Jun'ichirō's *In Praise of Shadows* (1933), is linked by a cut to the Zen garden at Ryōanji [Image 74]. Characteristically for Ozu, this culturally loaded association is counterbalanced by the sound of the father's snoring. Hou's vase shares with Ozu's ties to domesticity, generational passage, and the everydayness exemplified, in *A City of Sadness*, by the preceding scene of the Lin family meal [Image 75]. Also like *Late Spring*, the final shot of *A City of Sadness* is distinguished by its spatial geometry: the colored panes in the shrine harmonize with similar objects in the back left and back right as well as with the divided screens on the sides, which produces a seemingly contradictory impression of containment and expansiveness. The shot is equally notable for its focus on gradations of light, from the clearly positioned overhead lamps on the left to the partial illumination of the shrine to the flickering light in the back. That flickering light brings the film full circle, pointedly reminding the viewer of the multiple births – of the child Kang-ming ("Light") and of a fledg-

ing nation – in the opening scene, allowing the vase to suggest cyclicity as well as endurance [Image 76].

Ozu is, of course, the filmmaker with whom Hou is most frequently compared and the integrity of their cinematic worlds is secured by the habitual return to a small cluster of motifs that become increasingly resonant with each iteration.[33] Trees of various kinds are conspicuously present in Hou's films and several (*A Summer at Grandpa's; Daughter of the Nile*, 1987; *The Puppetmaster; Good Men, Good Women*; and *Goodbye South, Goodbye*) even include shots in which the camera slowly moves through dense boughs [Image 77]. Impervious to human affairs, trees embody a direct attachment to nature and these shots create a reflective distance on the narrative action. Although Hou's fascination with this imagery can hardly be attributed solely to the conventions of East Asian art, and he rarely uses the pine and cypress trees so central to Chinese and Japanese painting, his

32) Yoshida Kijū, *Ozu's Anti-Cinema* (Ann Arbor, MI: University of Michigan Center for Japanese Studies, 2003), 80

33) As Hou has explained on several occasions, he found the first Ozu film he saw (*An Autumn Afternoon*, 1962) boring, watched *I Was Born But…* at the recommendation of Marco Müller after finishing *A Time to Live and a Time to Die*, and became interested in Ozu's repetitions and variations several years later.

A City of Sadness [75–76]
Good Men, Good Women [77]

Late Spring, Ozu Yasujirō, 1949
[71–74]

A Summer at Grandpa's [80–81]

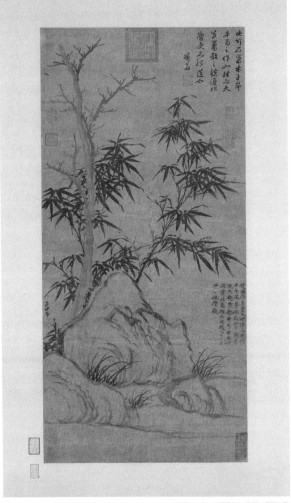

A Time to Live and a Time to Die [82]
Goodbye South, Goodbye [83]

Old Tree, Bamboo, and Rocks, Zhao Mengfu (Chao Meng-fu), 1254–1322,
The Collection of the National Palace Museum [78], A City of Sadness [79]

films assimilate the meanings customarily ascribed to certain tree types. The old, leafless trees in the final scenes of *A City of Sadness*, for example, gain added significance if the viewer is aware that the sentiments of loyalists during a period of foreign domination (such as the Yuan and Qing dynasties) could be represented in this way [Images 78–79].[34] Given the interweaving of the collective and private in Hou's work, it is both interesting and appropriate that the prevalence of trees may also be motivated by a childhood memory. In *HHH: A Portrait of Hou Hsiao-hsien* (Olivier Assayas, 1997), Hou says that he once climbed up a tree next to the residence of the county chief to eat stolen mangoes and had "an acute sense of space and time... a perspective on being" that informed his later filmmaking. The image of a figure seated in a tree is treated comically in Hou's first feature *Cute Girl* (1980) and it is central to a perceptually startling section of *A Summer at Grandpa's* in which the point of view seems to shift from shot to shot [Images 80–81]. This may also be the reason why Wen-ching in *A City of Sadness* is said to have lost his hearing after falling (like Han-tzu in *A Summer at Grandpa's*) from a tree.

While he was shooting *A Time to Live and a Time to Die*, Hou decided to film a tree in the rain that entranced him, without any clear idea what he would do with the footage.[35] Spontaneous and unassuming, the shot that appears in the film seems to effortlessly recover the "beauty of the wind in the trees" that D.W. Griffith saw as the greatest achievement of early cinema [Image 82].[36] The mobile train shots in many Hou films (especially *The Green, Green Grass of Home*; *A Summer at Grandpa's*; *Dust in the Wind*; *Goodbye South, Goodbye*; *Café Lumière*; and *Flight of the Red Balloon*) look even further back to the medium's nineteenth century origins [Image 83]. By positioning the camera at the front or back of a train car, Hou generates a visceral sensation of forward momentum not unlike that created by the "phantom ride" films popular in cinema's first decade

34) Richard Barnhart, *Wintry Forests, Old Trees: Some Landscape Themes in Chinese Paintings* (New York: China Institute in America, 1972), 7–11. In a similar way, Jerome Silbergeld argues that, in line with earlier models established by painters and writers ranging from Muqi to Ah Cheng, the trees in *Good Men, Good Women* function as "an instrument of moral measure" (*Hitchcock with a Chinese Face: Cinematic Doubles, Oedipal Triangles, and China's Moral Voice*, Seattle, WA: University of Washington Press, 2004, 113).

35) *The Taiwan New Cinema*

36) Ezra Goodman, "Flash-Back to Griffith," *PM*, May 19, 1948, M12–M13, reprinted in Anthony Slide, ed., *D.W. Griffith: Interviews* (Jackson, MI: University Press of Mississippi, 2012), 217

Dust in the Wind [84]
The Kiss in the Tunnel, G. A. Smith, 1899 [85]
Café Lumière [86]
The Arrival of a Train at La Ciotat,
Auguste and Louis Lumière, 1896 [87]

[Images 84–85]. This film historical lineage is embedded in the English title of the train-besotted *Café Lumière*, which points to both the mythic 1895 premiere of the *cinématographe* at the Grand Café in Paris and to the director's abiding obsession with the most fundamental elements of filmmaking (the original Japanese title, 珈琲時光, emphasizes these by juxtaposing the characters for time, 時, and light, 光) [Images 86–87].[37] Interviews with many of Hou's collaborators attest to his strong preference for contingency and a method requiring continual adaptation from everyone involved. Resistant, like Bresson, to affectation, actorly mannerisms, and storyboards, he "shoots his films like documentaries."[38] As the lead actor of *Café Lumière* (Asano Tadanobu) observed, however, Hou "knew what kind of images he wanted" and would reshoot covertly filmed train scenes many times to capture the desired effects.[39]

Like *Café Lumière*, the recent short *La Belle Epoque* (2011) combines Hou's signature motifs, with black-and-white shots of a moving train midway through and a color shot of a giant tree at the beginning and end [Image 88–89]. In "The Unmarried Women," Wen Tien-hsiang argues that the idealized image of female purity in Hou's earlier work is complicated by these

La Belle Epoque [88–89]

two filmbuns. They could also be paired through their stress on the invisible legacies that mark objects and places, which encourages the viewer to consider what the past has bequeathed to the present. The heirlooms passed on in *La Belle Epoque* include a piece of jewelry brought over after travel from China was permitted and gold bars, from the time of the young protagonist's grandparents and great-grandparents, that are indirectly related to mining systems developed during the Japanese colonial period.[40] *Café Lumière* reverses this trajectory through Yōko's research into colonial Taiwanese composer Jiang Wen-ye, who won honorable mention at the 1936 Olympic Art Competition in Berlin under his Japanese name Kō Bun'ya. In one striking scene, Jiang's music appears on the soundtrack as Yōko and her friend look for a Ginza café that the composer used to frequent, which has since been replaced by a modern multi-story building. Yōko takes pictures of this and other spaces previously visited by Jiang and photographs provide the primary point of entry to the past during her encounter with Jiang's Japanese widow. That these histories are so prominent in Hou's homage to Ozu should come as no surprise. The irony of the clip from *Late Spring* shown on a

37) Despite its iconic status, *The Arrival of a Train at La Ciotat* (1896) does not appear to have been presented at the public premiere of the Lumière *cinématographe* in December 1895. Claims about the terror supposedly created by the first screenings of this film may derive from Maxim Gorky's description of a *cinématographe* program in Moscow ("On a Visit to the Kingdom of Shadows," translated and reprinted in Jay Leyda, *Kino: A History of the Russian and Soviet Film*, Princeton, NJ: Princeton University Press, 1983, 407–409).

38) Lorenzo Codelli, "Entretien avec Chang Chen," *Positif*, Number 537 (November 2005), 22

39) "Interview with Asano Tadanobu" on the Shochiku DVD of *Café Lumière*

40) This is evident, but by no means obvious, from the conversation about the changing value of gold (and it is reinforced by the implied generational dating).

Good Men, Good Women [90]
Late Spring [91]

TV screen in *Good Men, Good Women* derives above all from the fact that it comes from a cinema under occupation; the bike ride shown on-screen in Hou's film is followed in Ozu's almost immediately by a shot of a Coca-Cola sign [Images 90–91]. Hou began a 1993 interview about Ozu by talking about Chiufen [Jiufen], a town in the North of Taiwan famous for its preserved Japanese architecture and its former status as a hub for gold mining.[41] In a documentary about the making of *Café Lumière* ten years later, Hou mentions that he lived in a house with *tatami* mats as a child and was exposed to the Japanese language through the

words absorbed into Taiwanese. He continues by saying that he is not interested in assessing the merits of Japanese society, but only in understanding how it developed and "why there was a Second World War."[42]

Questions of cultural heritage are broached in a very different way in *The Puppetmaster*, which opens with a title card declaring that Taiwan was ceded to Japan in the 1895 Treaty of Shimonoseki. The sound of puppet performance starts in the credits and continues largely unabated through a series of vignettes representing Li Tien-lu's childhood (accompanied by the real Li's offscreen narration) and into the first visual demonstrations of puppetry more than four minutes in. This unusual use of off-screen sound establishes an inextricable link between theater and colonialism and suggests

41) Chiufen, also known during the colonial period by the Japanese name Kyūfun, became a tourist destination after it was used in *A City of Sadness*. It was the model for the town in Miyazaki Hayao's *Spirited Away* (2001).

42) *Métro Lumière: Hou Hsiao-hsien à la rencontre de Yasujirō Ozu*

43) Camera movement in *The Puppetmaster* is very limited, generally consisting only of slight reframings. Hou compensates by emphasizing the movement of figures along the z-axis. In the interview included here, Mark Lee explains that he shot material involving more active camera movement, which Hou decided to excise at the editing stage.

The Puppetmaster [92–93]
The Lady from Shanghai, Orson Welles, 1947 [94]
The Story of the Last Chrysanthemums,
Mizoguchi Kenji, 1939 [95]

that Taiwanese history is itself a sort of performance. The fictional Li deepens these implications when he explains why his puppet troupe was named "Also like Life:" "Puppets in performance are like people, so puppet plays are also like life." Indeed, Hou shoots the puppet performances, which serve as punctuation marks in the narrative and metaphorically comment upon dramatic changes in Li's situation, in long takes from a fixed camera position, the same way he shoots most of the human interactions.[43] Much as Hou's characters pass in and out of doorways within the same shot, moving through the space demarcated by the camera, Li's puppets move through their covered gateways, passing through the spaces demarcated by the stage (in her essay, Jean Ma notes a parallel with the silent chase genre). The proscenium framing of the performance scenes, markedly different from the montage-oriented angularity of similar shots in films by Orson Welles and Mizoguchi, strengthens the association with the presentational modes of early cinema and the historical concurrence implicit in the opening title – with 1895 as the inauguration of motion pictures and Japanese rule [Images 92–95].

The ubiquity of Japanese authority figures at public events in *The Puppetmaster* is Hou's way

The Puppetmaster [96–97]

of acknowledging the realities of Taiwan's most overtly imperialist regime. In one particularly effective sequence, a group of officers comes to the protagonist's family home and tells the residents that they will get free tickets to an opera if they remove their queues. What follows is a series of shots in which, no matter the setting, an officer generally occupies the center of the frame, highlighting the quiet insidiousness of the mechanisms of control [Images 96–97]. In other ways, however, Hou subtly inverts colonial assumptions. Beginning with the Meiji era writings of authors like Shiga Shigetaka, Taiwan was portrayed as a romantic landscape, the Japanese equivalent to "Italy, Spain, or Egypt."[44] Works by influential artists like Ishikawa Kin'ichirō prioritized the heat, light, and "characteristic colors of a Southern Country."[45] By contrast, *The Puppetmaster* is extraordinarily reliant on darkness and chiaroscuro, with several scenes hovering at the edge of visibility [Image 98]. Like many things in Hou's work, the visual palette of *The Puppetmaster* is rooted in realism, accurately re-

flecting a period in which artificial light was scarce, but it also contributes to a beguiling atmosphere in which mundane and epochal incidents, the "drama, dream, and life" in the Chinese title (戲夢人生), are indelibly mixed.

Far from the polemicist some of his critics apparently want him to be, Hou remains content to explore history in all its complexity, upending expectations and refusing facile judgment.[46] Near the end of *The Puppetmaster*, Li recounts a moment when one of his postwar performances was interrupted by a group of Taiwanese villagers accusing Japanese of hoarding rice, but what, at first, seems like a predictable story of revenge is soon revealed to be a gross misunderstanding: "If they had distributed it, they would have been heroes of the neighborhood. But they didn't. Instead, they gathered all the rice up and burned it. I went and asked the Japanese soldiers why they had done this. They explained that the rice had been in storage a long time. It had turned black, and wasn't edible. It had to be burned, and it was only after I explained this to people that

The Puppetmaster [98 and 99]

they stopped beating them." Li moves almost immediately into a discussion of a time when he saw airplanes that had been sabotaged with acid being dismantled and asked why junk collectors had been brought in. "Where do you think we're getting the money to pay you? The money from your performances comes from this scrap metal. You know, our gods answer our prayers. That's why we've asked you to perform for them," Li was told. "And that was the reason why Taiwan was finally liberated from Japan," he concludes, as Hou transitions to a pair of shots that depict the dismantling with increasing distance. The most remote shot [Image 99] includes observers in multiple planes, with figures and oxen crossing laterally and the sound of rolling carts intermingled with the elegiac music. As perfect an ending as any in cinema, the final section of *The Puppetmaster* makes the movement of history palpable and presents artistic performance – of dancing puppets and electric shadows – as the vouchsafe of memory, a fleeting simulation of continuity salvaged from the detritus of an ever-changing world.

44) Painter Miyake Kokki's comparison was reiterated by other Japanese artists and writers (Hsin-tien Liao discusses a number of these in "The Beauty of the Untamed: Exploration and Travel in Colonial Taiwanese Landscape Painting" in Yūko Kikuchi, ed., *Refracted Modernity: Visual Culture and Identity in Colonial Taiwan*, Honolulu, HI: University of Hawaii Press, 2007, 46–51). Shiga Shigetaka's most influential book was *The Landscape of Japan* (1894), but his ideas about the colonial situation were also developed in *South Seas Affairs* (1897).

45) Toshio Watanabe, "Japanese Landscape Painting and Taiwan: Modernity, Colonialism, and National Identity" in Kikuchi, 74. Ishikawa published a famous aesthetic treatise about the Taiwanese landscape called "The South Chair" in 1929 (Yen Chuan-ying summarizes Ishikawa's ideas in "Colonial Taiwan and the Construction of Landscape Painting" in Liao Ping-hui and David Der-wei Wang, eds., *Taiwan Under Japanese Colonial Rule, 1895–1945: History, Culture, Memory*, New York: Columbia University Press, 2006, 252–254).

46) Critiques of the ambiguity and alleged lack of political commitment in Hou's work were collected in Mi Tsou and Liang Hsin-hua, eds., *Death of the New Cinema* (Taipei: Tang-shan Publishing Company, 1991).

Peggy Chiao (Hsiung-ping)

In Search of Taiwan's Identity

Nativism and Traditional Aesthetics in A City of Sadness

Taiwan is located on the east side of China, separated from the mainland by the Taiwan Strait. Over the last 300 years, mass immigration from China to Taiwan has resulted in the Han people becoming the majority in Taiwan. In its short political history, the island had been ruled by political regimes as diverse as the Netherlands, Spain (in Northern Taiwan), the Han Chinese Ming Dynasty, the Manchurian Qing Dynasty, Imperial Japan and the Kuomintang (KMT, the Nationalist Party) of the Republic of China. This complicated political and social history constitutes the special background of Taiwanese culture: "[Taiwan] has been ruled by five different regimes, notably by the Japanese Empire and the authoritarian KMT...Taiwan includes the cultures of Middle China, Fukien [Fujian] and Canton [Guangzhou], the Southern Islands, etc. In this particular historical time and space, Taiwan cultivated a diverse, rich and unique ocean culture."[1]

Through frequent commerce with foreign countries, the introduction of modern Western thought during the Japanese occupation, and the infusion of American culture in recent decades, Taiwan has developed a complex and hybrid character. Yet, true to its population, Taiwanese society is predominantly China-centric.

Taiwan was returned to China after the Second World War. However, the reinstatement of Chinese rule fostered immediate resentment because of the KMT's overbearing and often violent takeover measures. Adding fuel to the fire were the many economic and social problems typical of the immediate postwar era, gravely intensifying the negative views of the ruling Nationalist party by the so-called Native Taiwanese (those Chinese that immigrated from the seventeenth century to the end of the Japanese colonial period). Accordingly, the so-called Mainlanders (Han Chinese who immigrated to Taiwan after 1945 or fled there after the Communist victory in 1949) and the Native Taiwanese were embroiled in frequent conflicts and even violent clashes, resulting in over forty years of increasingly bitter political discord: "Postwar Taiwan, already wearied and beleaguered, was plunged into devastating turmoil by the February 28 [228] Incident, ignited by the police's heavy-handed crackdown on black market cigarettes. The government announced Martial Law the following year, citing the gravity of the situation. It provided over-

1) Tai Pao-tsun, "Taiwan is the Focus of 'Taiwan Study:' a Summary of Research into Taiwan History," *China Tribune*, Oct 25, 1989, 7

Poster for *A City of Sadness*, 1989

reaching power to intelligence agencies led by the police, eliminated freedoms of speech, publication, assembly, and organization of the people… Intelligence agents could question, arrest, and investigate any civilian at any given time. People disappeared in the middle of the night. The effect of this White Terror was a society in fear of politics. Matters of national concern were not discussed on a personal level and, especially, in education and academic research. People could discuss the issue of China, but 'Taiwan' was taboo, to be avoided at all costs."[2]

The enactment of Martial Law in 1947 was followed in 1949 by the Nationalist government's retreat to Taiwan along with two million refugees. Taipei became, in name, the site where the "government of China" was located and Mandarin was imposed as the official language, setting the tone for the political climate of the next four decades. During that time, the KMT insisted on sovereignty over all of China, creating forty years of Cold War between Taiwan (the Republic of China) and the government of the People's Republic of China (PRC). Due to fears of Communism and indigenous opposition, the politicians (legislators, national representatives, and Committee Members of the Control Yuan) who were voted into office in 1948 on the mainland would permanently retain their seats. The Nationalist Party propagandized using slogans like "regaining mainland China," and suppressed development of any local Taiwan consciousness. Academic research in this area was under stiff control: "Taiwan research can only be a part of China research. It cannot survive as an area of independent study. Academia Sinica, the premier academic organization in Taiwan, has an institute devoted to the study of American culture but, up until the time of this essay [1989], it has not been allowed to establish an institute focusing on Taiwan's history, society, and culture."[3]

Still wounded from the traumatic experience of losing the mainland, the KMT shifted the blame onto failed socioeconomic policies. In Taiwan, it implemented vigorous land reforms consisting of tax reductions, land rewards to farmers, and the transformation of a largely agricultural society into an industrial one. With the outbreak of the Korean War in the early 1950s, the United States began pumping annual aid of US$20 million into Taiwan, propelling a

2) Liu Huang-yueh, "The New Garden Out of Ruins: Research on the Society of Postwar Taiwan," *China Tribune*, Oct 25, 1989, 30

3) Wang Chen-huang, "The Study of Taiwan Society After the 1980s," *China Tribune*, Oct 25, 1989, 27

new economy based on the manufacturing of consumer products. From 1962 to 1972, Taiwan enjoyed a golden age of economic growth. GDP increased by 9.8% annually, with an inflation rate of only 2.9%.[4]

Taiwan suffered a series of diplomatic setbacks in the 1970s. The heartbreaking expulsion from the United Nations in 1971 was followed by the severance of an official relationship with the United States in 1978, when the Carter administration established formal diplomacy with the PRC. Many other countries followed suit, recognizing China and breaking off ties with Taiwan. Taiwan was forced to find self-affirmation through other means, notably economic accomplishments. In 1978, Taiwan miraculously registered an economic growth of 14%, breaking its own record; exports growth soared to a best-of-the-world 35.7%. While denied diplomatic recognition by most countries, an enterprising free-market Taiwan managed to gain a foothold in the global economic system – the thirteenth largest economy in the world, with a foreign reserve of US$760 million and an

average income of US$6,000.[5] The small island, with a population density lower than Bangladesh, became the second richest country in Asia (after Japan).

CHANGES IN THE 1980s

As Taiwan became more affluent in the 1980s, its social problems became more serious: an uneven distribution of wealth; broken social harmony; a widening gap between urban and rural communities; the sluggish development of public infrastructure; low investment; and crazes in the stock market, real estate, and even in lottery sales. Especially critical were the breakdowns in public transportation, environmental conditions, and public safety. Some of the issues arising for the first time since the onset of KMT rule included:

— The exchange rate of New Taiwan dollars (NTD) to United States dollars remained unchanged from 1963 to 1987. An enormous trade surplus forced the NTD to appreciate at a rate of roughly 30% in two years.

— Martial Law was lifted forty years after it was established, leading to the formation of opposition parties and a rise in public rallies.

— In 1987, the KMT lifted the ban on visiting relatives on the mainland and communication by mail and telephone was legalized the fol-

4) *Global Views Monthly,* Aug 15, 1989, 30

5) Ibid, 59

lowing year. Frequent travels across the Straits occurred after several decades of broken contact during the Cold War.

The many changes led to widespread maladjustment. Society was soon besieged by divisiveness and enmeshed in clashes of conflicting interests. Internationally, Taiwan managed to foster formal diplomatic relationships with only twenty-three nations, but continued to trade with 150. Domestically, confrontational debates were rampant between KMT loyalists, followers of an independence movement, and those who advocated unification with China. Economically, Taiwan evolved from a backwater semi-agrarian society into a modern urban society with metropolitan centers like Taipei. Culturally, it remained the embodiment of traditional Chinese values while also integrating influences from the developed world, especially America and Japan.

The inevitable result was identity confusion. What is Taiwan? Is it the "Republic of China" as the KMT said? "Free China," as citizens of the island liked to believe? "Formosa," after the colonial name given by the Portuguese? "Chinese, Taipei," the official country name used at international events like the Olympics? An economic miracle? A colony of Japan or America? One of the provinces of China? In a similar vein, who are the Taiwanese – the aborigines, the Native Taiwanese, or the Mainlanders? These identity issues became popular fodder for literature and art. Before the 1970s, creative works were notable mainly for their escapism. Reality was evaded at all costs. In the 1970s and 1980s, however, the search for identity became essential to the Nativist movement in literature and Taiwan's New Cinema.

THE BURGEONING OF NATIVE CONSCIOUSNESS

New Cinema inherited the spirit of Nativist Literature, which was driven by left-wing Chinese nationalism and triggered by the modernism that was then popular in Taiwan. Although the movement evolved into a rigid political force of confrontation, its realistic exploration of the changes in Taiwanese society was clearly picked up by the New Cinema through the use of colorful slang and the sympathetic treatment of the plight of "little people," those who had been displaced or reduced to petty crime by industrialization. A prominent example is the early New Cinema classic *The Sandwich Man* (1983), a portmanteau film directed by Hou Hsiao-hsien, Tseng Chuang-hsiang, and Wan Jen. The film was adapted from three short stories by Huang Chun-ming, a leading Nativist author. It appropriated the realism of

Huang's writing, what Chen Ying-chen once described as Huang's delineation of "the tragic conditions of villagers during rural Taiwan's transition from old to new."

Son's Big Doll, Hou's contribution to *The Sandwich Man*, focuses on an endangered occupation (a small town sandwich man – a mobile advertisement, with a man walking around draped between two movie posters pasted on plywood), a metaphor for the helplessness felt by those confronted with modern technology. The second part, *Vicky's Hat* (directed by Tseng Chuang-hsiang), offers a sharp criticism of Japan's economic invasion, while *The Taste of Apple* (directed by Wan Jen) uses a car accident in which a poor laborer is hit by a car driven by an American serviceman to examine the physical and psychological traumas suffered by the Taiwanese people. The critical and commercial success of the film spawned a host of films adapted from Nativist literature. Writings by key figures such as Wang Chen-ho, Yang Ching-chu and Chi-teng Sheng [Liu Wu-hsiung] were favorites.

The autobiographical tone of New Cinema echoes the quest for everyday realism in Nativist literature. Most of the filmmakers were in their 30s and 40s. They grew up at the very moment that Taiwan was going through its most drastic social changes. The personal memories depicted in their films represented not only a realism never before encountered in Taiwan's films, but also a collective search for identity. *In Our Time* (1982), widely regarded as the first film of the New Cinema, was a portmanteau work directed by newcomers Tao Te-chen, Edward Yang, Ko I-cheng, and Chang Yi. The stories were set in Taipei in 1960, 1967, 1971, and 1982, and it is interesting that the four parts correspond to a Taiwan growing from radio days to the television era to a metropolitan center sprouting with apartment buildings. The theme of growing up was found in many films including most of Hou's 1980s features; Yang's *That Day, on the Beach* (1983) and *Taipei Story* (1985); Chen Kun-hou's *Growing up* (1983) and *The Matrimony* (1985); Chang Yi's *Kuei-mei, a Woman* (1985) and *This Love of Mine* (1985); Wan Jen's *Ah Fei* (1983) and *Super Citizen* (1985); Wang Tung's *A Flower in the Rainy Night* (1983), *Strawman* (1987), and *Banana Paradise* (1989); even in TV movies like Tsai Ming-liang's *All the Corners of the World* (1989) that tried to establish New Cinema on the broadcast medium. They all appeared within the short span of six years.

The experiences depicted in these films constitute a collective document of Taiwan's cultural, economic, and political history over several decades, a vivid mosaic that captures and narrativizes the changing faces of modern Taiwan. *A Time to Live and a Time to Die* (Hou Hsiao-hsien, 1985) and *Banana Paradise* explore the complex relationship between Taiwan and China in their portrayal of the tragic lives of Mainlanders who followed the KMT to Taiwan after the civil war. *Dust in the Wind* (Hou Hsiao-hsien, 1986), *Taipei Story, Super Citizen, The Terrorizers* (Edward Yang, 1986), and *Daughter of the Nile* (Hou Hsiao-hsien, 1987) paint pictures of the economic and social changes of metropolitan Taipei. *Ah Fei* and *Kuei-mei, a Woman* depict the structural changes in Taiwanese society through the lives of female characters and their families.

Many of these films, including *The Sandwich Man, Old Mo's Second Spring* (Lee You-ning, 1984), *Daughter of the Nile*, and *A City of Sadness* (Hou Hsiao-hsien, 1989) were victims of censorship. For several decades, fear of severe political censorship motivated the pervasive escapism of the film industry. The anti-Communist propaganda films of the 1950s, the melodramas exalting the government's agricultural policies of the 1960s, and the romance and martial arts pictures of the 1970s were far removed from everyday reality. By contrast, New Cinema films made after the lifting of Martial Law like *A City of Sadness* and *Banana Paradise* boldly tread on political taboos, demonstrating the potential of films to explore the real identity of Taiwan.

During this time, filmmakers also tried to break away from classical modes of storytelling and the Hollywood-esque star system. They opted instead to look for new ways to express themselves aesthetically: elliptical structures and ambiguous narratives, long takes, real locations, complex approaches to space and *mise-en-scène*, natural lighting, non-professional actors, the creative use of language and sound, etc. As a result, the New Cinema altered the film industry irrevocably and put Taiwan on the international map. Among the New Cinema directors, Hou Hsiao-hsien was especially devoted to documenting Taiwan's social changes. His works were motivated by a quest, on the level of form and content, for Taiwan's identity. *A City of Sadness* represents the pinnacle of this search and marked the true maturity of the New Cinema.

"TAIWAN" IN HOU HSIAO-HSIEN'S FILMS

Hou's early work was marked by a conscious effort to cinematically express specific living conditions in Taiwan's recent past. *The Boys from Fengkuei* (1983) tells the story of several young boys from the Penghu Islands wandering around the city of Kaohsiung before the military draft;. *A Summer at Grandpa's* (1984) contrasts urban and rural life in the 1980s in a story that waves goodbye to childhood while stepping into adolescence. *A Time to Live and a Time to Die* traces the gradual demise of the Mainlanders who immigrated to Taiwan (together with their "Mainland Complex") as well as the growth and maturity of their descendents (together with the rise of their indigenous identity). *Dust in the Wind* depicts the social changes of the 1970s – the extreme split between urban and country cultures – and the adjustment difficulties of growing up. *Daughter of the Nile* examines the depravity of a city in the 1980s and the nihilistic pessimism of the young people who live there.

Hou's documentary impulse is even more evident in *A City of Sadness*. The immediate postwar years, from 1945 to 1949, were critical in dictating the future of Taiwan and Hou plunged headlong into this period, determined to find the key that could unlock the political myth. The film portrays Taiwan from the end of the Japanese occupation to the establishment of the Kuomintang regime. Such a structure corresponds to the pattern of changing rulers

(Portuguese, Spaniards, and Manchurians) throughout Taiwan's history. In other words, the 228 Incident in the film is only the background on which the broader issue of Taiwan identity is projected. In a land where political rulers changed frequently, it is only natural that crises and contradictions in identity have political, social, cultural, and even racial aspects.

A City of Sadness focuses on the process of transferring power. With a tragic disposition, it depicts the overwhelming victory of the Nationalists from multiple perspectives – it was a time when new political forces arose, when traditional village orders eroded, and when the romantic ideals of the intelligentsia towards the motherland (China) gradually faded into despair. Structurally, Hou uses a multilayered narrative to portray this transitional period. The power shift from the Japanese to the KMT is expressed through dialogue, music (songs and the score), images, and metaphors, all informed by a sense of fate and irony. Early in the film, such notions as "light," "motherland," and "rebirth" are evoked through childbirth, the return of Taiwan to China, and the return of electricity after a blackout, creating a sense of optimism, idealism, and joyfulness. Multiple events signifying the prospects of a new life and new ideals are presented: the radio broadcast of Emperor Hirohito's surrender speech, the birth of a child when light returns, the opening of a new restaurant named "Little Shanghai" (ironically, the Lins will later be persecuted by Shanghai people), new jobs, and aspirations for the future. Hinomi's voiceover when she arrives is characteristic: "To think that I will see such beautiful scenery every day fills my heart with happiness." ... All of these convey the jubilation and expectation that accompanied Taiwan's "rebirth" as it returned to the bosom of the motherland.

The light mood is soon wiped out by the relentless trauma and death that follows, sinking all the way to the dark, gloomy realm of sadness at the end – inside Little Shanghai, the lighting is dark and gloomy while the stained glass glows with dense colors. The stifled, repressed feeling of the confined space contrasts sharply with the intimations of freedom and possibility in the beginning. During the transfer of power from one sovereignty to another, two sons are lost to the Lin family (one killed by the Shanghai gang, the other arrested by the KMT), and another becomes an invalid (his brain damaged when interrogated by KMT agents). Only women and children remain, living on in muffled silence.

The film is seldom one-dimensional in its method, lingering instead on the intricate relationship linking Taiwan, China, and Japan. For example, when the school principal Ogawa and his daughter Shizuko are about to be sent back to Japan after the war, the strong-willed old man resists being sent back, insisting instead on visiting friends in the south. His daughter bids farewell to Taiwan in apologetic words, leaving to her friends her favorite kimono and the bamboo sword of a brother who died in the war. Awkward and melancholic, the love between Hinoe and Shizuko is terminated because of political changes. This episode exudes forgiveness and understanding. The second Lin son may have died while serving in the Japanese military, political changes may have resulted in oppositions between Japan and Taiwan, but human relationships transcend the divide of nationality and international politics. The attachment of Ogawa and Shizuko to Taiwan allows us to understand the tragedy on the Japanese side (Ogawa's loss of sanity and Shizuko's loss of love). In celebrating Taiwan's return to the motherland, Hou has not put Japan on a sacrificial altar.

As Japan's influence fades, China's rises. Chants of "The Exile Trilogy" (an anti-Japanese song widely sung after the occupation of Manchuria) can be heard through the window

A City of Sadness

right after a group of intellectuals joke about the Chinese and Japanese flags. The scenery outside is shrouded in dusk and they rise up to open the window and sign along: "What year... What month... Will we return to our wonderful hometown?" The men's longing for their homeland is at once romantic and abstract, and the song lingers into the next shot showing the hills at the harbor city, with the distant thunder sounds whispering warnings for their quixotic feelings towards China. Rain is about to pour and Hinomi collects the clothes drying on the laundry line while the third son has a tear running down his face, lost in memory (a translator for the Japanese in Shanghai, he was arrested and tortured after the war as a collaborator).

This passage reveals the complexity of the relationship between Taiwan and China. The intellectuals once had high hopes for China and could have become socialists, opponents of the KMT. Instead, the fate of Taiwan is decided, as always, by outsiders: "It was the Qing Dynasty who sold us out to Japan. When they signed the Treaty of Shimonoseki, did they consult us?" laments Old Wu. The Taiwanese who had to shoulder the burdens of historical mistakes were actually treated as collaborators simply for being used by Japan. Slowly but surely, the KMT gained civil and official control of Taiwan. In much the same way that the Shanghai gang, with close ties to the ruling party, used their political power to eradicate the local gang, Chen Yi's new government wiped out dissident intellectuals through enticement and persecution. When the fourth son's letter – written in blood, "You must live with dignity. Father is innocent." – arrives, his widow weeps and the song "Spring Flower Looks for the Dew" can be heard along with the voiceover. The song was originally about the longing of Taiwan women for husbands who were drafted to fight for Japan in Indochina. Here, it is cited to express the grief brought onto a Taiwan woman by the KMT.

Similarly complex details can be found throughout the film. "History" takes on multiple meanings. Through words, images and sounds, a complex interpretive framework is established between historical discourse and author/audience. History is in fact a narrative recorded by language (words) that is shaped by culture, ideology, and genre. Three levels of history can be found in *A City of Sadness*:

I. VERBAL TEXT

Words take on special significance in the film, in the form of title cards and superimposed text. At the beginning and end of the film, "objective" captions appear: "On August 15, 1945, Japan announced its unconditional surrender. Taiwan was liberated following fifty years of Japanese occupation" and "In December 1949, mainland China is lost. The Nationalist government moves to Taiwan and Taipei becomes provisional capital." There are also entire paragraphs of poetic prose ("Cherry Blossoms of the same fate, Fly as much as you wish, I will follow you later") or the myth of Lorelei explained.

Words appear in the form of text without grammatical pronouns (me, you, etc.), putting the audience into a state of objective substitution and amplifying the sense of narrative multiplicity. Written text is often found in the works of French New Wave directors like Jean-Luc Godard, where it is used largely to block audience identification and to establish dialectical relationships between literature and film. In *A City of Sadness*, the inserted text is presented in the manner of traditional Chinese poetry, asking the audience to adopt an empathetic and subjective point of view. Artist and critic Chiang Hsun once remarked that, in the Southern Song Dynasty, artists juxtaposed painting and poetry, leaving empty spaces in compositions for text. Written words are used in *A City*

of Sadness not only to express emotion, but also as a modernist device designed to disrupt the continuity so typical of Hollywood cinema.

2. AUDIO TEXT

This is used mostly in Hinomi's diary, Shizuko's voiceover, and Ah-shue's letters. These three women serve as narrators on the soundtrack; they also maintain harmony and provide the spiritual power that enables their families to persist. They add to the multiplicity of perspectives in the film and also give independent voice to the women who were denied expression in a patriarchal society. Female voices are also respected in Hou's other films, which contain a degree of empathy and understanding for the plight and repression of women that is rare in Chinese film history.

The female voices are more lyrical. Hinomi's narrations are in diary from, yet the style is poetic, with descriptions of scenery used to express her emotions. For example, her mood as she rides in a sedan chair up a hill is represented by the voiceover: "The hill already has the feel of autumn. To think that I will see such beautiful scenery every day fills my heart with happiness." Similar language is employed in a letter to Ah-shue near the end of the film: "Chiufen [Jiufen] is getting chilly. The Mang flowers bloom, making the entire hill white, like snow."

The projection of subjectivity onto the outer world, resulting in the convergence of emotions and environment, follows the Chinese poetic tradition of becoming one with objects of the world: "I look, therefore all things are tinted with my color." The author's subjective views are concealed in outer objects, thereby avoiding overly direct and simplistic expressions of emotions.

3. VISUAL TEXT

Protagonist Wen-ching, the fourth son of the Lin family, is deaf and mute (to some degree a metaphor for the repression of the Taiwanese). He works as a photographer, instantaneously documenting history with snapshots and providing a way to review it introspectively. In this way, *A City of Sadness* takes issue with various facets of presumed historical meaning. The frequent appearance of photographs, negatives, and the act of refining images on negatives suggests a conscious rumination about the nature of the medium. At the end of the film, Wen-ching takes a self-portrait of his family in the studio, posing with props – sofa, furnace, and flowers – that represent comfort and affluence. The reality is quite the opposite; he is about to

be arrested and separated from his family. Capturing profound sentiments with deep irony, the photograph becomes the most prominent metaphor of the film, with the figures looking out into disillusion (of images, history, political ideals, and family ties). Moreover, real historical details are integrated into the drama.

For example, the character Teacher Lin is based on the brother of novelist Chung Li-ho and Ho the journalist is a reference to the *Ta Kung Pao* reporter Ho Kang. The counterfeit case involving the underworld, Chen Yi's broadcast about the 228 Incident, and the "I am innocent" blood letter containing the lines "away from motherland when I am alive, return to motherland when I die, everything is destined, no longings or regrets" are all based on historical facts. Audiences who are familiar with this history are able to develop a complex reading of the film: it is a mixture of history, memory, drama, and verisimilitude. The viewing experience is based on the dialectic between illusion and reality.

CHALLENGE TO THE SENSITIVITY OF THE AUDIENCE: SOUND

The formal originality of *A City of Sadness* was unprecedented for Taiwan's cinema. Hou's combination of extremely long takes, elliptical editing, and in-depth spatial arrangements was radically new, as was his use of the repetition of camera angles as a visual motif, the mixing of traditions from poetry and painting, the metaphoric and metonymic use of sound, and the political connotations of language and music. The aesthetic and narrative approach of the film expanded the metaphysical potential of cinema. It also presented challenges to audiences, requiring the active pursuit of information and the reconstruction of meanings.

Creating the soundtrack alone was a monumental task. Five languages and dialects are used in the film: Mandarin, Taiwanese, Shanghainese, Cantonese, and Japanese. Recorded with synchronized sound, the film provides an auditory portrait of the diverse linguistic system of the period. This diversity is also representative of the complicated sociopolitical background of the story and the difficulties in communication caused by cultural differences.

The score, songs, and operatic performances further exemplify these diverse sociopolitical backgrounds while also generating meaning through irony, contrast, emotional pitch, and ideological expression. As mentioned above, the use of songs such as "Exile Trilogy" and "Spring Flowers Looking for Dew" has complex connotations. Before she leaves Taiwan,

Shizuko is shown in a classroom with her students. Bathed in over-exposed lighting, she plays the organ and sings "Red Dragonfly," a Japanese children's song popular in Taiwan, with them. The purity and innocence of the moment, with Hinomi's brother quietly watching on the side, beautifully articulates the sense of loss represented by a romance doomed for political reasons. Later, when Wen-ching bids goodbye to the cellmates who are about to be executed, other cellmates start chanting "Song of the Covered Wagon," a Japanese farewell song that was also popular in Taiwan at the time. The lyrics narrate the situation of watching a friend leave in a covered wagon, gradually fading away on the cobble road, a farewell that lasts forever. In addition to mourning the death of the prisoners, this singing also expresses the disappointment the intelligentsia felt about the Nationalist government (the contrast between the earlier patriotic song in Mandarin, "September 18," and this song in Japanese is derived from the writings of Lan Po-chou).

Opera and folk songs are used effectively to enrich the sonic environment as well as to enhance emotional development. The Taiwanese opera Wen-ching was so fond of while growing up is paralleled by the mainland opera that the Shanghai gang leader listens to after setting a trap for Wen-leung. When the intellectuals become disillusioned with the KMT, they listen to folk songs marked by melancholy (the first son Wen-hsiung even smashes a *huqin* violin, demonstrating the rash temper that will lead to his death by the Shanghai gang). The most inspiring of the songs is "Lorelei." In one scene, intellectuals gather in a restaurant criticizing the government for inflation and low salaries; "Something bad is bound to happen. When can the Taiwanese people see the light of day?" Wen-ching and Hinomi are shown listening to a record of "Lorelei," discussing the romantic fatalism of the old German folk tale. At this point, the film suddenly switches to a narrative within a narrative, telling the story of Lorelei. Wen-ching details how the boatman listens to the beautiful song and sees the siren; in a joyful trance, he cares little if his boat is about to crash. "The boat turned over and the boatman died." The story seemingly has no relevance to the intellectuals in the room, yet, in juxtaposition, it presages the intelligentsia's fate, that they would soon fall victim to their romantic ideals. Meanwhile, Wen-ching switches from listening to music to remembering his childhood. Hinomi affectionately listens, a tear in her eyes, as insert shots of Taiwanese opera and children in a tutoring class appear. This sequence, informed by Romanticism, provides a contrast between radical and forgiving sentiments, with the music reinforcing the complex narrative structure. The intellectuals' penchant for classical music and the third son's fondness for Beethoven are also examples of the refined taste learned from the Japanese.

In many instances, sound becomes the essential connecting link between scenes, filling in the omission of time and space while also delivering drama in condensed form. Hou was already using offscreen sound to complement his long takes, but his use of it became increasingly original and imaginative from *A Time to Live and a Time to Die* to *Dust in the Wind* to *Daughter of the Nile* and *A City of Sadness*. For example, when Wen-ching is behind bars, the soundtrack includes the clinking of the cell door and the footsteps of cellmates walking away; later, two shots can be heard. Another example of the brilliant use of sound is the layering of Chen Yi's announcement of Martial Law over the "empty" shot of Wen-leung's arrest at night. At the end of the film, the sound and the visuals are not synchronized, changing the viewer's perception of time. The images appear to flash forward to foretell the arrest of the protagonist.

LONG TAKE / SPACE / STRUCTURE

Hou is fond of saying that his use of long takes was a result of there being "too few professional actors and a deficiency of sets and locations." His editor Liao Ching-sung maintains that Hou's explanation of his aesthetics is "too modest." Liao has argued that long takes are difficult to use properly. Unless they are fully charged with emotion or narrative tension, long takes can be very pretentious (as is the case in many New Cinema films). By contrast, the use of the long take in *A City of Sadness* is rarely dull. Hou managed to sustain interest through the skillful arrangement of the entrances and exits of his characters, the reframing of *mise-en-scène*, contrasts between visual planes, and the careful use of offscreen sound. This is amply demonstrated in the scenes in Little Shanghai, where the sophisticated composition creates multiple focal points.

Structurally, the long takes are enhanced by an editing scheme that follows traditional Chinese poetry in its rhythm, tempo, and metaphors. The omission of grammatical "pronouns" in the film's text (a practice that emulates classical poetry) is echoed in the perspective of Hou's shots. Often, the subjective source of the shot is not established. Whose view is this? Is this an objective point of view or the memory of a character? When Hinomi's brother Hinoe first brought Ho and Teacher Lin to see Wen-ching, the latter inquires about Ogawa's plight and Hinoe replies: "Mr. Ogawa was sick, but he insisted on going out. He calmed down after shots. Ms. Shizuko was sad." The image we are shown is of Shizuko standing beside a hill with her father. We are not sure whether this is an objective shot, Hinoe's memory, Wen-ching's imagination, or Shizuko's projection (her voiceover begins during this shot).

Shots without controlling subjects or points of view are abundant. Sometimes, they seem fragmented. Parallels to this form of non-linear juxtaposition can be found in poetry. Chinese poetry is full of disparate, seemingly unrelated impressions. More often than not, when the last image appears, the entire picture suddenly seems to be organized in a unified way. Ma Zhiyuan's Yuan dynasty poem "Autumn Thoughts" provides a perfect example:

> *Dry vine, old trees, night crows*
> *Small bridge, running creek, cottage huts*
> *Old path, west wind, lean horse*
> *Evening sun setting west*
> *A heart-torn man wanders at the edge of*
> *the world.*

This poem is composed of fragments and it is only when the final image appears that we realize the subject is a traveler longing for his hometown. The montage effect of unrelated visuals is similar to the treatment of metaphoric images in *A City of Sadness*. The key idea transcends the actual images or narratives, aspiring to a suggestiveness that goes beyond the surface.

The use of ellipses, inserts, fragmented images, synchronized or non-synchronized sounds and images all suggest a conscious effort to disregard classical Hollywood storytelling, giving *A City of Sadness* a sense of modernity. This strategy also has affinities with traditional Chinese literature and art. Hou's elliptical narrative echoes the notion of *liu bai* in Chinese art – the act of leaving empty spaces in paintings, especially in literati paintings completed in a freehand style, rendering verisimilitude unnecessary and relying on audience imagination to conjure the "unpainted" and the "unsaid."

Many other connections to Chinese traditions can be found in *A City of Sadness*, such as the emphasis on rituals of life or death, weddings, festival celebrations, and the rotations of seasons, all of which reflect the cyclical pattern of life and the resilient nature of the Chinese people. The treatment of everyday details like daily meals and sleep habits is also deeply Chinese. On the other hand, the dinner table at or around which much of the film takes place is also an embodiment of patriarchal practices. The film combines a Taoist belief in harmony with fate and nature with a Confucian adherence to patriarchal orders.

A City of Sadness is at once modern and traditional, reflecting the complexity of Taiwan's culture. It is a work that testifies to the history of Taiwan, not only in its subject matter but also in its very historical position, emerging at a time when cries of "New Cinema is dead" were heard. It proved that news of the Cinema's death was premature, setting the stage for the artistic flourishing that followed.

Translated by Sam Ho

Ni Zhen

Transcending Local Consciousness

The Significance of Hou's Films for Asian Cinema

Since the 1980s, the films of Hou Hsiao-hsien have been landmarks in Asian cinema. The interconnection of local Taiwanese issues with the history of mainland China and of social change and the fate of the individual is as unique as the composed, reflective style of his narratives. Even though Asian cinema has had many developments over the past twenty years, and countless young talents have emerged, Hou has confidently retained the same position and continued his explorations of culture and history. The vitality of Hou's body of work is undoubtedly related to his personal cultivation and self-awareness while its ability to transcend local Taiwanese consciousness and speak broadly to the intelligence of Asian culture has made a decisive contribution to the world.

Linked by ethnicity, Taiwanese and Mainlanders also share a long-standing cultural tradition that is both diverse and united. Colonization has gone on for three centuries and this has created elements of resistance that have not yet ceased, but the Taiwanese have always considered themselves part of the Chinese community. Traditions in Chinese culture are mutually recognized by Mainlanders and Taiwanese. The history of Taiwanese cinema over the past hundred years has given substance to them.

The emergence of the New Cinema of the 1980s is one of the most significant moments in Taiwanese culture. The New Cinema's ultimate goals were to reflect on the past, to reassess Taiwanese identity, and to reconstruct the language of cinema. Some would even go so far as to say that the New Cinema was committed to redefining the history of Taiwan and to establishing a unique culture of its own. However, when we look back on the works of the New Cinema, whether comprehensively or individually, it is clear that most of the works are associated with Chinese culture and Chinese history. Hou's films are representative of the period and they also embody the moral stance, aesthetic perspective, and sentiments of Chinese culture. At the same time, his films also reflect a more diffuse, multicultural point of view. In this way, they transcend the boundaries of Taiwan and constitute a sustained cinematic exploration of, and speculation on, the cultural heritage of Asia.

~

TAIWANESE CONSCIOUSNESS AND CHINESE THOUGHT IN THE "TRILOGY OF SADNESS"[1]

A Time to Live and a Time to Die (1985), *A City of Sadness* (1989), and *Good Men, Good Women* (1995) are rich in historical contexts and meanings that have been the subject most thoroughly addressed by critics. Through these three films, Hou depicted the spectrum of Taiwanese history across three generations of mainland immigrants, showing the development of their emotional attachment to and identification with Taiwan, the tragedies that resulted from the first transfer of Nationalist (KMT) sovereignty to Taiwan, and the hardships the general public faced during the Japanese colonial period. Some critics state that these three films have "constructed an innovative national cinematic context" for Taiwan.[2] In an era marked by freedom of interpretation and diverse voices, this phenomenon is indeed nothing special. However, interpretations driven by polarized ideologies are opposed to the intentions of Hou's films. As his body of work has demonstrated, he has adopted a neutral stance in order to document and disclose the complicated relationships with Chinese culture manifested by different generations of Taiwanese, aiming to reexamine Chinese history and to reassess the self-image of Taiwan over the course

of its changing history. The "Trilogy of Sadness" reveals Hou's objective attitude towards Taiwan's blood ties with mainland China and its historical evolutions while also recording the history of Taiwan and searching for a Taiwanese identity.

A Time to Live and a Time to Die is rooted in Hou's personal experience as a Chinese immigrant attempting to fit into Taiwanese society. It is the inception of his Taiwan Trilogy and also the introduction of his mature period as a director. In the words of Peggy Chiao: "*A Time to Live and a Time to Die* is Hou's autobiography, but thanks to its outstanding cinematic approach and profound message, it has created a language appropriate to the politics, economics, and social changes in Taiwan over the past few decades, and it has become one of the towering masterpieces in the history of Taiwan cinema."[3]

---

1) Editor's note: Many critics refer instead to *A City of Sadness*, *The Puppetmaster* (1993), and *Good Men, Good Women* as Hou's "Trilogy." The substitution of *A Time to Live and a Time to Die* for *The Puppetmaster* gives a different inflection to the arguments in this essay.

2) Lin Wenchi, Shen Shiao-ying, and Li Chen-ya, eds., *Passionate Detachment: Critical Essays on Hou Hsiao-hsien* (Taipei: Rye Field Publishing Company, 2000), 291

3) Chen Fei-bao, *The Art of Taiwan Film Directors* (Taipei: Ya-tai Publishing Company, 2000), 145

Good Men, Good Women, 1995

Lee Daw-ming claims that "this film, with enormous scope and breadth, attempts to juxtapose the 'Mainland Experience' and 'Mainland Complex' of the older immigrants from China with those of the younger generations born after the retrocession of Taiwan."[4] Hou was born in Guangdong in 1947 and moved to Taiwan with his parents in 1948.

From the perspectives of Taiwanese aborigines and the much earlier immigrants, Hou is considered a "Mainlander." He was not yet in Taiwan at the time of the "228 Incident" [1947]. However, it is precisely because he is an immigrant from a later generation that he has been so committed to inspecting the history of Taiwan and reflecting on its political tragedy. *A City of Sadness*, which addresses the injustice, was released after Martial Law was abolished, and it is once again because of his position as a Mainlander that Hou does not ignore the "Mainland Complex." He uses his personal experience, as well as those of his parents and grandparents, to delineate his Taiwanese life and identity, in the process evoking, retracing, and ultimately transforming the "Mainland Complex." The political, historical, and cultural links between Taiwan and mainland China exist objectively. They can never be denied or eliminated, even if one wants to. Some film critics misleadingly analyze Hou's films by using them as the grounds for political statements that run contrary to the historical and cultural perspectives embedded in his work.

Through the exploration of death in *A Time to Live and a Time to Die*, Hou accomplished his filial mission as a son/grandson to bid farewell to the mainland culture his grandparents and parents embraced. It is a story of growing up from childhood to adolescence that also contains, through its portrayal of the loss of the preceding generations, a fable of tradition (Hou also constructed stories around the theme of death in subsequent films). The history of family love and inherited ties shared by Taiwanese and Mainlanders is shown here authentically. Both the storyline and the ethics of *A Time to Live and a Time to Die* are structured around rituals of mourning. The parents and grandparents physically depart, but their mentality inescapably shapes the young protagonist. The name given by the grandmother, Ah-ha-gu (阿孝咕), contains the character for filial piety (孝). The father's filial piety, the mother's love,

---

4) Ibid

5) Editor's note: As Chen Huai-en explains in the interview included here, the central family in *A City of Sadness* would have originated in Keelung historically. The film was largely shot in the area around Chiufen [Jiufen].

A Summer at Grandpa's,
1984

and the descendants' self-condemnation and remorse all indicate that this deeply rooted traditional virtue does not die with the older generation, but is instead inherited by the later generations growing up on the island.

With the 228 Incident as the background, *A City of Sadness* is an epic film that depicts the transformation of Taiwanese society from 1945 to 1949, during the transition from Japanese political/cultural dominance to KMT sovereignty. Through the stories of life, departure, death, and separation in a family from Keelung, the film provides a despairing history of Taiwan during this transformative period.[5] The eldest of the four Lin brothers, Wen-heung, is a leader in the criminal underworld. He is devoted to his comrades, to supporting his family, and to the observance of filial piety, but he eventually dies in a gang war. The second brother was recruited as a military physician in Southeast Asia. He lost contact and never re-

turned. The third brother, Wen-leung, was forced to act as an interpreter for the Japanese; he is imprisoned after the war as a traitor and finally goes insane. Wen-ching, the youngest brother, is a mute running a photo studio. He is an intellectual with a critical mind and his own opinions. Although he cannot speak, he is a perspicacious observer of the world, which he documents with his camera. He exemplifies the silent witnesses of Taiwan's history, but he still could not escape from the darkness of the era and, in the end, he is devoured by the "228" tragedy.

A City of Sadness is an outstanding aesthetic achievement and its political and historical value lies in the way that it unwinds Chiang Kai-shek's shroud in its depiction of the injustice of "228." It digs into history, discloses the truth, and delineates the experiences of different Taiwanese communities. The film's epic historical narrative does not undercut its artistry, but instead extends its range, raising the level of Asian cinema through its profound humanistic implications. Even as it unveils the historical truth of this repressed moment in Taiwanese history, the film demonstrates Taiwan's historical attachment to China. As Chen Ru-shou has argued: "The attitude of the Taiwanese to China is always oscillating. Taiwanese culture is truly part of Chinese culture, but, at the same time, Taiwan still hopes to have its own unique culture acknowledged... Only when the Chinese from mainland China present themselves as the new conquerors of Taiwan and treat the Taiwanese (with their Japanese education) as second-class citizens will the close ties between Taiwanese culture and Chinese culture be severed. This results in the master-slave dynamic that made the 228 Incident inevitable."[6]

The film allows us to consider the trauma, origins, and consequences of the 228 Incident.

Hou portrays people from different social strata in *A City of Sadness*. In the first part of the film, there is a scene in which a group of Taiwanese intellectuals sing an anti-Japanese song together in a tavern. They had aspirations – for victory in the war with Japan and for the retrocession of Taiwan – that would be torn apart by politics. Wen-heung at one point says, "We are deprived by everyone, dominated by everyone, but looked after by no one." It is a complaint characteristic of the time that speaks to resentment at Taiwan's multiple roles in history. What does "everyone" mean? Who does it indicate? The Spanish or the Dutch colonialists, the Qing government, the brutal rule of the Japanese, or the corrupt tyranny of the KMT. Those who are not Taiwanese can hardly understand the situation of being repressed and enslaved under the political conditions of the Japanese colonial period [1895–1945]. Mainland China endured an eight year War of Resistance [1937–1945] and experienced the complexities of occupation and the contradictions of the anti-Japanese struggle. However, this is completely different from the colonial situation in Taiwan during the fifty years of Japanese domination. In his analysis of *A City of Sadness*, Chen Ru-shou opposes official history and collective memory: "...the public's memory can be multi-dimensional... Hou's perspective is only one facet, but what he presents is worth paying attention to, because the 228 Incident in *A City of Sadness* is no longer simply a life-and-death battle between the Taiwanese and the Chinese, but a battle among perceived social hierarchies. In other words, the Chinese from the powerful upper class repress the powerless Chinese masses and all Taiwanese. Those sacrificed during the 228 Incident and the subsequent White Terror include not only Taiwanese, but also those Chinese 'nobodies' who just wanted to survive in a turbulent world."[7]

In excavating the period between Taiwan's retrocession and the retreat of the KMT, Hou scrutinizes the relationship between Taiwan and China.

Hou continues his exploration in *Good Men, Good Women*, where he considers the repression of progressive intellectuals in the 1950s. Although the film's *mise-en-abyme* parallels the modern women of the 1990s with the patriotic youth fighting against Japan, the true focus remains on the tragic destiny of the Taiwanese intellectuals, dedicated to their country, who were murdered during the White Terror. The film is inspired by real figures in history: Chung Hao-tung and Chiang Pi-yu [Chiang Bi-yu]. In *A City of Sadness* historical characters are fictionalized and absorbed within an overall artistic creation, but an attempt is made in *Good Men, Good Women* to represent the experiences of particular individuals.

Good Men, Good Women depicts the patriotic Taiwanese who, despite the danger, returned to mainland China to join the guerrilla war against the Japanese, resulting in suspicion from the Nationalists that culminated in ridiculous trials. Although they become resentful ghosts, their self-assurance as Chinese and their faith in the Chinese nation are presented clearly. Whatever the filmmakers' intentions may have been in contrasting two generations of Taiwanese, the national identity of Taiwanese progressives like Chiang Pi-yu and Chung Hao-tung does not waver despite persecution and the miscarriage of justice. In Chung's will, he writes, "I was born on my homeland and I will die on my homeland. Death is destined and I shall have no thought about it." Their hope is that the Chinese island of Taiwan will be liberated from the Japanese invaders so that the promise of a democratic, independent, and equitable China will be fulfilled. Some critics have argued that this "reconstruction of the past" indicates "the challenge presented by the emerging 'Republic of Taiwan' to the mystery of Greater China."[8] This political reading, predicated on the idea that history can be interpreted subjectively,

6) Chen Ru-shou, *The Historical-Cultural Experiences of Taiwan New Cinema* (Taipei: Variety Publishing Company, 1994), 74

7) Ibid, 86

8) Lin, Shen, and Li, 291

distorts the history of the anti-Japanese struggle in Taiwan and also exaggerates the ideological element in Hou's films. No matter what happened later, the fact is that all of China, including the Taiwanese, rose up in the 1930s and 1940s to fight against the Japanese.

In examining the significant changes in the history of Taiwan over the course of a half century, Hou's "Trilogy of Sadness" demonstrates that Taiwanese identity is a product of the dispute of different political forces. At the same time, the moral heritage connecting the cultures of China and Taiwan are shown to be part of that identity. The emotions and relationships of the leading characters in all three films are entangled with Chinese politics, Chinese culture, and the "Mainland Complex." This is nevertheless complicated by the infiltration of foreign cultures and colonial practices. As Chen Ru-shou has argued: "... the social structure, the language, and the customs in Taiwan are not significantly different from those in mainland China. Confucianism is the principle of life. After all, the ancestors are mostly from the other side of the [Taiwan Strait]. If the island had passed directly from the Qing dynasty to the Republic of China, the variations would be negligible. However, the fifty years of Japanese dominance have given Taiwan a different his-

tory. The development of politics, society, economics, and other aspects of culture diverged along with the attitudes, virtues, and customs that accompany them."[9]

The political connotations and cultural perspectives embedded in this passage mirror those in Hou's films.

By emphasizing the viewpoints of the general public and depicting their experiences through an almost documentary-like cinematic language, Hou articulates the pathos of their social position. The leading characters in *A Time to Live and a Time to Die* and *A City of Sadness* are from the bottom of society, living in violence and turmoil and suffering from their cruel destiny. The puppet artist in *The Puppetmaster* (1993) emerges from an even more plebeian situation. Through these characters, Hou has given form to the powerless, helpless public's tolerance, resilience, self-esteem, and composure in the face of the ebbs and flows of time.

However, there are other analyses of Hou's "Trilogy of Sadness," informed by different historical perspectives and values that are worthy of attention. For instance: "Although most Taiwanese are Chinese immigrants migrated from the 'homeland' hundreds of years ago, 'the return' [to China in 1945] ... is not as simple as a slogan ... The several scenes about Japan in *A*

City of Sadness indicate that Taiwanese identify themselves as Chinese by considering Japan as a 'foreign nation' and 'other country.' However, having been dominated for fifty years, Taiwan established a closer relationship with Japan than with China. In the film, extremely bright light and alluring compositions are used in the scenes about Japan... and the reminiscences of days with Japanese friends... Even the Japanese film critic, Tamura Shizue claims that 'the Japan depicted in the film is way too beautiful. It is excessively embellished.' Such embellishment of Japanese culture and Taiwanese friendship with Japan suggests the feelings of loss and separation that accompanied the end of Japanese governance."[10]

The complications of political influence and cultural heritage continue to produce conflicts in historical interpretation. During the Japanese colonial period, some Taiwanese were murdered, repressed, or even forced to serve as barricades for the Japanese military. Others died from excessive work as laborers mining or constructing railroads. Still others resisted silently, sowing the seeds of resistance in their minds. There were also some people who

9) Chen Ru-shou, 57
10) Lin, Shen, and Li, 169

could not help but cooperate with the invaders. In the first half of the twentieth century, these invaders were the occupiers of Taiwan, treating Taiwanese as second-class colonial citizens. This internationally acknowledged historical truth can neither be changed nor obscured.

Nevertheless, some critics have mentioned a residual yearning for the Japanese colonial period. Regarding *The Puppetmaster*, for example, it has been argued that: "Taiwanese still retain a contradictory, complicated affection – juxtaposed with discrete hostility, repressed nostalgia, and jealousy – for Japan and Japanese culture. Only by considering the memories of the Japanese colonial period can we understand such a complicated love-hate relationship. The brutality towards, and discrimination against, the Taiwanese is undeniable, but the colonial government's development of infrastructure in Taiwan created the postwar economic miracle. Politically speaking, the Japanese were the enemies during the colonial period. However, on an individual level, Japanese colonialists established stable working relationships or even friendships with some Taiwanese during this period... Political struggle is unpractical... [and] political incidents are meaningless to the general public. They do not have time to reflect upon the meaning of Japan's surrender or

Taiwan's 'retrocession,' simply because they are busy surviving."[11]

For this critic, the above statements about brutality and discrimination are empty. They are simply a compulsory foreword that one has to make before making an argument. People only strive to "survive," and the sense of ethnic belonging or national identity is, for them, "meaningless." However, if the Japanese surrender did not have any meaning, if Japanese imperialism had continued and they continued to occupy Taiwan, what would it be like today to "be busy surviving?" Would the *kōminka* movement [a campaign launched in 1937 to eliminate Chinese culture in Taiwan] still continue now?

Social relationships between families are the basis of Hou's cinematic narratives. In traditional Chinese society, the family is a stable unit that maintains unity and the ethics of respect for seniority. It is the essential unit of social relations. However, Hou's films differ from the moral melodrama of conventional Chinese films in that the dramatic conflicts among members of a family are intentionally diminished or obscured. The relationships between self, others, and social incidents create the radius of the drama, enabling the family to play a more important role in the representation of

history. By downplaying melodramatic domestic struggles, the fate of each family member is able to suggest a more individualized conflict with society. Sometimes, eliding the direct presentation of an event creates a narrative gap, which sustains emotions by linking dramatic and calmer scenes. This is, along with his extremely long shots, one of the defining components of Hou's poetic and meditative style. Yet the philosophical value of Hou's approach goes beyond questions of cinematic style. His films emphasize historical reflection by encouraging the viewer to connect disjointed plots and thereby to consider layers of embedded meaning. The omission of Wen-ching's end in *A City of Sadness*, the abruptness of the deaths in *A Time to Live and a Time to Die*, and the lengthy depiction of Chiang Pi-yu's mourning for her husband coupled with the elision of the suffering of other victims can all be seen as manifestations of Hou's historical consciousness. He chose to pursue this course rather than to distract the viewer with simplistic entertainment and easy visual stimulation.

11) Ibid, 282

12) Chen Kuan-hsing, Hou Hsiao-hsien, and Wei Ti, "Visual Production and Political Involvement: an Interview with Hou Hsiao-hsien," *Dushu*, Number 8 (2006), 8

ASIAN CULTURE AND NOSTALGIA

Hou's early creations pivot around the theme of adolescent growth and the recognition of the local history of Taiwan. These two subjects are closely intertwined, which gives Hou's cinematic narratives a unique perspective marked by the amalgamation of personal history and ethnic development. Since the late 1990s, Hou has demonstrated groundbreaking ambition in his artistic interests and selection of material, allowing his considerations of, and nostalgia for, Asian culture to transcend the boundaries of Taiwan. The outstanding examples are *Flowers of Shanghai* (1998), the adaptation of a Chinese novel from the end of the Qing dynasty, and *Café Lumière* (2003), made in celebration of Japanese director Ozu Yasujirō's one hundredth birthday.

Hou explores his blood ties with traditional Chinese culture in *Flowers of Shanghai*, while showing his understanding of Japanese culture in *Café Lumière*. This complex cultural positioning is indicative of the Taiwanese director's consciousness of geopolitics and historical accretion. In Hou's personal experience and cultural inheritance, the marks of Chinese culture and ethics are extremely noticeable. His films clearly reinforce this. In a recent interview, he described this realization: "I think that if you have enough knowledge of Chinese culture, you will have more energy to express yourself when you reach to the West, and this approach is very different from the one in the West. I have started to wonder why Chinese films are supposed to do what European or American films do. You can never outshine simply by imitation. We have a completely different background. They have absorbed their traditions, logic, and abstract thinking since childhood, and ours are different."[12]

However, due to the influence of the half-century of Japanese colonization, the relationship between the cultures of Taiwan and Japan is extraordinary. The historical viewpoint embedded in Hou's films also reflects this. The interpretation of the culture and mentality of Japan in *Café Lumière* is antithetical to the one used in a film like *Hiroshima mon amour* (Alain Resnais, 1959) and it is not an exaggeration to claim that there is an affective stream flowing seamlessly between Japan and Taiwan. As Chen Ru-shou once observed when cataloguing the elements of Taiwanese culture, "the third feature is open-mindedness and a tolerance of foreign cultures. Deeply influenced by Chinese culture, Taiwanese culture simultaneously embraces Dutch, Qing/Manchu, Japanese, and, currently, American cultures. Such a fusion of influences is rarely seen in the world."[13] Modern Taiwan has been nourished by multiple cultures, among which that of the Japanese colonial period is the most prominent.

One of the most significant aspects of Hou's films is that they constitute a broad reflection on Asian history and culture, as demonstrated by their treatment of diverse influences. This reflection is neither superficial, an attempt to secure adulation through attractive images, nor demagogic, defined by emphatic mannerisms. Hou's consideration of Asian culture is connected to his nostalgic exploration of humanity. History inevitably provides the backbone and support for Hou's narratives. Some people claim that the Hou films that are set in a city or focused upon the languishing behavior of contemporary lovers are unsettled or incoherent. Such criticism is based on the idea that the spectators can see more than the players.

The Sing-song Girls of Shanghai is a novel written in Wu Chinese by the intellectual Han Bangqing in 1894. Difficulties in understanding the Shanghai dialect limited the reach of the novel and it was almost destroyed. However, it started to broadly circulate when Eileen Chang completed her Mandarin translation, and it has become one of the most valued works from this period of Chinese literature. Screenwritten by Chu Tien-wen, the film *Flowers of Shanghai* undoubtedly recalls the self-centered, talented Eileen Chang and simultaneously presents itself as a continuation of the history of Chinese women writers. Although Hou applied his characteristically equitable approach in adapting the story cinematically, a decisive contribution to the film's visual impact was made by the imaginative set and costume designs of Hwarng Wern-ying. They transform the plainness, simplicity, and unadorned realism characteristic of Hou's earlier films into a meditation on the Orientalist expressionism of late nineteenth century artists such as Gustav Klimt.[14] In this way, two female "authors," Chu Tien-wen and Hwarng Wern-ying, introduced significant female elements into a nostalgic film adapted from a late Qing novel, contributing an aesthetic delicacy that was not previously associated with Hou's films.

13) Chen Ru-shou, 56

14) The symbolic and decorative paintings of Gustav Klimt are famous for extensively applying "Oriental" techniques.

15) Editor's note: The performers indicated are stars from Hong Kong (Tony Leung, Michelle Reis, and Carina Lau) or Japan (Hada Michiko).

16) Editor's note: Ni Zhen was the screenwriter for *Raise the Red Lantern*, which was executive produced by Hou Hsiao-hsien.

Raise the Red Lantern,
Zhang Yimou, 1991

Flowers of Shanghai presents the lives and customs of old China, and it undoubtedly gave Hou a chance to express his ideas about Chinese culture. Set in a brothel in the foreign enclaves of Shanghai, the novel depicts the characteristics and mentalities of people from various backgrounds. Due to the novel's length, the film adaptation focused on the wealthy men Wang (played by Tony Leung), Hong, Luo, and the courtesans Crimson (played by Hada Michiko), Emerald (played by Michelle Reis), and Pearl (played by Carina Lau).[15] Most works on the lives of courtesans attempt to critique the repression and persecution of women, aiming to reclaim justice and reprimand the dark forces in feudal society. No matter how ambivalent or indirect the artistic language is, the social issues can never be ignored. By uniting critique with sensuousness, *Flowers of Shanghai* laments and empathizes with the misfortune of the courtesans while simultaneously eliciting amusement and appreciation. The level of visual display in *Flowers of Shanghai* – from the splendid, extravagant brothel to the luxurious costumes – far exceeds that of *Raise the Red Lantern* (Zhang Yimou, 1991) or *Farewell, My Concubine* (Chen Kaige, 1993).[16] It is not an overstatement to claim that *Flowers of Shanghai* applies Oriental customs and feminine attributes to cater to the curiosity of European viewers.

Flowers of Shanghai shows how women were able to free themselves from constraints and resist male dominance. For example, Emerald redeems herself and lives independently, and Pearl uses poison on the fifth junior master to avenge herself and protest his fraudulent marriage proposals. Although such protests do not necessarily change their fate – even after redeeming herself, a courtesan may end up resuming her old profession or becoming another's concubine – they do demonstrate women's yearning for freedom. The ending of the film, with its depiction of a brief respite after the ripples of still water, demonstrates sharp insight into the vanity fair of Shanghai in the waning days of feudalism.

In the same way that *The Puppetmaster* evokes and reflects upon the historical memories of Taiwan, *Flowers of Shanghai* demonstrates Hou's imaginative conception of China through its representation of the customs of the late Qing dynasty. The extravagant feasting

Flowers of Shanghai, 1998

and revelry of a *changsan* brothel and the self-indulgent life in the self-constrained building are Hou's metaphors for the dreams of old Shanghai. If, for Hou, the exploration of Taiwanese history entails the reproduction of an image that is as close as possible to reality, then his speculation on Chinese history is completely the opposite. The remote fantasy, the extravagant buildings, the elegant costumes, and the splendid feasts all reflect the ancient China in his imagination. The sentiment this induces is like that of a Han dynasty stele or a piece of Chinese ceramics – a representation that is familiar yet strange, nostalgic yet alien. It suggests a freeze frame of history, a spatial construction without temporality.

Although similar in its nostalgic tone and exploration of vanished eras, *Café Lumière* is done in another style. In this tribute film to Ozu, Hou applied his customary realist methods to a story about a modern woman retracing history. Unlike *Flowers of Shanghai*, *Café Lumière* suggests spatiotemporal fusion and the merger of memory and reality. Both films recall the work of older artists. *Flowers of Shanghai* is saturated with emotional resonances that suggest the writing of Eileen Chang. *Café Lumière* communes directly with *Tokyo Story* (Ozu Yasujirō, 1953) and *An Autumn Afternoon* (Ozu Yasujirō, 1962) through its imagery and cinematic language. The significance of this to Hou's body of work is abundantly clear.

Café Lumière uses its story of young Japanese writer Yōko's journey in search of Taiwanese composer Jiang Wen-ye's history living in Japan to establish a spiritual connection between past and present. However, the context for this is that Yōko came to Taiwan to be a Japanese teacher, fell in love with a young Taiwanese man, and became pregnant, thereby establishing a physical connection. Yōko spends a great deal of time studying this Taiwanese musician. Despite being pregnant, she refuses to marry her Taiwanese lover and spends her "coffee hours" on books and music, in the company of a Japanese man. The film makes Japan's links to Taiwan visible and there is a spatiotemporal realization of this relationship. Through the exploration of history, Japan and Taiwan are spiritually bridged in the present, which reflects Hou's orientation towards Asian culture.

Hou's narrative style is made to resonate with Ozu's in *Café Lumière*. The sympathetic depiction of family, the gentle but always silent father, the kind and virtuous mother, Yōko's mannerisms and her spiritual bond with her Japanese lover... these all suggest a reflexive and substantive dialogue with Ozu's cinema. By adopting an Ozu-like narrative and cinematic language and elaborating on the reserved, indefinite silences of his work, Hou affirms his status as a filmmaker dedicated to merging different Asian film cultures.

Café Lumière imbues its realistic silences with implied meanings. Yōko's perpetual train journey, traveling back and forth, suggests her incessant but futile pursuit as well as the collective experience of the Japanese public. The trains crisscrossing Tokyo Bridge evoke a uniquely Japanese sense of space. However, Yōko's Japanese boyfriend uses these trains to construct an imprisoning metal barricade in one of his graphic designs. The overlapping train cars surround the solitary human figure at the center, implying the constraints of modern life and explaining why the past is always

remembered during "coffee hours" with melodious music and fairytale fantasies.

In 2005, Hou directed *Three Times*, in which he compared the early twentieth century, the 1960s, and the contemporary moment. He explained, "I have a long-term project, which is called 'the best moments'... which is not about how good those moments are, but about the irrecoverable past. I will make a series on this time that will include documentaries aiming to authentically present history with various perspectives and different kinds of people."[17] It is difficult for Hou to extract history from his films, since it has long been their subject matter and focus, beginning in Taiwan and extending out to all of Asia.

THE REALISTIC IMAGE AND THE POETIC HUMANIST FILM

Hou's films are unique in their fusion of extremely realistic imagery and poetic narratives. These narratives are informed by historical reflection as well as a desire for self-expression and by aesthetic considerations. Abandoning conventional plot exposition, Hou combines the poetic representation of quotidian trifles with realistic images, thereby embodying "a humanist cinema that always embraces compassion for others."[18] He once explained that his

17) Chen Ru-shou, 56

18) Edmond Wong, *In Search of Humanist Films* (Taipei: Yuan-liou Publishing Company, 1990), 61

films are seen as unusual in Europe: "... not only because of the long shots, but also because of the style and structure of the story, that is, the perspective. This perspective and treatment of space cannot be found in other countries. My films are close to Taoism. There is no answer, it is just an expression of an individual or an incident. Put another way, they are simply a feeling, a reflection."[19]

Hou's cinematic style has been broadly studied. The consensus is that his films feature a poetic style and that his poetics are centered on the human essence, thereby leading to self-examination.

Taiwanese critic Peggy Chiao points out that Hou is not only an artist with self-awareness, but also a historian with a sense of commitment. Cinema is his writing tool. This has helped him make a unique contribution to cinematic language. Many Western scholars and critics have shown special interests in this cinematic language. For example, Vincent Canby of *The New York Times* wrote that "Hou's cinematic language is rather similar to that of [Jean-Luc] Godard in his early days. *A Summer at Grandpa's* [1984] seems to be influenced by [François] Truffaut. *Daughter of the Nile* [1987] reminds us of Godard and Ozu."[20] Many reviews have juxtaposed Hou's films with Ozu's.

This is because Hou and Ozu prefer establishing long shots and find inspiration in details of quotidian life, and also because their works embody an Asian philosophy. Chiao has explained that Hou tends to construct elliptical narratives and uses the extension of time in his long takes to transform the meaning of "realism." This style is influenced less by Western films than by Chinese philosophy / religion and Hou's reflection on the aesthetics of Chinese poetry.

Many of these reviews focus only on Hou's early films, but the continuity and stability of his cinematic language and artistic style has always been remarkable. Hou's poetic narrative approach is rooted in historical interpretation and an awareness of the place of human destiny in the context of historical evolution. The films depict states of being by obsessively fixating upon the minutiae of life. Passing, quotidian details are transformed by the solicitous contemplation of the long take, which lets time accumulate, extending its fluid nature, and prompting reflection and evocation. Hou often combines these with long shots, providing a more detached and distanced view of narrative events. He seldom switches to closer shots – refusing to manipulate viewers or abuse their emotions – and strives to retain an unperturbed, observational stance.

Extreme long shots appear frequently in Hou's films. These shots emphasize the relationship between tiny characters and their surroundings, natural elements, and sometimes the expression of deep emotions. Essential components of Hou's cinematic language, extreme long shots demonstrate the connections between humans and nature and his attitude to life. Through them, his films are able to convey the Asian poetic idea of continuity, like the water under the bridge.

Long shots situate narrative development and social relationships within a more complete space. Combining them with long takes makes it possible to present the evolution of a life through small details, creating a unified spatiotemporal reality. Long shots force viewers to view story more objectively and to contemplate its development more deeply. Bertolt Brecht coerced a feeling of "alienation" in order to force spectators to withhold their emotions and reflect upon what is presented. Hou instead pursues a moderate, distinctively Asian approach to *mise-en-scène*, intermingling sentiment and reason to facilitate both observation and realization, as if the viewer were both an outsider and a participant.

The long shot opens up space so that crucial actions and strong conflicts happen deep within the image (e.g. the soldier's arrests and the death of Wen-heung in *A City of Sadness*).

The avoidance of medium or close-up shots to embellish effects sets Hou's work apart, encouraging viewers to focus on moral judgments and social conflicts, while still remaining strongly affected by dramatic action. Shots stress relationships among groups or between two individuals. In conversation scenes, the shot / countershot method used in most films is replaced by long or medium shots. "The tutor code of classical cinema," the alternation of medium shots of individuals, is generally applied throughout the entirety of most American films, concealing the presence of the filmmaker.[21] Hou's two shot method does the opposite. It clearly designates a third vantage point. This position suggests a non-participating attitude, a point from which conversations and emotions can be observed without disruption. The meaning of life, the feeling of helplessness, memories of family love, and natural landscapes are all contained within these lin-

19) Chen Fei-bao, 159

20) Lin, Shen, and Li, 26

21) Editor's note: "The Tutor Code of Classical Cinema" is the title of an essay by French theorist Daniel Dayan that was originally published in *Film Quarterly* in 1975 and translated into Chinese in 1987.

gering shots. These shots are the fullest and most evident manifestations of Hou's cinematic language and his greatest contribution to Chinese cinema. They also reflect his understanding of the ideas about external objects central to Chinese philosophy.[22]

There are obvious differences of philosophical orientation, artistic form, and genre separating Western and Asian cinemas. Over the past century, Asian cinema has developed unique styles and has made a contribution to global film culture. Asian cinema consists of two streams – the spectacular and the elegant – and Hou's films undoubtedly belong to the latter. In the decades since the 1980s, his firm but gentle epics have been a very important phenomenon in Asian cinema, encouraging dialogue between different generations of Asian filmmakers. Early models for his style would include Fei Mu and Wu Yonggang from China, Lee Hsing from Taiwan, and Ozu and perhaps Naruse Mikio from Japan. Other directors closer to Hou's era – for instance, Heo Jin-ho from South Korea, Tran Anh Hung from Vietnam, and Huo Jiangqi from China, along with many other emerging talents – have revealed their interest in his elegant style in various ways. Emerging film talents are continuously coming into view and it is clear that Hou's films

have influenced, and continue to influence, Asian filmmakers. Through Hou's work, Asian cinema has extended its impact, and developed its cultural meaning, worldwide. Hou is still creating films and their interactions with currents in Asian cinema will continue to be a subject of discussion. There is great anticipation for new works by Hou Hsiao-hsien.

Translated by Dennis Li

22) In an interview about *Flowers of Shanghai*, Hou states: "From *The Boys from Fengkuei* [1983] to *Flowers of Shanghai*, my transformation is that I used to think the camera has to be zoomed out so that an elevated, indifferent viewpoint could be presented. However, in *Flowers of Shanghai*, I realized that this is not necessarily true. The position should be decided according to the way the characters are being presented. If you are very calm in the right spot, you can like them, love them, and be with them, but you also have a pair of eyes on the side to observe them. No matter how close the shot is, you can still create that kind of effect" (Lin, Shen, and Li, 344). This explains why Hou changed his approach mid-career.

Jean-Michel Frodon

Unexpected but Fertile Convergence

This is the story of an unpredictable convergence, about how two complex worlds, which ostensibly had very little in common, met. It is the story of a personal adventure experienced, and accomplished, by Hou Hsiao-hsien, but also of a larger cultural achievement. And it is a promise. As in a Hou film, the story can, and should, be told from different points of view – as it happened to the one who was its agent, and as it was received by those who, against all odds, engaged with it. They did so as the result of a long process with complex cinematic, cultural, and geopolitical backgrounds.

GENEALOGY

When Hou began to direct movies, at the end of the 1970s, he was an ambitious young man who believed that this job was likely to provide money and an easy life. More than his studies at the National Taiwan College of Arts, the mentorship of veteran director Lee Hsing taught him how to become a skillful mainstream filmmaker. He had successfully directed three sentimental comedies when something happened. This "something" is rooted in Hou's personal experience as well as the changing nature of Taiwanese society. The essence of this turning can be summed up through two decisive encounters.

The first was with a young and already famous female writer, Chu Tien-wen. They met because she was the author of a short story from which the director wrote a script. This will generate the film known as *Growing Up* (1983), directed by Chen Kun-hou, but in the making of which Hou was actively involved. Later, he would often mention this film as a sort of transition between his early career in cinema and his "real" debut. At first, the meeting of Chu and Hou personified the meeting of literature and cinema. She was a writer who knew nothing about movies (and did not care at all), he was a filmmaker who knew very little about books (and was fine with that). It became much more, however, as a result of what Chu was able to contribute.

Chu's own biography embodies the ambivalent situation of being a "Chinese/Taiwanese" writer, a situation that is fundamental to so many modern Taiwanese artists: her father was a mainland Chinese writer actively involved with the Nationalists during the anti-Japanese war, her mother was a descendant of a well-known family of the Taiwanese intelligentsia. Like her two sisters, Chu began to write and publish when she was very young, rapidly becoming a celebrated writer. When Hou decided to adapt one of her first short stories,

75

"The Story of Little Bi," the source of *Growing Up*, they became friends. She introduced him to traditional and modern Chinese and Taiwanese literature, and to the depths of Chinese culture, thanks to her extensive knowledge of painting, music, stage arts, and calligraphy.

She deeply influenced his style, as he has often acknowledged, from the time he made the first feature of his new career, *The Boys from Fengkuei* (1983). As he recalled: "I did not know how to film *The Boys from Fengkuei*. Chu Tien-wen gave me the autobiography of the writer Shen Congwen. Reading it gave me solutions for directing. I got acquainted with the idea of 'looking from afar,' as if watching the world's disorders in a detached way. While shooting *The Boys from Fengkuei*, I kept saying to the director of photography [Chen Kun-hou]: 'Move backward. Further away.' I intended to look at things from as far away as possible, with the coldest attitude."[1]

This "attitude," and among other things, the "move backward" would decisively affect the future direction of his work.

The second major encounter took place at almost the same time, or immediately after. Hou got in touch with a group of young would-be filmmakers returning from the United States: Tao Te-chen, Ko I-cheng, Chang Yi, Wan Jen, Tseng Chuang-hsiang, and, most importantly, Edward Yang. Not only was Yang bright, energetic, and talented, he also had the most extensive background and training. The others were film students, but (after a disappointing attempt to enter a film studies department) Yang had studied electronics and had worked as a high level engineer in Seattle during most of the 1970s. He was one of the first to explore the possibility of converting Chinese ideograms into computer language. He had also been exposed, enthusiastically, to the West Coast counterculture, and he became an expert in European New Wave cinemas, able to show (on videotapes), to explain, and to discuss endlessly films by Jean-Luc Godard, Michelangelo Antonioni, Werner Herzog or Milos Forman. Soon after he came back to Taipei, his house on Tsinan Road became a sort of permanent film school as well as the headquarters of the emerging Taiwanese New Cinema. The movement was launched with two omnibus films, *In Our Time* (1982) made of four shorts, of which Yang's *Expectations* is obviously the most significant, and *The Sandwich Man* (1983), where Hou's contribution is by far the most accomplished and promising.

FILMOGRAPHY

For three decades, Hou's work has explored an extraordinary range of artistic propositions: the interactions between individual and collective history, the relationship between China and Taiwan, the link between Time and Space, and the loss of reference points in a world driven by ultra-fast capitalist development, lack of democracy, submission to standardized ways of life, globalization, and new technology. Set in the present and the past, circulating between ages (*Good Men, Good Women*, 1995; *Three Times*, 2005) and even into the future (*Millennium Mambo*, 2001), foreign locations (*Café Lumière*, 2003, *Flight of the Red Balloon*, 2007), and dreams, his films constitute a singular universe. This singularity can be described, to a large extent, as the innovative and very personal translation of the canons of traditional Chinese culture

into cinematic language. Of course, Hou is certainly not the only one to have achieved such a translation. One might cite Fei Mu as a front-runner, and, with important references to the Chinese artistic tradition, the mainland Fifth Generation provided a bold and creative reinvention of Chinese cinema after the Cultural Revolution. Just as a very simple example, the opening shot of Chen Kaige's *Yellow Earth* (1984) openly evokes traditional Chinese painting, with the importance given to Void spaces, the minimization of the human presence in the landscape, and the prioritization of a graphic treatment of nature and emotion. The use of sound and the symbolism of the color red (far removed from the official use) also contribute to this process.[2] In totally different ways, many art movies have adapted some aspects of Chinese aesthetics into cinematic language. However, very few (if any) have so persistently and so creatively reconceived cinematic language through a "Chinese *Weltanschauung*" or vision of the world. By some apparently inexplicable process, none of the others have received such enthusiastic support from Western cinephiles (who remain almost completely ignorant about Chinese culture).

Since *The Boys from Fengkuei* and especially since *A City of Sadness* (1989), Hou's cinema has

1) Extract of *The China Times* (November 19, 1984), translated from Chinese by Mimi Tan and Peggy Chiao

2) This has been widely exposed and discussed, for instance in Xudong Zhang, *Chinese Modernism in the Era of Reforms: Cultural Fever, Avant-garde Fiction, and the New Chinese Cinema* (Durham, NC: Duke University Press, 1997) or in the Chinese section of Linda Ehrlich and David Desser, eds., *Cinematic Landscapes: Observations on the Visual Arts and Cinema of China and Japan* (Austin, TX: University of Texas Press, 1994), especially in Ni Zhen's text, "Classical Chinese Painting and Cinematographic Signification," 63–80.

Three Times, 2005

moved away from any form of classical drama-
turgy. It does not seem to relate to the rhetorical systems the Western world has been
brought up with, for millennia, with what we
used to call a *story* – whether told, written,
staged, or filmed. Hou's cinema suggests a
relationship to both reality and imagination
that does not correspond to the Greek and
Judeo-Christian patterns that are the core of
Western civilization. Instead, Hou's cinema develops connections between part and whole,
the flow of time and the organization of space,
reality and representation, the inside and the
outside, that relate to a completely different
conceptual system – a different philosophy, a
different cosmology, a different aesthetic, a
different ethic – than the one dominant in the
Western world.[3] This is manifested in numerous ways, the most explicit being the non-sepa
rated world(s) of word and image in the
ideogram, which is at the same time drawing
and writing. One might recall the visionary,

though partially distorted, meditation by Sergei
Eisenstein about the proximity and difference
of cinematic montage and Chinese ideograms
in "The Cinematographic Principle and the
Ideogram."[4] Eisenstein points out that ideo-
grammatic writing establishes a totally different
relationship between reality, meaning, and
representation than the Western paradigm
through which the language of cinema has
been understood since the beginning.

PHILOSOPHY AND EDITING

Hou's cinema, more deeply and with a
stronger power of seduction than that of any
other Chinese filmmaker, responds to another
conception of the world, in the largest sense
possible. His works challenge the classical cinematic language elaborated by D. W. Griffith
and Eisenstein. Since the time of the Founding
Fathers, this classical syntax has benefitted
from inventions in many directions; one might
even argue that a major cineaste is someone
who opens up, at least for himself, a new way
of organizing images, frames, sounds, rhythms,
characters, etc. They do so, however, always as
variations within a framework that inherited
the storytelling patterns established by the
Bible, Homer, Aristotle, and all those who
came after. Although it is immensely complex

3) This has also been acknowledged by Chinese critics and
film academics such as Ni Zhen, Li Tuo or Meng
Hungfeng (quoted and discussed by James Udden in
No Man an Island: The Cinema of Hou Hsiao-hsien,
Hong Kong: Hong Kong University Press, 2009, 1).

4) Sergei Eisenstein, *Film Form* (New York: Harcourt Brace,
1949), 28–44.

and rich, this general schema can be encapsulated by the basic principle known in philosophy, in logics, in mathematics, and in the physical sciences, as the *"tertium non datur,"* the Law of the Excluded Middle: something is or is not.

From a Chinese point of view, this is a totally alien way of thinking. As François Jullien's extensive comparison of Chinese and Western modes of thought has enlighteningly demonstrated, this difference – so vast and complex it certainly cannot be discussed here – testifies both to the fact that the Western approach is only one option, and to the immense resources accessible through the acknowledgement of the multiplicity of options. No rule says that the Western and the Chinese models are the only two possibilities.[5]

Among the many alternative possibilities opened up for a Westerner by an encounter with the Chinese vision of the world lies the important concept of Void, or Vacuity.[6] One of its major formal expressions can be found in traditional Chinese painting, where the unpainted (more precisely, un-inked) white paper not only occupies the majority of the surface, but contains the essential strengths and beauty the work is meant to convey. There are a number of formal, visual and narrative equivalences

to the idea of Void in Hou's cinema, most notably the systematic decision to move the camera backward, to enlarge the frame to a point where environment (not only the place, or the landscape, but the cosmos itself) becomes at least as important as what is being done by this or that character. Hou himself grounded this strategy in traditional Chinese philosophy when he quoted Confucius – "Watch and don't interact," "Observe and don't judge" – to explain its origins.[7] Among the many examples from his films, one might identify as particularly significant the killing in *A City of Sadness*, which is seen from a distance by a fixed camera that embraces the whole landscape, minimizing human actions and especially violent attempts to transform the world. Similar strategies are used in the same film when the battle

5) François Jullien's works translated in English include: *The Propensity of Things: Toward a History of Efficacy in China* (New York: Zone Books, 1995), *Detour and Access: Strategies of Meaning in China and Greece* (New York: Zone Books, 2000), *A Treatise on Efficacy: Between Western and Chinese Thinking* (Honolulu, HI: University of Hawaii Press, 2004), *In Praise of Blandness: Proceeding from Chinese Thought and Aesthetics* (New York: Zone Books, 2004), *The Impossible Nude: Chinese Art and Western Aesthetics* (Chicago: University of Chicago Press, 2007), *Vital Nourishment: Departing from Happiness* (New York: Zone Books, 2007), *The Great Image Has No Form, or, On the Nonobject through Painting* (Chicago: University of Chicago Press, 2009).

inside the gangsters' house is continued outdoors, as a very small event in a silent city. In *The Puppetmaster* (1993), dramatic events are sometimes shot from so far back that the viewer can hardly be aware of them, generating a very special feeling afterwards, the awareness that something happened without an immediate understanding of the details – which, in fact, gives the event an underlying meaning that goes beyond the specifics. Rhythmic choices – oriented partially, but not exclusively, around sequence shots – also demonstrate this kind of equivalence.

There is something else, possibly even more significant, that cinema owes to Hou Hsiaohsien alone (although others came later on the same tracks): editing. Editing here should be understood in its real and complex meaning,

which goes far beyond the idea of cutting and pasting shots in a certain order and at a certain length. Editing is actually another name for *mise-en-scène*, in the sense that it refers to the ways in which filmic elements are related to each other – within the same shot, from one shot to the next, or in the relation between image and sound (since there is, of course, sound editing, and mixing is nothing more than editing images with sounds). In this sense – only in this sense – editing is the language of cinema itself.

Quite naturally, this language has been developed according to the basics of the culture its founders came from, this immense body of implicit assumptions that organizes a certain perception of "things" (reality, imagination, ideas) as if it was the only possible way to do so. These assumptions, to a large extent based on the *tertium non datur* schema, are, notwithstanding gigantic areas of difference and their extraordinary personal creativity, common to Griffith, Orson Welles, Alfred Hitchcock, Eisenstein, Dziga Vertov, Fritz Lang, Roberto Rossellini, Ingmar Bergman, Godard... The basic framework has been appropriated, with limited changes, by such great non-Western cinema artists as Ozu Yasujirō, Satyajit Ray, and Ousmane Sembène.

6) See, for instance: "When it is understood that the Vacuity, the Void, is nothing but material force, then existence and nonexistence, the hidden and the manifested, spirit and eternal transformation, and human nature and destiny are all one and not a duality. He who apprehends integration and disintegration, form and absence of form, and trace them to their source, penetrates the secret of Change" (Wing-tsit Chan, ed., *A Source Book in Chinese Philosophy*, Princeton, NJ: Princeton University Press, 1963, 502).

7) Emmanuel Burdeau, "Rencontre avec Hou Hsiao-hsien" in Jean-Michel Frodon, ed., *Hou Hsiao-hsien*, Second Edition (Paris: Éditions Cahiers du cinéma, 2005), 76

For reasons that relate mainly to his double background (the Chinese aesthetic and visual tradition; the modern cinema's questioning of existing rules), Hou's approach to editing would precipitate a major shift, whose effect could be compared with the non-Euclidian revolution. A very simple and explicit example is offered by the crazy grandmother in *A Time to Live and a Time to Die* (1985). She continuously tries to walk home, that is to walk from the remote town on the island of Taiwan where she now lives to her former home in mainland China, which she believes is within walking range. She is "crazy" since she ignores, or refuses to acknowledge, the partition of the world imposed not so much by geography as by history – history that has broken the continuity of the universe, the very same continuity that, in geopolitical terms, maintained the unity of the Chinese Empire for more than thirty centuries. The title of James Udden's important study of Hou's work is appropriately titled *No Man an Island*, which refers to the widely discussed fact that Hou's films relate with his environment while also implicitly emphasizing the extent to which his characters are connected to each other, to landscapes, to the past, to entanglements of all kinds.

The old woman is literally haunted by the ancestral wisdom of an absolute immanence, the general co-presence of everything to everything. This goes beyond the (Western) opposition between rationalism and fantasy, it actually dismisses it. The Western Law of the Excluded Middle is the necessary basis for the notion of transcendence, a notion that does not have any conceptual relevance to the immense sociopolitical and cultural area that, appropriately, has been calling itself for millennia the "Kingdom of the Middle" (Zhongguo, the Chinese name of China). This acceptance of the possibility of the contiguity of all things – a contiguity that can be shown, dreamed, experienced, built – is the foundation of Hou's *mise-en-scène*. It eventually opens to the temporal vertigo of *Good Men, Good Women*, which interconnects different periods and different levels of reality in a way that suggests political interrogations, of the present as well as the past.

As he moves forward in his own career, Hou utilizes more and more intricate narrative elements, according to more and more integrated guidelines that finally seem to disappear, giving way to a continuum that directly mirrors the continuity of reality itself – a "seamless fabric of reality" that André Bazin could not have even dreamed of, a process without beginning

A Time to Live and a Time to Die, 1985

or end (like history itself).[8] This mode of composition discards, to a certain extent, Gilles Deleuze's opposition of the Movement Image and the Time Image. Hou has also made increasing use of the resources of sound, including voiceover, then voices-over, and even, in the mesmerizing opening sequence of *Millennium Mambo* where the female character speaks from 2011 in 2001, a voiceover from the future. Though hardly recognizable to Western ears, the impression of co-presence is also created by the interweaving of various Chinese languages (Taiwanese, Mandarin, Cantonese, Shanghainese, etc.). Music is also part of this process. For instance, in *Flowers of Shanghai* (1998), the multilayered score composed by musician Hanno Yoshihiro and sound designer Tu Duu-chih, Hou's master accomplice, replicates, in an even more complex manner, the atmosphere of seduction, betrayal, dedication, and despair created by the film.

FROM THE EAST, FROM THE WEST

We already know how this became possible. In addition to the creativity and the sensibility of this single man nicknamed HHH, the phenomenon derives from the double genealogy discussed above, the encounters, at almost the same moment, with traditional Chinese culture and the experiments of modern European cinema. This very particular situation was unique.[9] It happened to a director who proved able not only to embody this fusion, but also to use it to move forward, constantly learning from it. Although each of Hou's films clearly bears his signature, and reflects this collision of worlds, they are all significantly different from one another.

In recent years, a few very talented and open-minded younger directors from the same cultural and geographical area – Tsai Ming-liang, Jia Zhang-ke, or Apichatpong Weerasethakul – have been able to achieve their own synthesis. What makes Hou so significant and influential, aside from the extraordinary artistic and politico-historical value of his work, is the way his cinema became a new bridge between East and West. If Hou's films are so informed by traditional Chinese art, why is it that Western film lovers were able to respond so strongly while remaining almost totally ignorant of this background?[10] The intensity of this response, at least among the dedicated lovers of the art of film, can be explained because they had some access to it. They had the keys to enter his world. This may have been, at least partly, the result of misunderstandings. If that is the case, so what? It could not have been a total misunderstanding, of course, because the modern European cinema is part of Hou's cinematic DNA. There is also a more mysterious, chal-lenging, and potentially encouraging, reason. Such talented hands made it clear that there actually are meeting points between Western modernity and Chinese tradition. Leaving aside simplistic binaries, it actually appears that modern Western artists – in various attempts to break or to rewrite the rules of narration and representation – sought, met, or found echoes in what was for centuries the way Chinese artists and thinkers had been composing *their* relation to the real and imaginary world. In this sense, Western modernity does have similarities with Chinese tradition.

This was not a total discovery. It did not come out of the blue. Situated within the whole Western history of the arts, this phenomenon can be related to the generative use of external stimuli, to, for example, the models

8) The expression, used by Bazin in his *Jean Renoir* (Paris: Éditions Champ libre, 1971, 84), became the motto of one of his basic theories, referring to the fundamental relation between spatiotemporal continuity and a certain idea of cinema that he repeatedly advocated. it is significant that one of the films that Bazin uses as an important example was Albert Lamorisse's 1956 *The Red Balloon* (in the essay "The Virtues and Limitations of Montage" in *What is Cinema?*, Volume 1, translated by Hugh Gray, Berkeley, CA: University of California Press, 1967, 41–52). The film inspired Hou's *Flight of the Red Balloon* (2007), testifying to a continuity, with obvious and more secret aspects, between Bazin's idea of cinema and Hou's cinematic practice.

9) The situations are too different to be compared, but one could argue that, to a certain extent, similar collisions gave birth to a few African films like Djibril Diop Mambéty's *Touki Bouki* (1973) or Souleymane Cissé's *Yeelen* (1987), two explicit fusions of the heritage of modern Europe and non-Western cultural backgrounds.

10) In the first Western festival where it was screened (the 1984 Festival of Three Continents in Nantes), *The Boys from Fengkuei* was awarded the number one prize, the Golden Montgolfiere.

85

provided to modern painters by Japanese, Arab, and African aesthetics. This type of interaction is rare in cinema. External influences can hardly be found in F. W. Murnau and Robert Flaherty's South Pacific (*Tabu*, 1931), in the India of Jean Renoir or Rossellini (*The River,* 1951; *India Matri Bhumi,* 1959), hardly more in the work of Pier Paolo Pasolini, despite his *Notes towards an African Orestes* (1970). There was Glauber Rocha, true, but he worked alone, ultimately doomed to solitude.

One might argue that if the greatest Western filmmakers did not find a way to take advantage of these resources – the films are excellent, of course, even if they do not significantly transform the already existing cinematic language – it may be because cinema relates too strongly to its cultural and geopolitical origin. It seems that, from a Western point of view, the impetus had to come from abroad, from afar – from another side of the world, so to speak.[11] It did come – not only, but much more strongly and consistently than from anywhere else – from China. It came during the early 1980s and continues even now.

The idea of changing cinema by relating Western modernity and Chinese tradition offers more than a strange analogy. It contains the promise of a potential renewal in storytelling and of formal invention, the opening of new cinematic horizons. And the name of the one who accomplished the most significant, and the most celebrated, part of this groundbreaking operation is Hou Hsiao-hsien.

11) Exploring similar issues from a different point of view, Hamid Naficy reaches a similar conclusion in *An Accented Cinema: Exilic and Diasporic Filmmaking* (Princeton, NJ: Princeton University Press, 2001).

Jean Ma

A Reinvention of Tradition

Hou Hsiao-hsien's The Puppetmaster

In an interview conducted shortly after the release of *The Puppetmaster* in 1993, director Hou Hsiao-hsien presents the film as a preservationist project, one aimed at "exploring the values of traditional culture which we have lost, particularly at this [materialist and technological] juncture of our existence."[1] These values are embodied in the film's subject, Li Tien-lu, a renowned performer in the arts of drama and indigenous hand puppet theater, or *budai xi*, whose true life story beginning with his birth in 1910 and ending with the moment of liberation in 1945 provides the source for the film's narrative. Hou describes him as a "living encyclopedia of Chinese tradition," someone who "preserves the values of traditional drama within himself," his words recall the honor of "National Living Treasure" bestowed upon Li Tien-lu in 1989 by Taiwan's government.[2] The contrast between modernity and a cultural tradition on the brink of disappearance is further emphasized in Hou's understanding of

his project in direct contradistinction to the Chinese modernity envisioned by the May Fourth movement which, as he puts it, "made a fetish of the West" as signifier of the new and "created an attitude that rejected tradition."[3]

Such a project seems to affirm the prevalent characterization of Hou Hsiao-hsien as a sentimental auteur in writings on the contemporary cinema of Taiwan. For many, his retrospective predisposition first manifested itself in the works of the 1980s that propelled him into the critical spotlight, several of which (*A Summer at Grandpa's*, 1984, *A Time to Live and a Time to Die*, 1985, and *Dust in the Wind*, 1986) explore the island's pre-industrial past through the coming-of-age narrative. The film trilogy on twentieth century history Hou embarked upon with *A City of Sadness* (1989) – of which *The Puppetmaster* comprised the second installment – further testified to the director's fixation on the past by earning him a reputation as Taiwan's premier cinematic historiographer. In accordance with such themes, nostalgia and melancholy have been identified as the affective signature of his films, accounting for their attention to "the earthy details of Taiwanese country life," their "antiquated, sentimental charm," and their "strong sense of the continu-

1) Peggy Chiao, "History's Subtle Shadows: Hou Hsiao-hsien's *The Puppetmaster*," *Cinemaya*, Number 21 (Autumn 1993), 11

2) Ibid, 4

3) Ibid, 5

ity of Chinese culture and history rooted in an agrarian sensibility."[4]

Moreover, this attraction to history has been construed as a response to modernity, precipitated by the radical social changes accompanying Taiwan's transformation from an agrarian economy to a key player in the global marketplace, changes which Hou's generation was positioned to witness and experience with special acuity. As the well-known Taiwanese film critic and producer Peggy Chiao notes of Hou and more generally of the New Cinema movement with which he was associated during the 1980s, "nostalgia for the past... is usually coupled with criticisms of the big city."[5] Similarly, William Tay has discussed the collision of values staged in Hou's work, wherein an "unstained and innocent countryside always remains in idealistic opposition to, if not an alternative to, the city, which is usually portrayed as the embodiment of deception, corruption, and exploitation."[6]

If readings in this vein provide important insights into an earlier period of Hou's films by calling attention to the social context informing his thematic proclivities and historicizing their historical impulse, as it were, the sentimentalist portrait of the director himself is tested by his more recent works, which tackle the subject of contemporary urban life. However, even in a film such as *The Puppetmaster* – with its focus upon an art with deep roots in regional tradition, social ritual and festival, and the rural life of an earlier time – modernity is a central if not immediately apparent concern, figuring symptomatically as the invisible stakes of tradition, hence as a sort of present absence. In the following analysis, I will approach the relationship between tradition and modernity by focusing upon, on the one hand, how *budai xi* is represented as a popular art capable of bringing the past into the present – that is, as a vehicle of history – and, on the other hand, how it serves as a reflexive meditation on the modern medium of cinema.

Accordingly, my discussion of the film's historicizing strategies will encompass its formal

4) Alvin Lu, "Hou and Pop!" *Cinema Scope*, Number 3 (Spring 2000), 32; [Emilie] Yeh Yueh-yu, "Politics and Poetics of Hou Hsiao-hsien's Films," *Post Script*, Volume 2, Numbers 2–3 (Winter/Spring and Summer 2001), 66; Nick Browne, "Introduction" in Nick Browne, Paul G. Pickowicz, Vivian Sobchack, and Esther Yau, eds., *New Chinese Cinemas: Forms, Identities, Politics* (Cambridge: Cambridge University Press, 1994), 5

5) Peggy Chiao, "Contrasting Images: Taiwan and Hong Kong Films," translated by Wendy Wong in *Free China Review*, Volume 38, Number 2 (February 1988), 12

6) William Tay, "The Ideology of Initiation: The Films of Hou Hsiao-Hsien" in Browne, Pickowicz, Sobchack, and Yau, 155

The Puppetmaster, 1993

as well as thematic attributes, addressing the ways in which it mimics the very structures of vernacular storytelling. At the intersection of cinema and *budai xi*, two media forms that can claim both aesthetic and entertainment value, what we find is not so much a collision of opposing cultural values rooted in modern and traditional life, respectively, but rather an attempt to reconcile the old with the new, to comprehend the past as a history of the present, and to negotiate between the continuity of tradition and the inevitability of change. These concerns pay homage to Li Tien-lu as not only a performing artist, but also as a survivor of history and "a link from the past to the present."[7]

BETWEEN POPULAR ART AND POPULAR HISTORY

The Puppetmaster is the centerpiece of a trilogy that can be described as a counterhistorical project, exploring a set of experiences occluded from the chronicles of official history until Taiwan's post-Martial Law era and bringing into the light of public discussion a past long suppressed by censorship.[8] The context of local history is explicitly marked in the film's opening intertitles: "The Treaty of Shimonoseki signed by the Manchu government in 1895 ceded Taiwan and the Pescadores to Japan. Subsequently, Japan controlled Taiwan for fifty years, until the end of the Second World War." Located between these two events is a colonial era for many years dismissed by the Nationalist regime as an aberration in the historical trajectory of the Chinese Republic.

Li Tien-lu's childhood and early adulthood overlap with this era, but colonial power is not the focus of the story. Instead, encounters between the Taiwanese and Japanese are woven into a panorama of mundane rural existence, taking place amid an assortment of everyday scenes and random moments. These "slices of life" convey a shift from the representation of history as grand narrative into a more minor key, with history mediated by ordinary life, its grand schemes overshadowed by the

7) Chiao, "History's Subtle Shadows," 4. Survival has the status of a running trope throughout the films of the trilogy. Typically associated with female characters whose loved ones have fallen prey to state violence and political conflict, it invites reflection on historical trauma, historiography, and the possibility of collective healing.

8) The Nationalist (KMT) regime imposed Martial Law shortly after its takeover of the island. It was not until the late 1980s that the decree was revoked in gradual stages. As the first popular work to address the violent events surrounding the transition to Chinese rule, Hou's *A City of Sadness* is often referred to as a signpost of Taiwan's post-Martial Law era, when the return to a repressed history became possible.

personal rather than vice versa. The symmetry of micro- and macrohistorical narratives is reproduced structurally in the film, for the informational intertitle is followed by a scene that takes place in the home of the Li family, as preparations are made for Li Tien-lu's one year birthday party. While the film thus opens with the personal event of the celebration of birth, it closes with Li's account of his whereabouts at the moment of Taiwan's liberation from Japan, interweaving his story with the more monumental occasion of the island's 1945 transfer to Chinese jurisdiction. The audience's sense of historical scale is thus anchored on one end in the transient fragments of individual life cycle, and on the other in a larger political past.

If the film presents Li as an embodiment of history, then, it is specifically of a minor history that addresses the experiences of the ordinary village inhabitants among whom he numbers and who constitute the main audience for his talents in puppetry. *Budai xi* – an art at the height of its popularity in the early period of colonialism, with some five hundred performing troupes active in Taiwan – is affiliated with this popular perspective, signifying at once vernacular authenticity and an older, and to a certain extent nostalgically idealized, social order. Evolving as an art of storytelling since its beginnings in the seventeenth century, when it was brought to the island by settlers from China's Fujian province, *budai xi* drew upon an archive of popular history, folklore, and legend for its narrative material.[9] Georgette Wang observes that "to common village people, largely illiterate peasants, laborers, and small businessmen puppet shows introduced the world of literature and history… As one man suggested, watching puppet shows was like taking history lessons." In this regard, puppeteers can be characterized as transmitters of popular history and "effective communicators in the pre-mass media era."[10] Their stories were either transmitted orally or transcribed by hand in synoptic form; the practice therefore demanded an

9) Unlike the leather puppets used in Chinese shadowplay or wooden marionettes used in string puppetry – both older forms dating back at least to the tenth century – hand puppets consisted of carved wooden heads mounted on bodies constructed of fabric; hence the name "cloth sack [*budai*] drama [*xi*]." Alternatively, some researchers have suggested that the "cloth sack" actually refers to the container used to transport the puppets.

10) Georgette Wang, "Televised Puppetry in Taiwan – An Example of the Marriage Between a Modern Medium and a Folk Medium" in Georgette Wang and Wimal Dissanayake, eds., *Continuity and Change in Communication Systems: An Asian Perspective* (Norwood, NJ: Ablex Publishing, 1984), 171

adeptness at oral performances spun extemporaneously out of memory rather than recited from a script, as the head puppeteer simultaneously manipulated the puppets and spoke their lines.

Budai xi is represented in six scenes in *The Puppetmaster*, occasioned by social rituals such as Li's birthday party, funerals, seasonal festivals, and religious offerings where performances were staged for the pleasure of the gods as much as for earthly audiences in acknowledgment of fulfilled prayers. In all of these scenes, the plays take place in outdoor locations such as the marketplace, the temple courtyard, and the open air spaces of the countryside. With this emphasis on the traditional venues of *budai xi*, which was performed by itinerant troupes that traveled from village to village more often than in permanent indoor venues, the film calls attention to the communal quality of its shows and situates it within a *mise-en-scène* that is above all a public space of sociality, in which ordinary people work, eat, and shop together. For instance, the opening scene of the celebration is followed by an excerpt from *Three Immortals Celebrating a Birth*, a play customarily performed at birthday celebrations. Before we are offered a view of the puppets on the stage, however, the sequence is introduced by a much longer shot encompassing the audience assembled before the stage and the pastoral setting of the performance. Most of the other *budai xi* scenes also end with a similarly composed long shot, thus offering a vision of the viewing collectives organized by traditional entertainment, its staging of a community as well as a show, in a space that is public, face-to-face, and organically rooted in the preexisting social structure of rural life.

To the extent that such an audience looks different from a film audience, the film's representation of puppet theater replays a nostalgic populist fantasy, offering an idealized restaging of the sort of viewing community the cinema has rendered obsolete. Thus, *The Puppetmaster* displays a tendency manifested in the cinema throughout its history to subsume and re-orchestrate earlier cultural media and institutions in the very process of displacing them. Also notable in this regard is the complete absence of technologically mediated communication in this film, in contrast to the marked presence of the radio in *A City of Sadness* and the obtrusive ubiquity of telephones, cell phones, and fax machines in the final work of the trilogy, *Good Men, Good Women* (1995). This absence returns to the tenuous status of *budai xi* as a form of entertainment that addresses a physically proximate audience of intimate rather than mass proportions – which is to say, a status that threatens to become extinct with the development of modern mass media.

However, nostalgic cannibalization does not fully account for how *budai xi* figures within this historical narrative. To begin with, the many theatrical interludes included in the film consist of actual footage of professionally staged puppet plays. Providing a display of the art of extemporaneous indigenous performance, these inserts also counter the erosion of tradition by making *budai xi*'s ephemeral performances permanently available to film audiences. Hou highlights the importance of these disparate performance registers when he states that the film is divided among three points of view – his own, Li's, and that of "Chinese tradition" itself, of which the dramatic excerpts signify a "pure representation."[11] Here, he suggests a different way of conceiving the relationship of the two media, wherein the one-way dynamic of displacement is preempted by a less hierarchical, two-way model of transaction. His comments must be read not only as a claim to

multiple authorship – establishing a slippage between Li as master of puppets and Hou as master auteur – but also as a claim on behalf of cinema as a popular medium to inherit the very tradition it attempts to capture here through *budai xi*, and hence to participate in the project of reconstructing the past.

The Puppetmaster's intervention in history by way of *budai xi* also must be understood with reference to its temporal structures, in particular its deployment of the long take. As Robert Sklar has pointed out, the long shot durations that the viewer encounters in *The Puppetmaster* evoke a sense "of observing the action as if it were in a theatrical stage set" – that is, as if the film were formally duplicating the presentational format of puppet drama in addition to restaging it.[12] Duration thus marks a point of overlap between these two media and a means by which the one is interwoven with the other.

LEGEND OF THE WHITE SNAKE

Critics frequently describe Hou Hsiao-hsien's filmmaking in terms of a "static aesthetic," exemplified in his consistent and repeated use of the long take. The prevalence of this device in conjunction with Hou's elliptical editing procedures points to a non-classical realism that de-

11) Chiao, "History's Subtle Shadows," 6–7

12) Robert Sklar, "Time on a String," *Cinema Scope*, Number 3 (Spring 2000), 38

parts significantly from conventional modes of cinematic narrative and allies his work with the European art cinemas of the mid-century.[13] This is especially true of the sustained takes in *The Puppetmaster*, which would make an impression upon even the most casual viewer. The average shot length of the film is eighty-four seconds, with some shots lasting longer than five minutes. Some of the longest shots present stage views of puppet plays, composed with the space of the stage filling the frame to allow an optimal, unobstructed view of the performance.

One example can be found in the second *budai xi* sequence, which takes place shortly after the death of Li's mother. In it, Li's father performs the supernatural romantic drama *Legend of the White Snake* with the assistance of his young son. The scene opens with a frontally centered close view of the stage as a puppet clad in a richly decorated robe of bright yellow makes an entrance and announces, "It is the Qingming [Ching Ming] Festival, when we remember the dead," thus drawing a connection between the occasion for the play and the personal tragedy that has just transpired. The puppet identifies himself as Hanmun, the owner of a medicine store, and the action begins: on his way to visit West Lake, a storm

erupts and he flees for cover, encountering as he does so two ladies who are also enjoying a promenade, Miss Green and Miss White (actually human incarnations of the White and Green Snake Spirits). The three take shelter together, and when the storm eventually passes, Hanmun invites the ladies to a boat ride together on the lake.

This segment is the longest continuous shot of the three that comprise the entire, 165 second long, *Legend of the White Snake* sequence. The method of formally marking puppet performance by duration is repeated throughout the film, effectively encouraging the viewer to become absorbed in their dramas. For instance, the previous *Three Immortals Celebrating a Birth* sequence lasts 150 seconds, and the next insert lasts close to three minutes. The spatiotemporal unity of these scenes of performance lends them an autonomous quality within the body of the film and narratively privileges their "pure representation" – to return to Hou's description – of tradition. Additionally, the position of

13) Although many have construed this characteristic as evidence of a stylistic affinity with Italian Neorealism, the concept of realism requires more elaboration and theorization, particularly in light of the different socio-historic context in which Hou works. The director himself makes frequent reference to Jean-Luc Godard as a source of inspiration.

The Puppetmaster

the camera reinforces the centrality of this and other *budai xi* sequences, by capturing the stage performance from an ideally located, frontally centered point of view that is never attributed to any of the characters within the film.

The absence of an intermediary gaze not only endows the performance sequences with a floating quality within the body of the film, but also has the effect of acknowledging an imputed viewer to whom the drama is presented in an act of theatrical display that is only partially incorporated into the narrative. This effect has been noted by Robert Sklar as a gesture at not only theatrical perspective but also to "cinema in its earliest days," before the institutionalization of continuity editing during the period of Classical Hollywood cinema. If the dominance of the fixed camera and single shot over editing in the cinema predating 1916 entails a "presentational" format that has more in common with traditional theater than with cinema as we know it today, it also demands a different mode of spectatorship. The unbroken and dehierarchized tableau of the shot ensures that "the spectator must constantly observe and interrogate the full frame for activity and narrative meaning" instead of following the thread of attention pre-constituted in the sequence of shots.[14]

The unity of the shot emphasized by Sklar furthermore allows us to think about the intersection of film and drama by way of early cinema's proximity to theater, in various parts of the world.[15] This proximity encompasses not only the many examples of filmic adaptations of dramatic subjects or screen appearances by stage actors, but also a qualitatively different mode of address, one in which "theatrical display dominates over narrative absorption," affiliated with a cinema of, in Tom Gunning's words, "exhibitionist confrontation rather than diegetic integration."[16] Through much of film's history, the parallel between screen and proscenium was understood in terms of a derivative and "primitive" application of new technology, neglectful of its expressive possi-

14) Sklar, 37–8

15) The tendency to view the new medium of film as an extension of preexisting forms of drama is evident in China and Japan, the two central sources of Taiwan's culture in the period of cinema's emergence. Much of what remains of Japanese film from the early 1900s consists of film recordings of kabuki performances and screen adaptations of kabuki dramas. In China, this connection is imbedded in the very terminology of the cinema, translated into Chinese as *yingxi*, literally "shadowplay." Zhang Zhen has pointed out that the "play" in shadowplay refers not only to Chinese drama in the broad sense, but specifically to the popular art of shadow puppetry, which involved projecting the shadows of leather puppets onto a backlit screen.

bilities as "an entirely new independent art which must develop its own life conditions" and therefore hindering its self-realization as a modern medium.[17] However, the parallel between the frame and the proscenium in this contemporary use of shot duration can also be seen in a more positive light, where the return to beginnings holds in place the promise of potentiality and renewal, and "the number of roads not taken" evident in early cinema are resuscitated as "inspirations for new understandings of tradition."[18]

The implicit connection to early cinema takes a visible form in the White Snake sequence, which also contains a cinematic reference. As the puppets Hanmun, Miss Green, and Miss White dash to escape the rain, their jour-

ney across a distance exceeding the limitations of the proscenium is cleverly conveyed by an alternation of movement: the puppets each in turn quickly fly across the stage from right to left, disappearing behind the backdrop curtain at the left corner of the stage, with the same circular pattern of movement repeated for several turns. The representation of movement across distance in such a fashion effectively transforms the fixed space of the stage into a chain of contiguous spaces. While the puppets are literally running around in circles, the repetition of their actions dematerializes and mobilizes the space around them, leading the viewer to understand it as a serial set of locations seen from a mobile perspective instead of a singular, fixed locale. This simple yet clever technique visually inscribes a convergence of screen and puppet stage that goes beyond the unified, static tableau of the still shot. It produces a kinetic impression of space that, more readily associated with film than theater, could be compared to the panoramic traveling views of the actuality film or, perhaps more appropriately – given that the space is not only mobilized but also relativized as part of a larger abstract whole – the early genre of the chase film. With this display of an aspect of puppet theater that is strongly evocative of the cinematic medium,

Puppet theater, therefore, constitutes "the bedrock of the Chinese cinematic (un)conscious" (*An Amorous History of the Silver Screen: Shanghai Cinema, 1896–1937*, Chicago: University of Chicago Press, 2005, 98).

16) Tom Gunning, "The Cinema of Attractions: Early Film, Its Spectator and the Avant-garde" in Thomas Elsaesser, ed., *Early Cinema: Space, Frame, Narrative* (London: British Film Institute, 1990), 59

17) Hugo Münsterberg, *The Film: A Psychological Study* (New York: Dover Publications, 1970), 60

18) Tom Gunning, "An Unseen Energy Swallows Space" in John L. Fell, ed., *Film before Griffith* (Berkeley, CA: University of California Press, 1983), 366

the relationship of the two likewise comes full circle.[19]

The retrospection formally inscribed in these moments can also be extended to a specific point in time: the year 1895 which, as we have seen, marks the opening intertitle reference of the film as the first year of Japanese colonial occupation, but also the first public screening of the *cinématographe* at the Grand Café in Paris by the Lumière brothers. This coincidence, which has the status of a founding parable in Taiwan's film history, adds another significant dimension to the film's reflection on history. Just as the period of time in question here is figurally represented through Li and mediated by the tradition of *budai xi*, so it is furthermore identified at a metanarrative level with the history of the cinematic medium, in such a way that the film's thematic concerns overflow the frame of the film itself. The explicit mention of this date in the establishing intertitle of *The Puppetmaster* can therefore be seen as another autoreferential gesture, this time towards the cinema's own beginnings.

The coincidence between the birth of cinema and the birth of Japanese colonialism in Taiwan invites further reflection on the relationship between cultural tradition and the historical context in which it is situated. For instance, the vulnerability of native modes of expression during colonial rule becomes apparent later in the film, when Li recounts that he and thousands of other performing artists were deprived of their livelihood by the ban on outdoor performances imposed by Japan in 1937. The onset of the Second Sino-Japanese War brought about an important change in which Japan's earlier attitude of coexistence gave way to a policy of total cultural assimilation called *kōminka*, meaning literally "the imperialization of subject peoples."[20] Along with technology, then, colonial rule plays a role in the disintegration of tradition. However, despite his aspiration to eulogize and preserve local culture, Hou preempts such a reading, reminding us that "Taiwan has inherited a legacy of influences from Japanese culture – we had fifty years of existence as a Japanese colony after all." This legacy cannot be separated from the continuing legacy of modernity

19) The technique, not unique to *budai xi*, can also be found in Western forms of puppet performance; my thanks to Jacqueline Stewart for pointing this out.

20) George H. Kerr has written that *budai xi* became a special concern for the authorities when "it had been realized, at last, that under the guise of ancient Chinese stories, the puppeteers were caricaturing Japan and the Japanese armies in China in hilariously bawdy fashion" (*Formosa: Licensed Revolution and the Home Rule Movement*, 1895–1945, Honolulu, HI: University of Hawaii Press, 1974, 196).

itself, given the significant progress made by Japan towards developing the island's agriculture, industry, transportation, education, and social services during its fifty-year administration. Legacy itself thus becomes an equivocal term, wedged between the duress of colonialism and the desirability of modernization.

In response to such ambiguities, Hou suggests that the simple opposition between an authentic native culture and an oppressively contaminating foreign one might be superceded by a conception of cultural influence and mutation as a dynamic process. Instead of predicating popular value upon indigenous purity, he acknowledges the transformations exacted upon tradition through time, revealing the historical contingency of cultural forms. Such an understanding is reflected in the narrative art of the puppetmaster and displayed not only in the scenes of *budai xi* but also at several moments when Li himself appears in the film, directly addressing the camera as he turns his narrative skills to the events of his own life. This biographical framework brings into view the centrality of memory, which here serves as a channel between the act of storytelling and history; it is through Li's stories that history is sifted and reassembled, through his narration that it is passed on to an audience. The role of the pup-

petmaster as storyteller, then, carves an avenue through which to further explore the film's historicizing strategies.

STORYTELLING: A REINVENTION OF TRADITION

Hou's attribution of creative agency to his subject is confirmed by the puppetmaster's ubiquitous presence on the soundtrack; his voice, textured with age and speaking in Taiwanese dialogue, serves as a running first-person voiceover narration throughout the film. The disembodied voice is finally attached to a real body when he makes an appearance on the image track. Li appears in the film in a total of six scenes; the first takes place after his voiceover commences a lengthy story about his grandmother over a series of outdoor landscape images, followed by a shot of a house under construction by a group of villagers, with a pile of stones on the ground before it. A cut brings us to an image of Li in the same setting, seated upon the pile of stones. The shot is more tightly framed than the previous so that we see Li in medium view, and the space is now empty of people and activity, denoting a temporal ellipsis. The same combination of spatial continuity and temporal discontinuity characterizes his other incursions into the visual register of the film, with Li reposing within the spaces previously peopled by the younger actors who play his role, thus calling attention to the disjunction between person and character. Although the director has emphasized that *The Puppetmaster* does not purport to present a documentary portrait of Li – offering instead a fictional interpretation of his personal history and experiences – these appearances also function as moments of non-fictional representation.

Li's look at the camera as he tells his tale elicits an awareness of his narrative agency and the act of recollection structuring the story. As a result, various critics have described these appearances as Brechtian moments of distanciation that break the diegetic frame and undercut its illusionism. This description, however, requires some qualification. To begin with, the gaze at the camera is typically perceived as a direct address and reciprocated gaze – two properties associated, of course, with the presentational format of early cinema. Li's presence, as a fragment of empirical reality that exceeds the parameters of the fictional reenactment of his biography, is thus formally linked to the preceding *budai xi* sequences, likewise metanarratively situated at a remove from the main body of the film, a position that can be attributed to what Hou calls a different "perspective."[21] As in the puppet performance scenes, the relative au-

tonomy of Li's direct address to the camera is given weight by duration, with the shot lasting 224 seconds.

At the same time, while the gaze at the camera may signal a break or rupture in the fictive universe derived from his words, it is also true that he talks on as he gazes, continuing to construct this universe. His appearance, here and elsewhere, is more precisely described as a crease rather than a break in the fabric of the narrative, where representational and presentational modes of articulation become simultaneous and give way to one another. These scenes therefore crystallize the film's wavering status between historical truth and creative reinterpretation; the intrusion of Li's body as an index of a reality shared with the viewer serves both to factualize the story and to bring together two moments in time by linking the historical tense of its events with a present reality. In more ways than one, Li is "a link from the past to the present."[22]

Even as the verification provided by Li's image transports us beyond the world of diegesis and into the real, however, it simultaneously introduces another fictitious domain, one that we can identify with the work of the storyteller. This work, as part of the puppetmaster's profession, can be identified with his relay of the oral folk archive of *budai xi* drama, or to invoke Walter Benjamin's discussion of the storyteller, with "experience which is passed from mouth to mouth."[23] His phrase resonates with Hou's description of *budai xi* as a vehicle through which traditional values "have been disseminated to the people and integrated into their daily lives."[24] However, the story Li tells here is different from the popular dramas of puppet theater, given that the material which he crafts comes from his own past. This requires us accordingly to rethink the status of memory – a channel of retrieval, it now permeates the entirety of the storytelling process.

Again following Benjamin, we can say that "memory is not an instrument for exploring the past but its theater. It is the medium of past experience, just as the earth is the medium in which dead cities lie buried."[25]

Li's memory also saturates the production process of *The Puppetmaster*. As Hou describes it, Li initially orated the material from which the screenplay was drawn, then was asked to repeat his stories in front of the camera just prior to shooting. In the retelling, Hou claims, "what he said was invariably different from what I had in mind – from what I wanted to shoot."[26] These differences remain in the film, drawing the attention of the viewer as a collision between Li's word and Hou's image; for example, what Li describes very often does not directly correspond to what we see on the image track, although it might be tangentially related. Such inconsistency can readily be explained as a creative conflict, as the director notes that Li's impressive loquaciousness, which inspired the film in the first place, proved to be a difficulty during its making. In the course of answering a question set up by Hou, Li would stray further and further from the original question without ever answering it.[27] Hou's decision to include the traces of their conflict in the final product of their collaboration signifies a deference to Li

21) Chiao, "History's Subtle Shadows," 6

22) Ibid, 4

23) Walter Benjamin, *Illuminations: Essays and Reflections*, edited by Hannah Arendt and translated by Harry Zohn (New York: Schocken Books, 1968), 84

24) Chiao, "History's Subtle Shadows," 4

25) Michael W. Jennings, Howard Eiland, and Gary Smith, eds., *Walter Benjamin: Selected Writings, Volume 2*, 1927–1934 (Cambridge, MA: Harvard University Press, 1999), 611

26) Chiao, "History's Subtle Shadows," 6

27) "In a single breath, he would go on for ten minutes, going into the smallest details. Sometimes he strayed from my questions, and what he said would be very different from what I had in mind, but I didn't force him to respond to my questions. I just let him surprise me" (Michel Ciment, "Entretien avec Hou Hsiao-hsien," *Positif*, Number 394, December 1993, 10).

and an unwillingness to relegate him to the secondary role of a caption.

However, these problems can be traced to yet another, more fascinating cause: the storyteller's tendency towards variation, for as Hou further describes, Li "would have different versions of the same story, if he told it several times."[28] Li's inability, or unwillingness, to tell the same story twice reveals a fundamental difference between the functions of preservation and replication. The difference that arises in repetition here returns us to the particular notion of tradition at work in this film, a tradition whose continuity in time is spelled out in the pathways of mutation and resistance to the entropy of fixed values. The infidelity to the idea of the original evinced by the storyteller has consequences for the kind of history the film imagines, for it emphasizes the distance in time bridged by the act of storytelling. An account of the past emerges across a varying set of stories, and the inconsistencies and differences in this account remain visible. The past comes alive in the present by means of a "slow piling one on top of the other of thin, transparent layers which constitutes the most appropriate picture of the way in which the perfect narrative is revealed through the layers of a variety of retellings."[29] In the infidelity of word and image, we see the gap in time that separates Li's experience from Hou's interpretation of it.[30]

If betrayal constitutes but one way of conceptualizing a transmission of culture rooted in adaptation and variation, then we can return to the question of individual memory as the basis of history and examine forgetfulness as an alternative model. In this way, memory would figure neither as a means by which the past is unearthed as factual object nor as the representation of a subjective point of view. That is, Li's narrative revisions unveil memory as a double movement of remembering and forgetting, presenting a discourse marked by the "remem-

28) Jacques Morice, "La Mémoire impressionnée," *Cahiers du cinéma*, Number 474 (December 1993), 45

29) Benjamin, *Illuminations*, 93

30) In a discussion of what he identifies as a historical turn in late 1980s fiction writing in Taiwan, Chou Ying-hsiung draws a similar excavational analogy to describe the discontinuous and fragmentary sense of history that emerges in these works. As he puts it, "Past and present were no longer compatible, let alone continuous. Attempts had to be made, therefore, to play one against the other to make sense of either one... The past was unearthed not purely for its archaeological authenticity. Rather, living in the contemporary world... writers of the Eighties felt compelled to return to [an] imaginary homeland and retrieve whatever fragments made sense to them" ("Imaginary Homeland: Postwar Taiwan in Contemporary Political Fiction," *Modern Chinese Literature*, Volume 6, Numbers 1–2, Spring/Fall 1992, 36).

brance" of what was perhaps only imagined or a disavowal of what was actually experienced. In addition to the unfaithfulness of reiteration, we also encounter the complexity of retrospection, which unavoidably amalgamates the realms of the actual and the fictive. This is not only depicted within the frame of the narrative but at a discursive level as well, insofar as the film's reconstitution of the historical past through creative speculation – its placement of documentary on the terrain of fiction – mimics the movement of memory itself. Jacques Morice has noted that as a "cinematic memoir," *The Puppetmaster* displays for us a "seizure" of memory "in action."[31] In its interweaving of

reality and unreality, the film literalizes the contingent processes of remembrance as they recollect and reconstruct the past. The passage through time afforded by storytelling as the work of memory thus demands a surrender of history to an unstable imaginary.[32]

Benjamin, of course, could hardly have had Taiwanese puppetmasters in the back of his mind when he wrote his essay on Nikolai Leskov, nor is there reason to believe Hou was reading German critical philosophy when he filmed *The Puppetmaster*. Nonetheless, the two share a common sensibility, defined by a care for tradition in the context of historical rupture. Given the unevenness of modernization at the global scale, late twentieth century Taiwan might not differ significantly from early twentieth century Europe in its experience of industrialization and the growth of the city, and of the concomitant erosion of older modes of sociality and cultural expression. Indeed, the intense rapidity with which these change took place in Taiwan, augmented by the destabilizing effect of geographic dislocation for its mainland refugee population on the one hand, and of colonial suppression for its longtime residents on the other, indicates that the endangering of tradition – as a loss of history, a proper past, and hence a foreseeable future – is

---

31) Morice, 40

32) It should be apparent by my emphasis upon the processual and structural aspects of memory that my discussion of its importance in *The Puppetmaster* is not premised upon a psychologized explanation of the film. For an example of such a reading, see Tonglin Lu, *Confronting Modernity in the Cinemas of Taiwan and Mainland China* (Cambridge: Cambridge University Press, 2002). For Lu, Li's narrative agency works in a totalizing fashion to establish "an artificial continuity among chronologically discontinuous elements," a continuity anchored in his patriarchal status as a living font of culture (111). This argument, to my mind, overlooks both the disruptive effects of Li's appearances and the fragility of a subject-position predicated upon an ultimately unreliable memory.

infused with an urgency like that felt by Benjamin in his time. For him, the idea of tradition bears the burden of negotiating historical change and working through the very technologies that threaten to tear the very fabric of experience. The intersection of cinema and storytelling in *The Puppetmaster*, then, can perhaps also help us to not only "conserve the beauty of our own traditions," but also "disseminate them using the tools of our age and from our own perspective."[33] The interlacing of cinema and *budai xi* at various levels (formal, thematic, authorial) throughout *The Puppetmaster* speaks to the possibility that the medium of film will perpetuate what Benjamin calls "the chain of tradition which passes a happening on from generation to generation."[34] As much as the act of reinvention looks away from the past as a fixed locus of identity and authenticity, it looks forward to a future that did not previously exist.

In this vision we also find an alternative to the narrative of decline and deterioration implicit in nostalgia, broadly defined as a longing to return to a time that never existed in the first place, and for a past idealized in its very distance from an immediate reality. In the context of Taiwan's contemporary cinema, the irony of a "new" cultural movement's fascination with an older mode of existence is illustrative of the logical paradox of nostalgia as a symptom of modernity, cuing us to its status as a sentiment premised upon the impossibility of its own fulfillment. Thus, Susan Stewart defines nostalgia as an "inauthentic" desire, "hostile to history" insofar as "it does not take part in lived experience." As "a longing for an impossibly pure context of lived experience at a place of origin, nostalgia wears a distinctly utopian face, a face that turns toward a future-past, a past which has only ideological reality."[35] According to Rey Chow, beyond the Taiwanese context, nostalgia persists as an *idée fixe*, or even as "the episteme of Chinese cultural production in the 1980s and 1990s," common to "the otherwise diverse intellectual and artistic undertakings of the mainland, Taiwan, and Hong Kong."[36]

The centrality of contingency, infidelity, and forgetfulness within Hou's evocation of the past exposes the cracks in nostalgia's phantasmatic edifice. At the same time, however, the film retains nostalgia's utopic dimension, its attractiveness "as an alternative temporality for fantasizing a 'community' in a moment of social identity crisis."[37] Here, we can recall that the parallel between Li and Hou as producers of culture indicates the historical overdetermination of tradition versus modernity in *The Pup-*

petmaster, framed not only by the colonialism of Li's time, but also by the developments leading up to Taiwan's "economic miracle" of the 1980s. In this sense, tradition is dialectically interwoven with (a reaction against, yet constituted by) a modernity, attributed to prewar Japan as well as postwar America, caught between two sets of dislocations. The story of Hou's ascent as a star of the international art cinema, after all, is in many respects inseparable from the story of Taiwan's integration into a global marketplace.[38]

This situation also recasts the stakes of vernacular revivalism, adding issues of cultural translation to the question of the resuscitation of tradition in a post-traditional age. If Hou's reinvention of tradition is conditioned by an environment in which the juxtaposition of old and new, traditional and modern, has become an identifying topographical trope, it also suggests a way of mapping the movement of culture in an increasingly borderless world. In bringing together local culture and a global stylistic idiom, the everyday and the exceptional, his films demand a shift away from the bipolar hermeneutic of "native idiom versus foreign market culture" and towards what Miriam Hansen has described as "a more differentiated analysis of [their] stylistic hybridity" and variegated frames of reference.[39] The global success of *The Puppetmaster* and other films by Hou, then, testifies not to the emergence of a homogeneous monoculture – or, as some have claimed, a "parrot" cinema of colonial mimicry – but rather to a pluralization of boundaries along which hybridity must be discerned.[40]

33) Chiao, "History's Subtle Shadows," 5

34) Benjamin, *Illuminations*, 98

35) Susan Stewart, *On Longing: Narratives of the Miniature, the Gigantic, the Souvenir, the Collection* (Durham, NC: Duke University Press, 1984), 23

36) Rey Chow, *Ethics after Idealism: Theory–Culture–Ethnicity–Reading* (Bloomington, IN: Indiana University Press, 1998), 146

37) Ibid, 134

38) Upon its debut, *The Puppetmaster* received the Jury Prize at the Cannes International Film Festival, which at the time represented the most prestigious award received by a Taiwanese production.

39) Miram Hansen, "Fallen Women, Rising Stars, New Horizons: Shanghai Silent Film as Vernacular Modernism," *Film Quarterly*, Volume 54, Number 1 (Autumn 2000), 14

40) Chen Kuan-hsing, "Taiwanese New Cinema" in John Hill and Pamela Church Gibson, eds., *The Oxford Guide to Film Studies* (New York: Oxford University Press, 1998), 558

Hasumi Shigehiko

Who Can Put Out the Flame?

On Hou Hsiao-hsien's Flowers of Shanghai

ARTIFICIAL AND HYBRID

A magnificent film exists, a film shot in Taiwan at the twilight of the twentieth century that extinguishes all at once the film historical memory surrounding the mythical city called "Shanghai:" Hou Hsiao-hsien's *Flowers of Shanghai* (1998).[1] Other celebrated films that purport to be about Shanghai mostly seem to wither and fade in the face of this work. Not that Hou had such provocative intentions. On the contrary, his film insistently maintains an atmosphere of serenity. Anyone will be seduced by the elegant camera movement – so complex, yet because of its complexity appearing all the more simple – as it arcs in the film's opening section through the scenery of costumed men and women seated around a dining table enjoying lively conversation. Ruminating on this shot and its lingering power of attraction, I find myself at a loss over how to handle my memory of the scene from *Footlight Parade* (Lloyd Bacon, 1933), which I by no means disdain, where James Cagney and Ruby Keeler tap dance to the song "Shanghai Lil" on a bar counter. Things would be simple if we could draw a line and say: if this is a film, then that is not; or, if this is Shanghai, then that is not; but, when such divisions do not work, the situation becomes very inconvenient.

Certainly, the "Shanghai Lil" tap duet between Cagney and Ruby Keeler in *Footlight Parade* was something delightful. But Busby Berkeley's choreography in the ensemble dance number at the end of the film was spectacular without qualification, notwithstanding Susan Sontag's attempt to cast suspicion upon it. No less spectacular was the cinematography by Lee Garmes in *Shanghai Express* (Josef von Sternberg, 1932), while Boris Leven's art direction in *Shanghai Gesture* (Josef von Sternberg, 1941) reached breathless extremes of magnificence. Looking at scenes from these films, we cannot help but acknowledge that their contributions to film history are as exalted technical achievements, and therefore they should not be pigeonholed within the framework of "aesthetic Orientalism" surrounding the mythical city of "Shanghai." Nevertheless, upon witnessing a screening of *Flowers of Shanghai*, anyone will be prepared to say, if for the sake of this film that lets us taste an ecstasy sustained across two hours by Mark Lee's startling camerawork,

1) Editor's note: The original Japanese text consistently includes brackets around certain words. Since this stylistic device registers differently in English, quotation marks appear here only on first appearances or in sections where a level of conceptual abstraction is strongly implied.

Flowers of Shanghai, 1998

that it should not matter a bit if Marlene Dietrich's at once meaningful and ambiguous expressionlessness, Gene Tierney's moistened eyes, or the image of Cagney in that exotic sailor suit were all at once swept from the stock of film historical memory around Shanghai.

Of course, such a position is not the result of judging that the Shanghai depicted in *Flowers of Shanghai* is somehow authentic while that of *Footlight Parade, Shanghai Express,* or *Shanghai Gesture* is merely a coarse imitation. An authentic Shanghai does not exist anywhere in film history, and for this reason Orson Welles was able to give one of his films the dubious title *The Lady from Shanghai* (1947). In fact, even Cheng Bugao's *Old and New Shanghai* (1936), which was filmed during the golden era of Shanghai cinema, does not adequately capture the vibrant cosmopolitan atmosphere of Shanghai. Although the wartime street scenes portrayed in Naruse Mikio's Japanese film *Shanghai Moon* (1941) are far more vivid than what is to be found in Ang Lee's *Lust, Caution* (2007), which takes place in a Shanghai of basically the same historical period, it is a particularly cinematic inconvenience that even these scenes seem all the more fictional. The same obviously applies in the case of *Tokyo Drifter* (Suzuki Seijun, 1966), and even of *Tokyo Story* (Ozu Yasujirō, 1953),

where the "Tokyo" portrayed can hardly be called authentic. For such reasons, the "Shanghai" of *Flowers of Shanghai* is also not authentic.

Flowers of Shanghai opens abruptly and without any visual iconography of Shanghai on the aforementioned dining table scene, immediately following the film's opening titles, where the words "Based on Han Bangqing's novel *The Sing-song Girls of Shanghai*" appear in red lettering against a black background and a simple text explanation states that the setting is "a Flower House in the British concession of Shanghai at the end of the nineteenth century." While the viewer will be satisfied that the setting is probably in fact a "Flower House," no one will believe that the interior décor is actually from the "end of the nineteenth century." In fact, what we see is a set constructed in a suburb of Taipei at the end of the twentieth century, and the furnishings that fill its rooms are undoubtedly items procured in Taiwan. The "end of the nineteenth century" in China corresponds to the late Qing dynasty and the men who frequent this Flower House all wear their hair in historically accurate queues, the forehead neatly shaved and the hair at the back of the head braided into a long pigtail; however, we all know that this is probably not the actors' real hair. The costumed women, for their part, can be visually distinguished as "higher" or "lower" courtesans based on the luster of their clothing, but even Hou, who must have thoroughly researched materials pertaining to historical iconography, could not have determined the precise sartorial codes authentic to a "Flower House" in "Shanghai" during the "late Qing dynasty." In making a film set in Shanghai at the end of the nineteenth century, he must have been fully aware of the limits restricting the recreation of a lost period of time.

This film is not the first or only example in which Hou, who was born on the mainland but has spent most of his life in Taiwan, has trained his camera on such traditional sights as men with queues or the exclusive pleasures of the "house." For *The Puppetmaster* (1993), he went so far as to shoot the opening scene on location in China, committing to celluloid images of men of lower social standing who also wore queues. In *Three Times* (2005), there is an episode that portrays men with queues calling upon elegantly costumed courtesans in which the actor Chang Chen and the actress Shu Qi, who are fixtures in contemporary Taiwanese cinema, play a patron and a courtesan in the Taipei "pleasure quarters" of one hundred years ago.

However, circumstances are somewhat different in the case of *Flowers of Shanghai*. This is because Wang, a client of the Flower House, is played by Tony Leung, who we all know is an international Hong Kong star, while Jade, the courtesan who having failed to capture Wang's heart becomes consumed with worry, is played by the Japanese star Hada Michiko. Tony Leung had prior experience working with Hou on *A City of Sadness* (1989), but Hada Michiko not only had never worked with the director before this film, she also had not previously appeared in a foreign film. Moreover, she did not have a particularly good command of Chinese. In other words, in making this film set in a late nineteenth century Flower House in Shanghai, Hou cast two "foreigners" not especially adept in the language spoken in Shanghai in the two most important roles.

In light of these considerations, it should be clear how far from authentic the Shanghai of *Flowers of Shanghai* actually is. Hou's "Shanghai" is every bit as artificial and hybrid as Sternberg's, and can perhaps even be said to exceed Sternberg's in abstraction. The task facing us here is to investigate the reasons why this highly abstract artificiality and hybridity is so enchanting.

Flowers of Shanghai   *JLG / JLG*, Jean-Luc Godard, 1994

GUIDED BY LAMPS

Flowers of Shanghai depicts something highly concrete beyond the abstraction which is necessarily an element of any period film: namely, the lighting that illuminates the interiors of the Flower House. Since the ambience of a film changes depending on how the light that fills its settings is captured on celluloid, lighting is an unavoidable, concrete fact that determines the success or failure of a film. That Hou is extraordinarily sensitive to the subtle variation of natural light in outdoor locations needs no demonstration. The situation is completely different in this film, in which the narrative unfolds indoors from beginning to end, so that artificial lighting necessarily replaces sunlight. Of course, under such circumstances, it is customary for electric lights arranged off camera to supply the light that illuminates the scenery in front of the lens, but what is remarkable here is that the light source appears within the scene that it lights up. It is therefore also a prop, and is treated as a cinematic subject in its own right. Surrounded by its own artificial illumination, this light-source-as-cinematic-subject takes the

visual form of spirit lamps placed at the center of tables or at various points in the background of the scenery, and the little flames burning at the wicks of these lamps represent the historical and regional particularities of late nineteenth century "Shanghai."

It should be emphasized that the flames in this film are far more elegant as visual representations than the braided hairstyles or the lustrous silk garments that represent the "Qing." Each shot, in which lamps are arranged at the center or along the periphery of the composition, is a long take that invariably begins with a *fade in* and ends with a *fade out*. As a result, what first attracts the eye as each new shot begins are lamp flames emerging from darkness, just as what the eye sees last as each shot ends are lamp flames slowly sinking into the blackness of the screen. In the glow of these flames, the forms of men and women also emerge, but at a slight delay. Likewise, when these human figures are eventually extinguished from the screen with the fading of the image, the flames linger a little longer. This slight temporal dissonance spreads a fittingly ghostly atmosphere across the sur-

Rio Grande, John Ford, 1950   *How Green Was My Valley*, John Ford, 1941

face of the film. These flames – which, thanks to the exceptional handling of light, lead into and out of each scene as concrete cinematic subjects that slowly drift into and out of view – separate *Flowers of Shanghai* not only from Hou's other work, but also from the celebrated film historical examples of works that have taken Shanghai as a cinematic subject.

Numerous critics have already commented on the nearly hypnotic effect of these lamp flames that float onto the screen before any other subject has appeared and linger on the screen after every other subject has been extinguished, so we can proceed without repeating their observations. What I would like to address here is rather the subtlety with which the lamps are placed within the compositions. In the long dining scene that opens the film, which I have already touched upon above, two spirit lamps with tall transparent glass chimneys are placed on the center table; lamps can also be seen along the wall of the hallway visible through the open door to the rear, as well as on a table in a back room that comes into view when the camera pans slowly to the left.

What this placement brings to light is quite simply the lamp flames themselves, which determine the limits of the expansion of space in the Flower House and of the duration of the time that flows there. The camerawork of Mark Lee, which is characterized by such gentle slowness that it is difficult to detect when movements begin, consists of pans and tilts corresponding to the movements of the men and women lit up by the flames and produces rich scenes in which the existence of the camera mostly evades conscious awareness. As a rule, space in which there are no lamps does not attract his camera; as long as a given scene continues, the flames within it do not burn out.

Looking at these kinds of scenes, we cannot, in other words, help but notice how Hou trains his camera on lamps as both indirect light sources within the scene and as privileged cinematic subjects, as if he were connecting to a genealogy of "lamp films" that runs from John Ford to Jean-Luc Godard. Things are slightly different in the case of Godard since the light bulbs at which he directs his camera are always covered with lampshades, but it should not fail to surprise that the numerous lamps within the Flower House in Shanghai closely match the forms and arrangements of spirit lamps covered in tall transparent glass chimneys that are also to be found in Ford's westerns.

In fact, when men and women gather around dinner tables in Ford's frontier enclaves – think, for example, of John Wayne's gesture at the banquet hosted by J. Carrol Naish's General to welcome Maureen O'Hara in *Rio Grande* (John Ford, 1950) – lamp flames illuminate them, just like in the opening scene at the dining table in *Flowers of Shanghai*. This is not to say that Hou was in any way conscious of imitating Ford's handling of light. After all, film history is filled with provocations that surprise the viewer through chance resemblances that are independent of context. Just as Ford's men often enjoy a dinnertime smoke after lighting their cigars under the tall glass chimneys of lamps placed around the table, Hou's men inhale vapors through the long stems of water pipes after holding opium needles over the flames of small lamps, blowing on the heated substance to flare it up, and packing it into the pipe bowl.

Of course, the differences between Ford and Hou are also immediately recognizable. In Ford's world, a man can strike a match in empty darkness and light a lamp to reveal the form of a beloved woman standing close by – as in the classic example of the farewell scene between Walter Pidgeon and Maureen O'Hara in *How Green Was My Valley* (John Ford, 1941) – whereas in Hou's Shanghai, neither the courtesans nor their patrons ever so much as touch the lamps or adjust their flames. These flames have always already been lit by someone before the start of the scene, such that characters in the film seem even to be forbidden from touching the lamps, as if this were a "rule of the game." The consistency of this "rule" is precisely what lends a sense of unity to *Flowers of Shanghai*, a film otherwise characterized by a narrative that advances through the intertwining of different episodes.

The flames of these lamps that someone has so discreetly lit, as if it were forbidden to touch them, govern the space of the pleasure quarter through the very prohibition against touching that they represent, and thus constrain the behavior of the men and women who traverse it. Patrons and courtesans are equally subject to this control, and it is through nothing other than the absolute authority which the flames radiate throughout the space of the Flower House that this film can be decisively separated from Hou's other work, as well as from the many other films that have been made about

Shanghai. It could perhaps even be said that these flames thus impose a heavier shackle than the large financial debts that keep the courtesans imprisoned within their enclosed world. The reason why characters in this film cannot freely ignite or extinguish these flames is because, if they did so, the dramaturgical restriction that every shot must begin with a fade in and end with a fade out would not hold. The spatial setting of the Flower House in Shanghai is not the only thing that imprisons these women; they are also captive beings within the time of the film called *Flowers of Shanghai*.

A TRAGEDY OF FLAMES

Having earned praise around the world for autobiographical films like *A Time to Live and a Time to Die* (1985) and *Dust in the Wind* (1986) –

though the autobiographical subject of the latter film is notably the screenwriter Wu Nienjen – as well as for films like *City of Sadness* that deal with the modern history of Taiwan, why did Hou decide to make a film set in a "Flower House" in "Shanghai" at the "end of the nineteenth century?" He was probably attracted in part by the alluring prose of Eileen Chang, who had translated Han Bangqing's novel from the regional Wu dialect into contemporary Mandarin (and who also wrote the novel that became the source for *Lust, Caution*).[2] But we can easily surmise that he must also have been drawn to the subject by an interest in the intimate trade that characterized the pleasure quarters as a site, however "high class," where money was exchanged for sex. Hou must have wanted to explore in his own fashion the significance of that well-rehearsed Chinese tradition in which educated, financially privileged, and cultured men frequented Flower Houses. What possessed these men to visit the pleasure quarters every evening, and to spend their wealth with such abandon? To think that they did so solely with the purpose of engaging in a transaction, of trading their fortunes for the flesh of a favorite woman, is rather unsatisfying. What then was Hou seeking out when he trained his camera on this Flower House?

2) Editor's note: The dialogue in Han Bangqing's sixty-four chapter novel 海上花列傳 is written in Suzhou Wu. Widely considered to be one of the great achievements of Chinese literature, it was initially serialized in a pioneering literary magazine launched by the author in 1892. A shortened Mandarin translation by Shanghai-born Eileen Chang (Zhang Ailing) was published in Taiwan in 1983 and served as the primary source for the script of *Flowers of Shanghai*. Eileen Chang also worked on a complete English translation that, largely unpublished at the time of her death, was posthumously revised by Eva Hung and released as *The Sing-song Girls of Shanghai* (New York: Columbia University Press, 2005).

It is not that the creator of the film *Flowers of Shanghai* did not have any intention to critically examine, through the unhappiness of women, a historical moment in which it was taken for granted that a woman's role was to play, however unhappily, with the unconscious egoism of men. For such a critical view, we need only look to Mizoguchi Kenji, who beautifully depicted these kinds of tragedies in any number of films, from *Sisters of the Gion* (1936) to *A Geisha* (1953). In comparison to the "Gion" pleasure quarter of Kyoto that Mizoguchi portrayed as a microcosm of contemporary society, and as an insistently monochrome world, the historical Flower House in Hou's "Shanghai" is recreated in color, and is a more closed, austere, and alluring environment. In training his camera on this world, Hou seems to have imposed a certain fiction upon himself as a working hypothesis: the fiction that men more than women were seduced by the magnetism of the lamp flames that illuminated the enclosed space of the Flower House. Accordingly, his camera itself had to be guided not by the restrictiveness of Mizoguchi's one scene/one shot approach, but by a voluptuousness appropriate to the magnetism of the flames.

What is surprising upon viewing *Flowers of Shanghai*, which it seems can only have been filmed with a consciousness of such things, is the fact that Hou, who from the time he first became a self-aware filmmaker with *The Boys from Fengkuei* (1983) systematically went about recounting stories through the stabilizing medium of a fixed camera, here captures the expressions of men and women with a voluptuously moving camera, to the extent of compromising the perfection of his careful compositions. Of course, as is the case in his other films to this point, he still does not make use of close-ups, but the almost imperceptible fluidity of the camera when it tries to isolate a man and woman through reframing, in contrast to the communal compositions of men and women enjoying lively conversation around the dining table, seems to quarantine its subjects from surrounding space in ways that are not to be found in the earlier films shot with a stationary camera.

For example, at the moment when Jade first appears on screen, the first thing that meets the eye, from a position opposite the dining table and near the wall beside a bed – another piece of stage dressing with privileged status in the setting of the Flower House – is the flame of a small green lamp. As a rule, Hou does not film men and women in bed, and here as well it is not the bed but a chair that the courtesan occupies, sitting silently with her back to the lonely flame. The lamp continues to give off its dim light from behind Jade as she listens to the older woman declare her dissatisfaction with Jade's regular patron Wang. Watching its lonely flame, we cannot help but be convinced, without any particularly good reason, that this woman's love will only end unhappily.

The point, of course, is not to claim that the flame of the small lamp beside the bed "symbolizes" the unhappiness of Jade, whose room it illuminates, for it is hard to imagine a filmmaker who has gone farther than Hou in banishing visual symbols from the screen. Nevertheless, there is no denying the fact that the little lamp placed by the bed behind the courtesan, in contrast to the tall spirit lamps on the table crowded with men and women engaged in lively conversation, highlights her isolation with an elegance exceeding that of a mere prop. When the camera moves to the left, following the mistress as she stands there reproaching Wang's cold treatment of Jade, the large lamp placed on the table at the center of the room becomes visible, and when the figures of Wang and his associates next appear in the left corner of the picture, listening uncomfortably to the words of the mistress, another small lamp also emits a weak glow there. The

placement of these lamps unmistakably presages what might be called a tragedy of flames. For when Wang, persuaded by the words of the mistress, remains in the room after his friends depart, and when Jade sits beside him and begins to voice her sadness, the flame of the little lamp that radiates its dim light into the space between the two also impregnates the scene with an indeterminate atmosphere of anguish.

It is unclear why, after five years of patronage, Wang's relation to Jade unravels into uncertainty or why he begins visiting another courtesan. This is not because the staging of the drama is insufficiently expository; it is probably because the reasons why things have somehow turned out the way they have are unclear even to the couple in question. Even in the long opening scene in which the group of costumed men and women enjoy lively conversation while gathered around the dining table, Wang is portrayed sitting silently amongst the other regular patrons as a man who does not display his emotions and Jade, in turn, is depicted as being possessed of a gloomy disposition not befitting a courtesan. Nevertheless, looking at the scenes in which Jade energetically reproaches Wang for calling upon another woman, it becomes clear that the two remain strongly drawn to one another on a deep level. It is just that something has gone amiss, causing them to become incapable of behaving like partners to one another, and their situation has therefore proceeded to deteriorate. Perhaps in a Flower House where everything is settled with money, to love earnestly like Wang and Jade do is to flout the rules of the game. And perhaps it is with a vague realization of this that Wang tries to retreat from Jade. When he visits her for the last time, Jade mutters that, if she is to be abandoned by him, there is nothing left for her but to die and the flame of the lamp placed between them radiates an especially bewitching light, highlighting from the center of the screen the fact that things can only continue to progress in this way as the image fades to black.

By now, anyone can guess how the story of these two people will end. Should the moment arrive in which someone's hand puts out the flames of the spirit lamps that have remained untouched throughout, it will only mean the beginning of the end. It is as if this were a tacit rule of the game within this space. In fact, when – doubting Jade's love – Wang descends into a state of drunken, paranoid jealousy, he takes his leave of her by smashing the lamps burning in her room. This action forces his exit

from "Shanghai." With the lamp having been broken and the flame extinguished in her room, Jade too can no longer remain in the "Flower House."

It goes without saying that the tragic love between Wang and Jade is not the only story recounted in *Flowers of Shanghai*. There is also the courtesan who negotiates her independence and leaves the house, as well as the one who intercedes in all kinds of difficult problems within the house and earns the trust of the other women. Men gather around these radiant courtesans, enjoying lively conversation as the flames of lamps flicker on the tables that they encircle. However unhappy the parting of Wang and Jade, the Flower House continues to lure men with the flames of lamps just as if nothing had happened, and although the courtesans and their patrons gossip about Jade who has disappeared from their midst, no one is earnestly troubled over her situation.

It is clear that Hou could not have concluded this film without depicting a fading flame in Jade's proximity. In fact, matters could only have led us here, and thus we behold Jade sitting in a chair by the wall just as when she made her first appearance in the film, only now she entertains a man other than Wang in some shabby room in an undetermined location, looking defeated and expressionless. The two do not exchange words. Looking downward, she silently packs his pipe with opium. In the midst of this gesture, the scene begins to fade out, and after the flame at the tip of the little pipe in her hand has lingered a moment in the darkness, *Flowers of Shanghai* – a poignant tragedy to which only a flame could bear witness – draws to a close upon a completely black screen.

Although the film ends in a profound darkness that spreads across the screen, that very night there presumably will still be flames flickering around the table and lively conversations continuing uninterrupted at the Flower House, as if Wang's having smashed a lamp and extinguished its flame were nothing more than an insignificant mishap. Who then can conclu-sively put out these flames? Who can exercise such a privilege? Surely, this should not be the role of the individual Wang, who was unable to maintain his love with Jade. Instead, the task falls to "history." Only the impersonal subject of history can put out the flames burning in the Flower House. This is the conclusion that we are left murmuring after having witnessed the tragedy of flames of Wang and Jade who were guided by lamps. The profound darkness of the screen faded to black must therefore somehow intersect with history itself. This is the suggestion that Hou's *Flowers of Shanghai* finally plants, and, in doing so, it captures the heart more than any other film set in Shanghai and does not let go.

Translated by Ryan Cook

James Quandt

Three Times Three

A Certain Slant of Light in the Films of Hou Hsiao-hsien

Side-lit and glimmering, the billiard balls in the opening sequences of Hou Hsiao-hsien's *Three Times* (2005) appear like *objets d'art*, so aestheticized is the aura in which they exist – a hushed, radiant world of teal shantung, green baize, and crisp muslin. As if observing Emily Dickinson's instruction that "the Truth must dazzle gradually," the film initially hangs fire in that becalmed but fraught manner identified with Hou: time suspended, natural light, alive with iridescent motes, spilling from an open door into recollected space, a sense of reverie and yearning quietly cumulating in the idle air.[1] By film's end, the light that defines Hou's cinema – embodied in the preliminary shot of an overhead lamp from which the camera descends, rack focusing to impart form to the indefinite, and by the lantern that is lit at the outset of the film's second part and relit at the film's midway point – has become harsh and unforgiving, the chill blue glow of neon and computer screens casting a deathly pall on contemporary Taipei. "Smoke Gets in Your Eyes" warn The Platters in the sunny, romanticized mid-Sixties environs of the first of Hou's "three times," while in the afflicted modernity of the third, the blur of nocturnal *sfumato* and Jing's sung instruction, "Please open your eyes," ironically underline Hou's grim appraisal of the present – the

singer's imminent blindness, both actual and metaphoric, will soon extinguish the scrutinizing light. Similarly, the film's other motifs – transport and motion; written messages – transmute from the quest for an ideal love through rural Taiwan (by ferry, bicycle, train and bus) to a hurtling race through the city (on motorcycle) interrupted by a panic attack; from the open-hearted letters sent by Chen to his pool hostesses to Jing's anxiety-inducing cell phone texts from her girlfriend that accuse her of disloyalty and threaten suicide. Thus, Hou moves in the film's trajectory from sentimental nostalgist to punitive modernist, a shift that reflects the course of his previous career.

Returning to Taiwan after a sojourn in Tokyo to make his Ozu homage, *Café Lumière* (2003), Hou produced a portmanteau film that serves as a retrospective of his career, each of its three stories recalling a successive period of the director's cinematic development. That each tale is set in a different epoch (1966, 1911, 2005) of Taiwan's history and in a location (rural, cloistral, urban, respectively) that mirrors the temporal and geographic setting of an

1) This is a greatly revised and expanded version of the essay that first appeared in *Artforum International*, Volume XLIV, Number 2 (October 2005), 248–54

Three Times, 2005

important work in his hitherto career only re-inforces the film's function as conscious summa. Hou did not originally intend it as such. The omnibus form to which *Three Times* reverts was, of course, the hallmark of the Taiwanese New Cinema. Like such episodic films as *In Our Time* (1982) and *The Sandwich Man* (1983), *Three Times* was conceived as a trio of thematically related tales about "growing up," by Hou and two others, Hwarng Wern-ying and Peng Wen-chung – no doubt an update of the "initiation" films crucial to Hou's early career.[2] But funding for the project, which was to focus on the "musical memories" of each director and how they relate to love, fell through, and Hou rescued it by making all three stories, using the same actor and actress (Shu Qi and Chang Chen) to play similarly named characters (e.g., Chen; M. Chang; Zhen) in each.[3] He has referred to the resulting triptych as being about the "bliss" that comes from recollecting a wonderful time, lost and restorable only through memory – reflected in the original Chinese title which invokes, according to Hou, "the best of our times" – though only the first "panel" or tale seems to accord with that notion, the ensuing two hardly blissful in their accounts of various forms of immurement and alienation.

No director in contemporary cinema has so insistently defined life as an accrual of loss and injury, of broken or vanished ideals and irretrievable loves. Hou's early work *Dust in the Wind* (1986) suggests that as fated and ephemeral as life is – the very title intimates mortality – it also offers us the consolations of place and memory. But memory can become less solace than trap, as the tormented Liang Ching discovers in *Good Men, Good Women* (1995), when her past arrives every day, as pages of her stolen diary are anonymously faxed to her apartment, a reminder that she cannot live in the present, so wounding and utter is her memory of the man she loved and lost. And place, all important to Hou, poet of verdant landscapes, rural train stations, and mingy, inhospitable cities, cannot transcend the history that weighs on it. The port city Kaohsiung, the seaside town Chiufen [Jiufen], the bucolic hillside villages of Hou's autobiographical films, Shanghai, and the trio of settings in *Three Times* – Kaohsiung, Tataocheng [Dadaocheng], Taipei – are, in Hou's melancholy estimation, sites of stoic despair, all in some way "Cities of Sadness."

The first segment of *Three Times* returns to Hou's autobiographical early films, with their delicate, summery surfaces, rural or pastoral settings, comparatively linear narratives, mid-distance shots, and extended takes. (It has the longest average shot length of the three tales by at least ten seconds.) Its very title, "A Time for Love," echoes that of *A Time to Live and a Time to Die* (1985), filmed in the village in which Hou grew up, but it is *Dust in the Wind*, about two young people who move from their hill-side village to an inhospitable Taipei, that "A Time for Love" most resembles; its pool halls recall the Quemoy [Kinmen] billiards towards the end of *Dust in the Wind* where Wan learns that Huen is to marry someone else. Full of fugitive, unfulfilled hopes, *Dust in the Wind* reveals Hou's romantic attachment to the disappearing traditions and landscapes, the "paradise past," of Taiwan. A fixed shot of a grandfather, played by octogenarian actor Li Tien-lu, gazing into the serried green hills surrounding his village, captures in one rending image the director's vision of an eternal Taiwan, rooted in the land and centered on the family. Conversely,

"A Time for Love," set in 1966 in Kaohsiung, is all nomadic ramble.

Scouting locations for this segment, Hou discovered that traces of the mid-Sixties have largely disappeared from Taiwan, so he concentrated instead, he says, on character and story. But it is atmosphere – a gorgeous aura of melancholy and desire – that prevails in his account of an itinerant pool-hall hostess pursued by a lonely army conscript. She shuttles from town to town, hall to hall, never staying long, and briefly on leave he travels cross country to find her, road signs swimming out of the landscape to direct his detective quest. The recurrence of threes in "A Time for Love," including the street address of May's mother, seems too insistent not to be an in-joke; Hou likes his trios, trilogies, triptychs. Hou establishes a surprisingly Wongish vibe with the patterned glamour of Shu Qi's retro outfits, those Bakelite-looking pool balls, and the pop nostalgia of a music track that switch hits between "Smoke Gets in Your Eyes" and a persistently repeated "Rain and Tears" by Aphrodite's Child, a Baroque-pop classic improbably based on Pachelbel's canon that will surely lodge in your brainpan, if not your iPod, after its last insidious reiteration (though Hou's use of it stops short of Wong Kar-wai's over-roasting of Christmas

2) See William Tay, "The Ideology of Initiation: The Films of Hou Hsiao-hsien" in Nick Browne, Paul G. Pickowicz, Vivian Sobchack, and Esther Yau, eds., *New Chinese Cinemas: Forms, Identities, Politics* (Cambridge: Cambridge University Press, 1994), 151–160.

3) "Five Questions for Hou Hsiao-hsien," an interview with Tony Rayns conducted in Taipei and Seoul in May 2005, included in the pressbook for *Three Times*

chestnuts in *2046*, 2004). More astonishing, Hou gives his love story a happy ending, albeit tentative, bliss being provisional in his world of flux and farewell. The unabashedly romantic close-up of May and Chen's clasped hands prepares for a contrasting shot in the third part of Jing's hands clutched in panic.

Hou accords each of his three stories its own distinctive visual style and tone – each was assigned a different stylist, and has a markedly different average shot length (39.9, 24.8, and 29.5 seconds respectively).[4] In the second, longest, and most extraordinary of them, "A Time for Freedom," set in a society brothel in 1911, the director turns exigency into invention. The film's short production period forced Hou to forego the literary dialect then spoken in such a rarefied enclave, which would have taken too long for his actors to master. Instead of indulging in the anachronism of contemporary dialogue, the director made the bold choice to turn his period piece into a silent film. Hou's stylistic daring lies not only in his chosen form, but more in his refusal to recreate its traditional style or syntax. (Some critics have claimed that the segment faithfully reproduces the visual grammar of silent cinema, perhaps mistaking the proliferation of stately pans for antique authenticity.) The dialogue, presented as elaborate intertitles floating on a flocked gold-leaf background, achieves the desired formality of Hou's period setting, but at the occasional expense of stiltedness and over-freighting: "You mean Mr. Liang who fled to Japan after the Reform Movement failed?"; "In your articles, you always criticize the keeping of concubines. Are you acting against your own principles?" (M. Chang wants to start a newspaper, much as the partisans in *Good Men, Good Women* plan to launch *The Enlightenment* magazine to teach their countrymen about exploitation.)

4) Cinemetrics database (www.cinemetrics.lv)

Shu Qi plays a courtesan languishing in the lacquered world of the Tataocheng brothel secretly pining for the patron M. Chang (again Chang Chen) who talks poetry and politics with her. They both long for freedom, though of a different kind: he wants his imperiled isle to liberate itself from Japanese rule, while she yearns for the same liberty he has accorded a young concubine, by paying off her indentured debt. The ornate setting and dress recall Hou's amber-lit masterpiece *Flowers of Shanghai* (1998), whose clatter of mahjong tiles and hypnotic score are replaced here by silence, muted music – mostly soft solo piano – and two occasions of implied sound, in which Shu Qi sings a traditional song, accompanying herself on a stringed instrument. (One can almost hear the hiss and slither of silk, the sotto voce negotiations over the concubine's fate.) Cinematographer Mark Lee resists the clichéd halation of many period films, illuminating the confined spaces of the perfectly preserved wooden house with crisp, distilled twilight.

The segment employs eighteen fades-to-black as caesuras, recalling similar slow-fade hiatuses in *Flowers of Shanghai*, in a fastidiously linear chronology – "A Time for Love" uses only three such fades and begins with a premonitory sequence before (perhaps!) winding back in time. As materialist in its way as *Flowers*, though less heady and suggestive, "A Time for Freedom" is organized around a series of entrances and exits, oblique glances, and nebulous gestures; its world seems closed and immutable. (Departure is rendered as destabilizing: when M. Chang leaves, the camera gazes down the stairwell as he descends, the framed space split between a banister on the right and the stairway on the left, punctuated by a sliver of window downstairs and what turns out to be the continuation of the stairway in front of it.) The cloistered atmosphere of emotional privation, the gulf between the stanched passion of the courtesan and the obtuse fervor of the man who looks past her longing for autonomy to a wider realm of emancipation – historical, political, national – finally becomes allegorical, the freedom of the title bitterly ironic. Like Liang Ching in *Good Men, Good Women*, Shu Qi's courtesan seems trapped in a perpetual past. Immured among her mirrors, she covers both the large glass that M. Chang uses to dress, and the small oval mirror that later frames the face of the ten-year-old girl destined to become a concubine, with red embroidered curtains to avoid the reflection of evil spirits. By contrast, the brazen Liang Ching makes out with her lover Ah-wei before a full-length glass, narcissistically

inspecting herself as they have sex and then discussing whether she should have his child. A similar large mirror helps turn her apartment into a glassed-in enclosure, where she is imprisoned with her memories of Ah-wei.[5]

"A Time for Youth," the last segment of *Three Times*, set in present day Taipei, returns to the terrain of two of Hou's most controversial films, *Daughter of the Nile* (1987) and *Millennium Mambo* (2001), both traduced by critics as misguided ventures into contemporary pop culture. More than either, "A Time for Youth," one of Hou's few egregious lapses, presents contemporary Taipei as a forbidding locus of infirmity, alienation, and historical obliviousness. (Hou said that he wanted the episode to reflect the atmosphere of the 2004 elections, and the tensions between nationalists and those who desire rapprochement with the mainland.)[6] The bliss, retrieved through memory and music, that Hou has suggested was the inspiration and impetus for *Three Times*, is nowhere apparent in the amorphous, drifting lives of the couple – Jing, an afflicted singer-model and Zhen, a photographer enthralled by her fragility – whose "youth" is blighted by disease and anxiety. Jing seems a remake of Vicky, the rootless heroine of *Millennium Mambo*, also played by Shu Qi. (Although Hou told Tony Rayns that Part 3 was "a new beginning" for him, he also said it "takes off from what we did in *Millennium Mambo*.")[7] Attempting to capture the sheer weightlessness and inertia of contemporary Taipei, *Millennium Mambo* focuses on free-spirited bar hostess Vicky as she floats into the new millennium, seemingly unfettered by work, love, or family, drifting night to night, club to club, Ecstasy and techno fueling and flattening her abandon. Hou has said that heedless Vicky is a modern-day version of the courtesans in *Flowers of Shanghai*, free to choose what men she wants in her life, and she finally leaves the abusive addict Hao-hao for a gentle, older businessman.

Some of Hou's erstwhile champions felt baffled or betrayed by *Millennium Mambo*, by the incessant superficiality of its young characters and the film's lack of history and politics. One might argue that these voids are Hou's point and purpose; he is genuinely fascinated with Vicky's (non-)life, and he wants to get at its sadness, its seeming freedom. (The theme of entrapment carries over from *Flowers of Shanghai*.) The tranquil rhythms and deep focus, static, often symmetrical and extended shots for which Hou has been celebrated are replaced in *Millennium Mambo* by the throbbing, spectral beat of rave music and a nervously roving, claustrophobic camera, which employs narrow depth of field to capture a world he finds shallow, disconsolate. Hou describes his visual approach as that of a microscope, using an 85 mm lens to bring things close, so close in fact that they can be hazy, obscured, or oddly cropped, rendering Vicky's neon-lit world chaotic, indecipherable.[8] Hou's time sequences are often challenging, and *Mambo*'s has a confounding effect. A voiceover tells us at the beginning that the events "happened ten years ago in the year 2001," and the narration often announces what will happen a few scenes or sequences later, a spiral of time complicated by Vicky's sudden trip to Japan. Like Tsai Ming-liang's *What Time Is It There?* (2001), *Millennium Mambo* is a ghost story, but what has died is more than a single soul – history, memory, a sense of being and belonging.

Hou's aversion to the modernity of the alienated and unanchored, of compulsive consumerism and historical amnesia, apparent in *Daughter of the Nile* and *Millennium Mambo*, was already palpably evident in his Taiwan trilogy, which he has called his "Three Tragedies" – *A City of Sadness* (1989), *The Puppetmaster* (1993), and *Good Men, Good Women* – a monumental chronicle of his country's postwar history. Establishing the past by which the present is measured and found wanting, the first two films in the trilogy are perhaps Hou's greatest –

5) See the detailed discussion of Hou's use of mirrors in *Good Men, Good Women* in Jerome Silbergeld, *Hitchcock with a Chinese Face: Cinematic Doubles, Oedipal Triangles, and China's Moral Voice* (Seattle, WA: University of Washington Press, 2004), 88–93.

6) Michel Ciment and Yann Tobin, "Entretien avec Hou Hsiao-hsien: Nos meilleurs moments," *Positif*, Number 537 (November 2005), 16–18

7) "Five Questions for Hou Hsiao-hsien"

8) See Lee Ellickson, "Preparing to Live in the Present: An Interview with Hou Hsiao-hsien," *Cineaste*, Volume 27, Number 4 (Fall 2002), 15, where Hou confesses about the *Millennium Mambo* shoot, "I still feel much more comfortable filming the countryside than I do filming a city."

certainly his most complex and demanding. *A City of Sadness* was the first film to address the event that most deeply scarred postwar Taiwan's body politic, and which was left suppressed and suppurating in the national memory: the "228 Incident," as the Taiwanese call it, referring to February 28, 1947, the date on which a struggle between a policeman and a Taiwanese woman erupted into an island-wide conflagration. The rebellion was quickly crushed by the corrupt Kuomintang regime, whose forces, many dispatched from Nanjing [Nanking] by Chiang Kai-shek, massacred as many as thirty thousand Taiwanese natives and broke the independence movement. Hou's intimate epic focuses on an extended family, the Lins, in the years between Japan's defeat and subsequent withdrawal from Taiwan in 1945 and the 228 Incident and its aftermath. The Incident had been expunged from official history for many decades, and the polyphonic density of *A City of Sadness* seems as much an act of historical restitution as a formal approach: from enforced silence, a sudden, mournful pouring forth of voices. The indrawn, watchful quality of its compositions, all long takes and framed space, intensifies this sense of apprehensive disclosure; in Hou's typically oblique method, the Incident is not portrayed but only alluded to.

If the sprawling, abstruse *A City of Sadness* sometimes seems to require the full exegetical apparatus of family trees and background notes on Taiwanese history, *The Puppetmaster* – about Li Tien-lu, one of Taiwan's official "national treasures," whose life (1910–98) spanned the turbulent modern history of the island, from the early years of Japanese occupation through the coming of democracy – is even more difficult. After using Li as an actor (most memorably in *Dust in the Wind*), Hou decided to fashion the puppeteer's life into a film, focusing on the four decades under Japanese rule. Hou treats Li's craft (and craftiness), which was perfected despite strict censorship by the occupying forces, as an expression of Taiwanese identity and lovingly recreates some of the master's most vivid performances. The director characteristically employs modernist strategies to celebrate a traditional art form. As he would henceforth, Hou compresses time, sometimes conflating past and present within the same frame or leaping a decade in a single cut. Temporal shifts and caesuras between narrative events are abrupt, unmarked, or provisory. He elides central events or leaves them offscreen, collapses fact and fiction, history and performance, moves between a multitude of characters without transitional devices, and fills his compositions with so much quotidian detail that one's eye is left to roam a field of potential signifiers that may be mundane, even indifferent, but seem so implicative that they demand deciphering.

It is in the final panel of Hou's historical triptych, *Good Men, Good Women*, that his desolate view of contemporary Taiwan is most urgently expressed, repeatedly juxtaposing incidents from a heroic past with similar events in a dissipated present. The film explores another topic long taboo in Taiwan: the period known as the White Terror, during which '50s cold-war paranoia escalated into full-scale repression. The Chiang Kai-shek regime, now ensconced in Taiwan and abetted by the United States, imprisoned or executed thousands of leftists and nationalists and *Good Men, Good Women* examines the legacy of that brutal era. Hou is less interested in how "Red Scare" intensified into "White Terror" than in how the inhibition of political memory continues to exact a psychic toll decades after the event. His most wrenching film, which achieves a piercing threnody of grief in its concluding sequences, *Good Men, Good Women* is a tribute to Chiang Pi-yu [Chiang Bi-yu], a brave patriot who joined the anti-Japanese resistance in the '40s only to be imprisoned as a threat to the state in the '50s.

The film assertively braids past and present, art and history, to suggest that contemporary life has lost any sense of selfless purpose. Hou juxtaposes the story of Chiang Pi-yu (shot in black-and-white) with that of actress Liang Ching, previously a bar hostess, who is rehearsing to play the partisan in a film (in color). Hou further complicates his structure by layering another "past" into the contemporary story – the film has three time frames, much as *Three Times* does – which doubles and deepens his theme: good men and good women still exist in modern Taiwan, he suggests, but idealism, and commitment to anything but the immediate and the monetary, seem impossible. (Like Robert Bresson, to whom Hou would later pay homage in *The Electric Princess Picture House* [2007], Hou employs a modern gadget – in this case, a fax machine – as an infernal instrument, a kind of externalized, mechanical conscience for Liang Ching, as the tormentor who daily sends pages from her stolen diary to her remains unidentified.)

Perhaps because the idea for the final segment of *Three Times* came from another director who shared Hou's office and was working with a different actress who inspired the idea for Jing's character, the attenuated "A Time for Youth" lacks the conviction of either *Good Men,*

Good Women or *Millennium Mambo*, even as it extends their critique of modernity.[9] An unconvincing coda to *Three Times*, suffering from compression and tendentiousness, "A Time for Youth" appears both overloaded and thin. Even more than Liang Ching who drunkenly performs a karaoke song that summarizes her self-loathing – "All around I see gilded lives, but mine is tarnished… Why was I born under a bad star?" – Jing seems paralyzed by her ill fortune. An epileptic bisexual Goth art-song chanteuse born premature with broken bones and a hole in her heart, Jing arrives burnt out, losing her sight, and bedeviled by her jealous lesbian lover Micky whom she escapes to spend more time with her beau. (Her ex-girlfriend, we later find out, committed suicide, and one wonders if Hou cynically uses Jing's homosexuality as another symptom of her unstable state.) With a yen sign tattooed on her throat, Jing exhorts an "everything for sale" message: "Name your price. I want to sell my soul. No past, no future. Just a greedy present," recalling the guilt-ridden Liang Ching who takes hush or blood money to cover up the death of her lover Ah-wei.

In "A Time for Youth," text messaging has replaced the wistful letters of "A Time for Love" and the elegant calligraphy of "A Time for Freedom" – all is speed, media, and entropy in today's Taipei, every image alterable, every word (including Jing's broken English) depleted. The closed, composed worlds of the billiard hall and brothel give way to steely, anomic spaces whose geography often appears baffling, blurred and obscured by a shallow depth of field and rack focus. Early on, Hou revealed an Ozu-like eye for patterns and forms – e.g., the apertures that reappear throughout *Dust in the Wind*, from the opening train tunnel that forms a kind of iris shot to the window in the tailor's shop and the tunnel in the army barracks on Quemoy – and "A Time for Youth" predictably does not want for visual splendor. Everywhere one finds Hou's fondness for color effects (a late, ironic sunburst of lemon in a cab, a garbage truck, and workers' uniforms as Jing returns home to smoke and contemplate her fate) and his attention to texture (the soft pink shimmer of a glass-bead curtain in Jing's apart-

9) "Five Questions for Hou Hsiao-hsien"

ment). Among his many found symmetries, none is more striking than the wooden curvature on the transparent door to the club's washroom that frames the conversation between Jing and Micky, pressing the two together in the middle of the image, their centrality accentuated when another woman takes up frame right. And it is a measure of Hou's mastery that "Youth" manages to overcome its enervation in the symmetrical motorcycle drive that closes the episode (and the entire film), shot in long take, an onrushing reminder of similar wild rides to nowhere, especially in the final sequence of *Goodbye South, Goodbye* (1996). Jing and Zhen finally lose us, leaving the breathless camera behind as they proceed into their un-

certain future, unlike the good men and good women who advance toward us on their confident path to a prospect they imagine, wrongly, will only be brighter.

Three Times encapsulates a career, but hardly encompasses it. Patiently waiting for Hou's stories to coalesce out of floating, notational detail, for the relationships between his characters to emerge from a nimbus of uncertainty, for the muted and indistinct to slowly flare into incandescence – the votive fires at the end of *Good Men, Good Women* literalize this sensation – one knows precisely what Dickinson means by her edict about dazzle. Hou's is gradual, then engulfing.

James Udden

Dust in the Wind

A Definitive Hou/New Cinema Work

In the illustrious career of Hou Hsiao-hsien, *Dust in the Wind* (1986) is arguably the most overlooked film. In some respects, of course, this film failed to match its predecessors and successors. Both of the first two feature length projects Hou completed during Taiwan's New Cinema period – *The Boys from Fengkuei* (1983) and *A Summer at Grandpa's* (1984) – received the Golden Montgolfiere, the top prize at the Festival of Three Continents in Nantes, marking the true beginning of Hou's dazzling film festival career. As a result of these successes, Hou's next film *A Time to Live and a Time to Die* (1985) was screened at the Berlin International Film Festival in 1986, where it won a special prize in the Forum section.[1]

Three years later, in 1989, *A City of Sadness* earned a stunning triumph with a Golden Lion at Venice, proving that Hou and Taiwanese cinema had now reached the acme of the international festival world. *The Puppetmaster* then became the first Taiwanese film to be entered in the competition at Cannes in 1993, where it won a Jury Prize. In terms of festival success, *Dust in the Wind* also could not match another masterwork to come out of Taiwan in 1986: Edward Yang's *The Terrorizers*. That film at least came away with the Silver Leopard at Locarno, despite intense political pressure on

the festival from the PRC and the USSR to exclude it.[2]

By contrast, *Dust in the Wind* "merely" made a return to the Festival of Three Continents. While it managed to receive citations for Best Director, Best Cinematography and Best Music, Hou was not eligible for the Golden Montgolfiere because *Dust in the Wind* was shown outside of the competition. *Dust in the Wind* also failed to attract a sizeable domestic audience, a fate by then familiar to most New Cinema films, Hou's and Yang's included. It did nothing to allay the increasing criticisms of those who claimed that Hou was abandoning

1) In the 1980s, the "Big Three" Festivals (Cannes, Venice and Berlin) were especially skittish about showing films from Taiwan for geopolitical reasons. Probably out of fear of being passed over for films by the Fifth Generation in mainland China, they did not want to antagonize the People's Republic of China which was trying everything to prevent Taiwan from gaining international recognition as the Republic of China. Berlin had invited Hou to show two films outside of the competition in 1985, but then withdrew the invitation for unspecified reasons. After Hou won at Nantes two years in a row, the big festivals clearly decided they could no longer afford not to show films from Taiwan, but they were presented in the non-competitive sidebars. Venice finally took the plunge in 1989 by entering *A City of Sadness* in the competition. This changed the course of Taiwanese cinema, making it a true festival powerhouse in the 1990s.

2) Edward Yang, "We are Lonely Runners on a Marathon," *Long Take*, Number 3 (October 1987), 17–19

Dust in the Wind, 1986

his own audiences in favor of a foreign festival crowd. This should have been discouraging for Hou, who at the time claimed that festival success meant little to him, and that it was meaningless to make films that his own fellow citizens refused to see.[3] In addition, it is not clear that *Dust in the Wind* was the film Hou most wanted to make at the time; he was toying with three different ideas, including a never realized project to be made with funding from Germany's Channel 2 [ZDF] and another that eventually became *A City of Sadness*. Hou only decided to make *Dust in the Wind* on the advice of one of his most trusted advisors, Chan Hung-chih.[4]

If the film has been so overlooked, how can the claim here be that *Dust in the Wind* is nevertheless the "definitive" work by Hou, and of the New Cinema as a whole, when so many other Hou films seem to have garnered more attention? The answer lies largely in the aesthetics. The formal features of this one film come closest to fitting the various definitions used for Hou's films, the New Cinema as a movement, and even Taiwanese cinema as a whole. Moreover, most of the films made in the style of Asian art cinema from the 1990s onwards that has been described as "Asian Minimalism," a style Hou is largely responsible for

giving birth to, could have easily used *Dust in the Wind* as their primer. Put another way, *Dust in the Wind* marks the aesthetic culmination of the most definitive and cohesive period of Hou's career, thus forming the bedrock for the most formative movement in Taiwan's cinematic history. Much like Hou's career, the film's influence did not die out when the movement officially ended in early 1987, nor was that influence contained within Taiwan's borders.

DEFINING A NEW / NATIONAL CINEMA

Defining any national cinema, or even a notable movement within that national cinema, is fraught with conceptual difficulties. However, define we must. In the case of the New Cinema in Taiwan, one cohesive definition came from Chen Ru-shou in *The Historical-Cultural Experiences of Taiwan New Cinema*. Three of the more salient traits Chen lists – long takes, a static camera, history filtered through the personal memories of ordinary people – are better used to describe Hou's films than Edward Yang's films, or those of the movement as a whole.[5] Yang did use a static camera in many shots in *The Terrorizers*, but, on average, his shots were much shorter in duration (roughly fourteen seconds) than those in *Dust in the Wind* (thirty-three seconds). *The Terrorizers* is also set entirely in the present, unlike *Dust in the Wind,* which takes place in the early 1970s. The only New Cinema director who did match Hou in terms of shot duration is Chang Yi. Indeed, Chang's *Kuei-mei, A Woman* (1985) has a higher average shot length than Hou's *A Time to Live and a Time to Die,* but he was far less successful than Hou in his use of *static* long takes, largely because he was not able to stage his shots with anywhere near the complexity or intricacy that Hou was already showing signs of.

The New Cinema is usually said to have ended in 1987. Early in that year, nearly every major participant in the movement from filmmakers to critics published a joint statement requesting the government support "another kind of cinema." Never again would this group act in such a collective manner, and many would never make another film. However, some argue that the movement continued through the subsequent careers of Hou and Yang. There is one crucial difference between the two: Edward Yang edited more, and had less influence; Hou was the true long take master, everyone knew it, and many followed his path. What is undeniable is that Taiwanese cinema thereafter became largely identified with the long take *and* the static camera, and not everyone was pleased. In 1995, for example, Huang Ying-fen lashed out at the "festival style" that Taiwanese filmmakers then aspired to since there was no local market as it was. Huang's definition of that style can essentially be reduced to *long takes coupled with a static camera.*[6] David Bordwell has described this long take tendency as an "identifying tag" of the New Cinema in the 1980s which then became a "national brand" in the 1990s. Moreover, this did not remain a strictly national style, since it spread throughout Asia, "making 'Asian Minimalism' a festival cliché by the end of the 1990s."[7] Soon, there were examples of directors utilizing the static, long take in Japan, South Korea and even mainland China: Koreeda Hirokazu's *Maborosi* (1995), Lee Kwang-mo's *Spring in My Home Town* (1998), Wang Chao's

3) Chu Tien-wen, "Hou Hsiao-hsien's Choice" in Chu and Wu Nien-jen, *Dust in the Wind,* New Edition (Taipei: Yuan-liou Publishing Company, 1992), 17–18

4) Ibid, 15, 22

5) Chen Ru-shou, *The Historical-Cultural Experiences of Taiwan New Cinema,* Second Edition (Taipei: Variety Publishing Company, 1997), 47–52

6) Huang Ying-fen, "After the Mobile, Long Take: A Debate on the Aesthetic Tendencies in Contemporary Taiwanese Cinema," *Contemporary,* Number 116 (December, 1995), 78–83

7) David Bordwell, *Figures Traced in Light: On Cinematic Staging* (Berkeley, CA: University of California Press, 2005), 230–231

Orphans of Anyang (2001), and both Hong Sang-soo and Jia Zhang-ke in several films.[8] Some filmmakers took the long take/static camera style literally; both Tsai Ming-liang in Taiwan and Hong Sang-soo in South Korea have at least one film made up entirely of static long takes, without even slight reframings to follow minute shifts by the actors. Of all of these followers, however, Jia Zhang-ke seems to have best understood the spirit of what Hou was after. Jia has never treated the static long take as an end in and of itself. Nevertheless, this stylistic trait alone largely came to define an auteur, a movement, a national cinema, and a pan-Asian festival style, all at the same time.

This emphasis does not denigrate Yang's own aesthetic accomplishments. Intricate sound-image mismatches became one of his stylistic signatures, but nobody else in the movement seemed to follow suit (at least not until Hou also experimented with this in A City of Sadness and The Puppetmaster). Certainly, the radical ambiguity of the ending of The Terrorizers – most of all concerning what is objective and what is subjective – is a modernist tour de force. Once again, however, only Hou also attempted to create the same level of ambiguity, especially in the extraordinary sequence surrounding Wan's illness in Dust in the Wind.

At first glance, the images appear to be either Wan's own hallucinations or a dream, but the ontological status of many of the images cannot be reconciled with either interpretation. Did Wan suddenly recall a long and prolonged conversation between his father and grandfather when he was but a toddler (and also ill then) – a conversation he could not possibly have overheard or remembered? This sequence alone shows that Hou could be as much a modernist as Yang ever was, but for Hou this was a one-off experiment. In any case, nobody else in the New Cinema imitated Yang's particular daring. Thus, the salient traits of his films cannot be used to define an entire movement or a national cinema. The static, long take, on the other hand, does, whether justified or not.

DUST IN THE WIND AS A VISION REALIZED

The static long take is easily the most imitable aspect of Hou's style – indeed, by itself, this is easy for any director to emulate, which is why so many others have followed this same aesthetic path, sometimes down to the letter. Hou's intricate compositions and dense staging strategies are another matter entirely. Moreover, neither the static long take nor the com-

8) Ibid

plex compositions and staging were ever ends in themselves, but were instead means of achieving a particular vision of the world. In this regard, *Dust in the Wind* marks the first time Hou fully realized the vision he had been carefully developing during his previous films, making it a fitting end to the New Cinema stage of his career, and setting the groundwork for what was to follow.

At first glance, the film seems "light" compared to Hou's previous three films. Nobody actually dies, nor is there the life-threatening illness of a mother, which cast a dark shadow over the second half of *A Summer at Grandpa's*. Instead, the film follows a young couple (Wan and Huen) who move from a remote mining town to Taipei; Wan leaves to join the military, Huen ends up marrying a postman, and Wan returns home. The film ends with Wan discussing the crops and the weather with his grandfather. One reason the film is so deceptively lighthearted is that the story is by Wu Nien-jen, one of the most recognizable figures in Taiwan today (whether through hosting television shows, appearing in commercials, or, most recently, touring with his own theater productions). Wu is beloved for his wry humor, often able to find something funny about even the smallest details of Taiwanese

life. It is therefore little surprise that *Dust in the Wind* includes two grown, drunken men engaging in a rock moving competition or a mother scolding a son for eating their medicine. In addition, Li Tien-lu's indelible performance as the grandfather produces some of the funniest moments in this film, such as when he accidentally lights a firecracker after a power outage, thinking it was a candle. Considering these details alone, *Dust in the Wind* seems to float like a feather compared to Hou's previous films.

In truth, however, this is arguably the most profound film Hou had made up to that time. Despite a surface of seemingly random quotidian details derived from life in Taiwan in the 1970s, the film possesses a deep underlying structure woven together by a complex array of recurring motifs. Moreover, underneath all this seeming "fluff" lies a philosophical stance that Hou had been developing since the earliest days when he first joined the New Cinema movement in Taiwan, a worldview derived from an idiosyncratic corner of modern Chinese literature.

Nothing affected Hou more profoundly than when his long-trusted screenwriter, Chu Tien-wen, introduced him to Shen Congwen, a famed twentieth century novelist who is diffi-

Dust in the Wind

cult to categorize, but whose similarities to Hou are uncanny. Both men could draw from certain aspects of Chinese tradition and reject them at the same time; both are utterly idiosyncratic. Shen's unorthodox syntax and use of long sentences, for example, has been described as being "itself sufficient to keep his prose in a state of rebellion against all of China's literary traditions."[9] In his works of the 1930s, Shen tended to create "plotless, still landscapes of vivid sensory impressions."[10] Nevertheless, Hou claims that what he learned above all else from Shen was a way of seeing the world: "After reading [Shen's autobiography], my feelings and field of vision became quite broad. What I really sensed from him is a non-judgmental perspective. It is not sorrowful, and yet it possesses a deep sense of sadness. Shen Congwen does not look at people and human affairs from a particular point of view and criticize. Everything human, all that life and all that

death, becomes quite normal under his pen, and all are simply things under the sun."[11]

With each film during the New Cinema period, Hou seemed to develop this worldview more fully. By the time he made *Dust in the Wind*, he appears to have reached a point where he could go no further by relying on his own recollections or that of his entourage. Moving to the next stage, starting with *A City of Sadness*, would require him to transfer this vision more deeply onto Taiwan's peculiar historical past.

This perspective on the world affects the entire narrative structure of *Dust in the Wind*: cause and effect is not so much eradicated or deemphasized as cleverly *disguised*. Each scene includes a plethora of quotidian details. However, only in retrospect does it become clear that what first appeared to be but one quotidian detail among many is in reality a key *narrative* element. Hou was already conscious of this narrative strategy during the making of his previous film, noting in particular how a mark on a school desktop is not explained until a later scene.[12] Still, in *A Time to Live and a Time to Die*, such a retroactive causal structure remains localized. In *Dust in the Wind*, it becomes a global narrative strategy, one that takes some getting used to. The most serious detail to emerge in

9) Jeff Kinkley, *The Odyssey of Shen Congwen* (Stanford, CA: Stanford University Press, 1987), 137

10) Ibid, 166

11) Chang Jinn-pei, "Before *A City of Sadness*: A Talk with Hou Hsiao-hsien," *The Journal of the Beijing Film Academy*, Volume 13, Number 2 (1990), 69

12) Hou Hsiao-hsien interview by Peggy Chiao in *Cinema in the Republic of China Yearbook*, 1986 (Taipei: National Film Archive, 1986), 9

the opening scenes is that Wan's father has returned from the hospital on crutches. This is more than counterbalanced by other details that seem unimportant. Why is it that one younger brother will not eat, even when the grandfather tries to convince him he is serving "Western" food? Why does another brother seem willing to eat anything, including medicine from a cabinet? Some audience members will laugh at the Grandfather's antics; others may giggle when the mother goes after the brother with a stick. These moments meld perfectly with others – the arrival of Wan and Huen on a train after school or the scene where Wan and Huen return home with a bag of rice and notice that there will be an open-air film screening that evening. All these seem to be mere incidents, life and nothing more.

It is only later when Huen arrives in Taipei that these earlier scenes retrospectively take on a darker tinge. Deeper connections emerge during a remarkable eating scene on the day of Huen's arrival. The conversation between Wan, Huen, and their other friends is banal, especially when Huen suddenly remembers a gift for Wan from his father back home: a watch. Everyone admires the watch, talking about its waterproof qualities and its likely expense. They are so distracted by this new shining bauble that few notice that Wan has stopped eating and has even stopped moving. As the others speculate as to the cost of this watch, Wan suddenly storms out of the room. The friends are shocked as are we, the viewers. Shortly thereafter, Wan is shown soaking the watch in water while writing home. Wan has clearly come to accept the watch and its amazing waterproof qualities, yet in the letter he briefly expresses concern about the cost of the watch. Piecing the fragments together, it seems that Wan was most likely upset that day because it was an expensive watch and he worried that his father could not actually afford it. This delayed revelation puts all the preceding scenes in a new, darker light. The reason one boy was not eating while another was eating medicine is that the family is not entirely sure how they will find their next meal. Survival is a real issue for this family and certain details no longer seem innocuous once that is understood.

The core narrative event in the film, Wan and Huen's sudden breakup, is handled in the same way. There are some hints of trouble in the relationship, albeit much less than what is found in the published script.[13] However, there are an equal number of hints that this couple will stay together for life. For this reason, the breakup comes as a shock. No doubt the military draft is a chief cause of this relationship's end, but when Wan goes away to the military, he receives a letter from Huen saying that she is counting the days until his return. That same letter provides two other details that appear, at least in retrospect, contradictory. On the one hand, Huen includes tags from women's underwear, which at the time was a way for a young woman to indicate permanent commitment to a young man. On the other hand, she also mentions going to a film with friends, including a postman. (She even includes the ticket stubs as evidence.) The "climax" of the film includes an astonishing number of ellipses. Within less than ten minutes of screen time, we go from Wan reading a letter from Huen expressing how she is his forever to a letter from his own brother saying she has married someone else. Hou did little to prepare us for Huen marrying the postman; he had previously appeared only briefly in two shots, one of which

is an extreme long shot. At that point, he was merely a postman delivering mail with no idea who Huen was. We had no idea who he was, or that he would play such a significant narrative role.

In a sense, what Hou offers the viewer is not cause and effect, but rather effects almost drowned out by the endless details of everyday life. As a result, the causes are left for us to surmise. His extremely elliptical and oblique narration is risky to say the least, and yet what holds it all together is a complex weave of motifs, all of which resonate with each other. The first and last shots of *Dust in the Wind* include two core motifs: the train and the verdant landscapes. The last shot of the film is of clouds and sea mingling with mountain peaks, and yet, off-screen, a distant train whistle can be heard. Shots of clocks at the train station in turn connect to the all-important watch that Wan received from his father. In response to that, Wan writes a letter, one of many in the film. Letters in turn are connections bridging distances, just like trains; but, at the end of the film, letters also signal severances such as when Wan's letters to Huen are inexplicably returned, answered only by a letter from his brother (and to add motivic insult to injury, Huen married a *postman* no less!). This breakup connects with

13) The original script written by Wu Nien-jen and Chu Tien-wen makes clear that Wu wanted to be more explicit about problems in this relationship, which he actually experienced as a young man. One telling moment is a scene never filmed in which Huen works in a restaurant and Wan watches from a distance as male customers flirt with her. Later, she seems very familiar with one of her male coworkers, who she smiles at. While this is still suggestive at best, it was clearly far too direct for Hou's taste (See Chu and Wu, 95, 105).

another motif, movies. The countryside and the city may be connected by trains, but they are contrasted by open-air movie screens in the former versus claustrophobic indoor movie screens in the latter. In her letter to Wan while he is in the service, Huen includes ticket stubs after going to a movie with their mutual friends – *and a certain postman* – a meaningless detail at the time. Then, there is the most ubiquitous motif, one found even strewn on the train tracks or when a mainland fishing family is stranded at his post: food. Charles Tesson's essay on this film captures perfectly the symbolic significance of food in *Dust in the Wind,* encapsulated in the last scene when Wan listens to his grandfather speak of failed crops and capricious weather. As Tesson put it, "The boy, in returning home, has also returned to the source of food and is once again joined together with nature."[14] For Hou, these are the inescapable realities – food, landscapes, and nature all dwarf our histories, forming the fundamentals of human experience, whether in Taiwan or elsewhere. With food, Hou reaches for our primal core. He also expresses a core philosophy.

DUST IN THE WIND AS A RARIFIED STYLE FULLY REALIZED

Hou's unique vision of the world carefully and steadily evolved over the four feature length films of his New Cinema period from 1983 to 1986. So did all the hallmarks of his style, including what became the most imitated: the static long take. Yet a careful analysis of these films, including crude measurements such as average shot lengths and the percentage of shots that contain camera movements, reveal a surprising development. When one compares Hou to other long take masters, whether predecessors such as Mizoguchi Kenji or Jean Renoir, or contemporaries such as Theo Angelopoulos or Béla Tarr, Hou stands out in this respect: the longer his takes become on average, the more static they become. It is typical for long take masters to utilize a *mobile* camera almost as a substitute for editing. Indeed, the most memorable long takes of a master such as Tarr almost invariably involved incessant tracking shots. Typically, for most of these directors, the norm is for anywhere from 2/3 to 3/4 of the shots to have overt camera movement, often

14) Charles Tesson, "Dust in the Wind," *Hou Hsiao-hsien* (Taipei: National Film Archive, 2000), 174

15) Hou Hsiao-hsien interview by author, June 20, 2001

for the duration of the shot. The exceptions, such as Andy Warhol in some films or Chantal Akerman in the 1970s, very consciously employ the static long take almost as an end in itself.

Hou does nothing of the sort. In the earliest days of his career, when he was making commercial films in the Taiwanese film industry, Hou generally averaged around twelve seconds per shot. The average shot length (ASL) of his chapter of *The Sandwich Man*, his first foray as a New Cinema director, was sixteen seconds per shot. Gradually, the average duration of his shots for each film thereafter increased. Both *The Boys from Fengkuei* and *A Summer at Grandpa's* averaged around eighteen-nineteen seconds per shot, and with *A Time to Live and a Time to Die*, the average shot length increased to around twenty-four seconds. In *Dust in the Wind*, however, the average duration was over half a minute, a figure that rivals other long take masters such as Mizoguchi and Renoir. Yet, once again, what is particularly striking about Hou is that, as his shots became longer in duration, they also became *increasingly static*. Hou acknowledges that he first became aware of this particular tendency during the production of *A Summer at Grandpa's*. A daily siesta was imposed on the crew since they were shooting in a real, operating clinic; Hou fell in

love with the stilled atmosphere of those times of imposed silence, and tried to replicate it with an increasingly static camera.[15] In *The Boys from Fengkuei*, nearly half the shots still contained at least some camera movement. With *A Summer at* Grandpa's, despite having a nearly identical ASL, the percentage of shots with a mobile framing drops to 1/3. With *A Time to Live and a Time to Die*, despite a much longer shot length than its two predecessors, the percentage of shots with camera movement was reduced to roughly 1/4 of the shots. In the case of *Dust in the Wind*, which has many long takes, only about 1/5 of the shots have any sort of camera movement at all, and half of those camera movements are slight, momentary reframings at best.

Despite such radical stillness, however, Hou's shots are often teeming with life. His mostly static long takes do not necessarily lead to Brechtian alienation, and they feel nothing like the static long takes of Warhol in the 1960s or Akerman in the 1970s. This is largely because, while the camera does not, Hou's actors do move often. With each passing film, his staging techniques became more and more complex. Yet it is in *Dust in the Wind* that Hou first became truly stupendous at using complex staging in depth; indeed, in this film Hou seems to have, for the first time, perfected a technique that is rather difficult for any director to master. This is most evident in the eating and drinking scenes, such as when Wan storms out over the watch. Part of the reason viewers are so caught off guard by that moment is because the staging distracts us from his sullenness, forcing our attention to the others admiring the watch, not the brooding Wan. We can see Wan on the far end of the table, perfectly placed between the heads of those on the near side of the table in relation to the camera. However, the words and movements of the rest of the actors call for our attention as they pass the watch around, try it on, hold it up to their ears, or shake it. Moreover, this is one of those rare long takes with a slight camera movement at the end, a pan right for some reframing. But the purpose of this movement is clear after close analysis: it is designed along with the staging to distract us from Wan until he shockingly storms out. The eating/drinking scene when Wan gives Huen a significant stare is another telling example – rather than place most of the actors on one side of the table, Hou layers them so that the most minute movements by those in the foreground can occlude or draw attention to those in the background. When Wan gives that momentary look her way (we only find out later it is be-cause she drank with other men present), he is perfectly framed by those in the foreground whose heads are backed to the camera.

It is important to keep in mind that complex staging is only a small part of a much more complex style that is indelibly Hou Hsiao-hsien's. Hou never did this out of principle. Instead, it was the result of piecemeal experimentation done film by film, relying on his instinct along the way as he tried to find the cinematic equivalent to a Shen Congwen-like view of the world. Likewise, the static long take was but one piece of a larger picture, one that allowed him to employ these peculiar staging strategies. In fact, nearly every film Hou made up to *Dust in the Wind* represented a step ahead in terms of his peculiar stylistic development. Even in his commercial stage, Hou had already realized that one did not always need to edit. With *The Boys from Fengkuei*, he discovered distance. With *A Time to Live and a Time to Die*, he first became aware of a more retroactive narrative strategy. *Dust in the Wind*, on the other hand, is where Hou seems to have put everything together for the first time in a single package, one dressed with staging techniques that few in history have dared to attempt. Hou himself admits this was the film where he finally overcame the technical limitations of all his previous films.[16] Yet, as seen here, *Dust in the Wind* is not only the crowning technical achievement for Hou during the New Cinema period – it is also an aesthetic and philosophical milestone.

CONCLUSION

Dust in the Wind marks both the pinnacle and definitive end of the most cohesive period in Hou's career. It also marks a sort of end to the most definitive period in the history of Taiwanese cinema. Hou's next film in 1987, *Daughter of the Nile,* was an odd step sideways, precisely at a moment when most directors in the New Cinema movement found it difficult to continue their careers. Hou followed that with two masterpieces, *A City of Sadness* and *The Puppetmaster* (1993). In these two films, Hou seems to have taken the aesthetic and narrative strategies first fully employed in *Dust in the Wind* and applied them to two of the most pivotal eras in Taiwanese history: the Japanese colonial period (1895–1945) and its immediate aftermath. Thereafter, each of Hou's films would become

even more unpredictable. Even in 1995, Chu Tien-wen, who understands Hou best, predicted that from that point on Hou's career would be nothing more than "complications and twists and turns."[17] Subsequent developments have proven her right.

Given the difficult conditions under which the film was made, *Dust in the Wind* is a remarkable accomplishment for Hou. Indeed, it is remarkable that this film has not received more notice than it has. This was not lost on everyone. At the time, Wu Cheng-huan claimed this about *Dust in the Wind*: "With this film, Taiwan finally has a work of art that can compare with the 'economic miracle.'"[18] Perhaps if André Bazin had lived to a ripe old age and seen this film, *Dust in the Wind* would have received the credit it warrants. If this instead had been the last film Hou had ever made, it is still possible that an anthology like this would be warranted, and *Dust in the Wind* would be clearly seen as the crowning masterpiece of an entire career. Hou is lucky that he was born and raised in Taiwan, for it is unlikely that he could have even made a film like this anywhere else. Then again, Taiwan is lucky to have Hou, for it is unlikely that anyone else would have dared to attempt, and then nearly perfect, what he does in this one film.

16) Ibid

17) Chu Tien-wen, *Good Men, Good Women* (Taipei: Rye Field Publishing Company, 1995), 8

18) Wu Cheng-huan, "Dust in the Wind," *Cinema in the Republic of China Yearbook,* 1987 (Taipei: National Film Archive, 1987), 11

Wen Tien-hsiang

The Unmarried Women

This is an article on the unmarried women in Hou Hsiao-hsien's recent films in reverse chronological order. First, we talk about the female lead in Hou's short film, *La Belle Epoque*, a segment of the portmanteau film *10 + 10* (2011) with a nostalgic ambience. Hou's heroine does not follow the traditions (of Taiwanese society and of Hou's other films). Then, we turn to *Café Lumière*, a film Hou shot in Japan in 2003. In this film, we see that the character of the unmarried woman has already fully formed in his work. In the context of Hou's career, could the unconventionality of these two heroines signify a change in his attitude towards life?

10 + 10: LA BELLE EPOQUE

After completing *Flight of the Red Balloon* (2007), Hou was elected Chairman of the Taipei Golden Horse Film Festival Executive Committee in 2009. He has achieved several pioneering tasks during his term of office, including the establishment of the Golden Horse Film Academy. It aims to bring renowned filmmakers together to share their experience with groups of new directors who have made Chinese-language short films. Under the guidance of the experienced mentors, the young filmmakers collaborate on short films at the Academy workshop. Previous participants include the Burmese / Taiwanese director Midi Z, whose film was nominated for a Tiger Award at the International Film Festival Rotterdam, and the Singaporean director Anthony Chen who was awarded the Camera d'Or at the 2013 Cannes International Film Festival for his first feature film, *Ilo Ilo*. Subsequently, in 2010, the book *The River of Shadow and Light – 100 Greatest Chinese-language Films* was published in Chinese as well as English.[1] Selected and voted by filmmakers, academics, and film critics, the book is not only the most complete, but also the most important worldwide reference for research on Chinese-language cinema. Furthermore, in 2011, ten established directors and ten up-and-coming directors were invited to participate in *10 + 10* as part of Taiwan's centennial celebration. Each of them made a five minute segment depicting the "uniqueness of Taiwan" from their point of view. *10 + 10* was selected as the opening film of the 2011 Golden Horse Film Festival and travelled to film festivals in Berlin, Hong Kong, Busan, and London. Hou made *La Belle Epoque* as his contribution to the project.

1) *The River of Shadow and Light – 100 Greatest Chinese-language Films*, collaboratively edited by the Taipei Golden Horse Film Festival Executive Committee (Taipei: Garden City Publishers, 2011)

La Belle Epoque, 2011

and, moreover, it can be turned into financial support if it is needed in the future. However, in *La Belle Epoque*, there is no sign of an upcoming wedding, leading one to conclude that the mother has decided that "the moment has arrived" despite the fact that the daughter is not getting married. In their intimate conversation, the mother talks about how gold has always been used as a present to express people's gratitude and how gold jewelry has always been handled with care. This shows Hou's nostalgia for "the old world" and his "constancy." On the other hand, the daughter, dressed in a crisp white shirt and jeans, joins the family for the photo shoot with ease since her choice of remaining single is readily accepted by her family. This rather unconventional arrangement represents Hou's "change" and his acceptance of the "new world." This makes the shot of the big tree in front of the house, which appears in the beginning and the end of the film, even more significant. The tree provides shelter to

Audiences familiar with Hou's early works will immediately notice that the main location in *La Belle Epoque* is the same as in *A Summer at Grandpa's* (1984). It is the Chong-guang Clinic in Tongluo (Miaoli County), a historic building where Chu Tien-wen's grandfather lived.[2] Hou cuts from the children playing in the corridor to the mother and daughter talking in the room; one can infer that the film takes place at a family gathering. The mother (Mei Feng) hands pieces of jewelry and bars of gold to the daughter (Shu Qi). These presents are called *qiumui* in Taiwanese. Usually a mother gives her daughter the jewelry before her wedding. It signifies the mother's love and blessing for her daughter

2) Chu Tien-wen was an established novelist in Taiwan before moving into scriptwriting. In 1983, she and Hou turned her award-winning story into a screenplay, for *Growing Up* (directed by Chen Kun-hou), that won Best Adapted Screenplay at the Golden Horse Awards. Since *The Boys from Fengkuei* (1983), Chu has written all of Hou's films. She won Best Original Screenplay and Best Adapted Screenplay at the Golden Horse Awards for

everyone – it does not matter whether one chooses to marry or not. The tranquility in Hou's films embraces traditions, but respects changes; both the old and new bear testimony to the purity gold symbolizes.

Hou mentioned that the story of *La Belle Epoque* was inspired by the experience of his long-time collaborator, Hwarng Wern-ying.[3] However, a similar viewpoint can be found in *Café Lumière*, which he shot in Japan in 2003.

CAFÉ LUMIÈRE

Café Lumière was Hou's first foreign-language film. He was invited by Shochiku to make a film to commemorate the centenary of Ozu Yasujirō (1903–1963). Ozu has long been considered *the most Japanese* of all film directors and his works center around Japanese emotions and relationships. Although this sounds very similar to Hou's focus on Taiwanese families, the parallel comparison is rather arbitrary. For the scene of parents visiting daughter/daughter-in-law

A Time to Live and a Time to Die and *Good Men, Good Women*, respectively.

3) Hwarng Wern-ying has worked with Hou as art director and costume designer since *Good Men, Good Women*. She won Best Art Direction at the Golden Horse Awards for *Flowers of Shanghai* in 1998.

and the host borrowing sake from the neighbor, Hou used one single long take lasting 104 seconds in *Café Lumière*, while Ozu arranged seven shots in forty seconds in *Tokyo Story* (1953). Both films make similar use of scenes in which the families casually chat while waiting for sushi, but Hou films his in one long take lasting for approximately four minutes and Ozu uses at least twenty-four shots. The editing styles alone show the substantial difference between Ozu and Hou, so we can only say that both masters are very good at capturing the essence of daily life.

Shochiku had invested in a number of Hou's previous films. However, to make a Japanese film in Japan was completely different from having Japanese funding for a Taiwanese production. Liao Ching-sung, the editor and producer of *Café Lumière*, described the experience as like "Taoism (natural, fuzzy) meets Yangmingism (clear, organized)."[4] How the two would adapt to each other was an open question and people were even more curious about how Japan or Ozu's spirit would be treated in Hou's film.

The plot of *Café Lumière* is neither clear nor dramatic. In short, it tells the story of Inoue Yōko (Hitoto Yō). Yōko is doing research on Jiang Wen-ye, a Taiwanese composer who studied in Japan. She returns to Japan from Taiwan and, in a dream she has about a baby, we learn that she is carrying a child by her Taiwanese boyfriend, who she has decided not to marry. The camera follows Yōko as she gets on and off the train, drinks coffee, and carries on her research. In these seemingly trivial and insignificant details, Hou's observations on relationships between people and his attitude to life are clearly reflected. In addition to Yōko's parents, Takeuchi Hajime (Asano Tadanobu), who runs a second-hand bookshop, plays an important role in her life. His relationship with Yōko

seems, ambiguously, both distant and close. They spend a lot of time together, but it appears as if he lacks the courage to make a move.

Although Ozu was good at depicting family life in Japan, his works are not confined by old traditions. In *Tokyo Story*, he laments the fact that traditions are crumbling as the Japanese try to reconstruct their country. After her mother-in-law's funeral, Hirayama Noriko (Hara Setsuko), the embodiment of the perfect women, tells her sister-in-law (who despises her own sister and brother) that changes are inevitable and confesses that she sometimes finds herself lacking confidence. Noriko's sincerity and efforts give us a final glimpse into the beauty of Japanese traditions, however, since she needs to rethink her future, they also announce the inevitable move towards the "new world." Despite everything – including the estrangement of his children and a widowed daughter-in-law who could have left but still remains close to

4) Interview for the documentary *Métro Lumière: Hou Hsiao-hsien à la rencontre de Yasujirō Ozu* (Harold Manning, 2004). Liao Ching-sung is a veteran editor in Taiwan. He has directed two films and also works as producer on Hou's films. He was awarded Outstanding Taiwanese Filmmaker of the Year at the 2002 Golden Horse Awards. [Editor's note: Ming dynasty philosopher Wang Yangming (1472–1529) was an influential Neo-Confucian idealist associated with the School of Mind.]

him – the ageing father (Ryū Chishū) who always keeps silent must have reconciled himself to both the changed and the unchanged. I am more curious about whether he has thought about how to live with his youngest daughter, a single primary school teacher. My question is answered in Ozu's *Late Spring* (1949) and *An Autumn Afternoon* (1962).

It has been fifty years since Ozu passed away. Even if he was here to make a film about Yōko today, she would not be another Noriko. Hou's tribute to Ozu does not come through copies of the low-angle shots Ozu is known for, but rather through an imaginative and spiritual connection to the old master.

When looking at how Hou deals with the relationship between father and daughter in *Café Lumière*, the first image that comes to mind is of the father (Kobayashi Nenji) waiting for his daughter at the exit of the train station. The train has not arrived, and there is no dialogue, yet his silence reveals more than words as his body language speaks louder. We know that Yōko's father had worked away from home. He should know that his daughter no longer depends on him. Today, she contacts him and pays him a visit, and yet he does not really know how to talk with young women, let alone a woman who leads an independent life

in Tokyo. Expectation and nervousness are clearly suggested by his gestures. When Yōko finally appears, he walks up to her and helps her with the baggage. The only words he comes up with are, "How long will you stay this time?" "Just two or three days," she replies.

When they get home, the father sits on the *tatami* – reading newspapers, watching baseball games, and drinking beer – while the mother is busy preparing food. This sequence demonstrates the roles played by husband and wife in a traditional Japanese marriage. Yōko's relationship with her parents is, however, quite different. When she is back with her parents, she sleeps when she feels like it, ignoring dinnertime and offering no help. She wakes up in the middle of the night; while she is looking for food in the kitchen her mother gets up and cooks for her. This is when she breaks the news of her pregnancy to her mother.

How does the father learn the news? We do not get to see it in the film, but, in a long sequence shot with a fixed camera (Ozu would never have done it this way), we see Yōko (after having visited the graves of her ancestors) drink a cup of tea without saying a word to her father, borrow her mother's bicycle, and depart. The tension is evident. The mother pleads with her husband to talk to Yōko, but he remains silent. He changes his positions on the *tatami* and tries to go out, intentionally dodging the subject.

Obviously, the issue of "being single and pregnant" is not solved. When the father goes to Tokyo to attend his friend's funeral, he and his wife pay Yōko a visit. This "visit" makes a good comparison to the one in Ozu's *Tokyo Story*.

Tokyo Story depicts an old couple's rather disheartening visit to their children in Tokyo. Although their own children are occupied with their work and personal lives, the couple is somehow warmly welcomed by their widowed daughter-in-law in her apartment. In this film, Ozu shows the increasing number of working women in Japan after the Second World War. Moreover, through the scene in which the daughter-in-law borrows sake from her neighbor to treat her in-laws, Ozu portrays the lives of single women and nuclear families in detail. In *Café Lumière*, Yōko's parents come to her small apartment. As soon as they arrive, the mother busies herself with cleaning the fridge and heating up Yōko's favorite dish, stewed pork with potatoes. Yōko suddenly realizes that she does not have tea in her place, so she serves her parents chilled water. Hou shows that Yōko keeps a special blue mug for herself while

her parents drink from plain glasses, and this is an indication of Yōko's life as a single woman. In the following sequence, they borrow sake from the neighbor, much like the family in *Tokyo Story*. It seems to be a natural thing for Yōko, but her mother is so embarrassed that she insists on giving the neighbor something in return (at which point we finally understand the purpose of the present her mother has been carrying). While eating the stewed pork with potatoes, Yōko answers her mother's questions. She explains that she is three months pregnant and, although the father of the child is concerned, she refuses to work in her boyfriend's family business or to give up her research for her marriage. Yōko's father simply remains silent throughout the conversation.

Hou once mentioned that the actor declined to say the lines originally written for the character.[5] Therefore, Hou decided to turn this to his advantage and asked him to drink in silence instead. The silence expresses the father's worries better and makes the awkward situation the mother is facing even more prominent. The situation is exacerbated by the realization

5) *Métro Lumière: Hou Hsiao-hsien à la rencontre de Yasujirō Ozu*

halfway through the film that the character played by Yo Kimiko is actually Yōko's stepmother. I do not mean to suggest that her worries about Yōko are insincere; on the contrary, this detail makes us realize how difficult it is for her to act like a mother when she is not a real one. The scene in which they borrow sake from the neighbor reminds me of Ozu, but it is not the same. The fact that Yōko is single and pregnant and the fact that her relationship is with her stepmother make the film more modern and complicated.

Yōko loves old things, but she does not stick to the old rules. This is reflected in the fact that she keeps tracing every step of composer Jiang Wen-ye, but when she discovers that these places have either been turned into office buildings or slipped into oblivion, she does not seem upset. Her close friend, Hajime, loves old books and other old things, but he records the sounds of the trains with technologically advanced equipment and turns the recordings into computer-generated images. The old and the new, the traditional and the modern, Ozu and Hou can coexist with each other. In *Café Lumière*, we see many railway tracks and trains. Sometimes Yōko and Hajime ride past each other on different trains without seeing each other; sometimes he sees her but she fails to

notice him. Eventually, Yōko falls asleep on the train; Hajime walks up to her quietly, and then they get off the train together. Watching the trains driving past each other, separating, and moving on – oscillating between closeness and estrangement – is intriguing, suggesting the trace of our lives or the path of our fates. The trains are like people: they not only travel forward or in parallel with each other, they also turn around and meet up. Nevertheless, they will eventually go their separate ways. The beautiful moment could be regarded either as a fleeting instant or an eternity. It looks as if we do not need to worry too much about Yōko's future.

WOMEN IN HOU HSIAO-HSIEN'S FILMS

"Men are judged by their career, women by their marriage." Traditionally, in China and Taiwan, marriage is considered the most important decision in a woman's life. However, it is a decision that is not necessarily made by the woman herself. Very often, the parents or even the matchmaker have the final say.

Feng Fei-fei was the lead actress in Hou's first two films, *Cute Girl* (1980) and *Cheerful*

Wind (1981). In both films, she is courted by two men, one (Kenny Bee) representing the love she yearns for and the other (Anthony Chan) meeting the expectations of her family. *Cute Girl* gives a straightforward solution to this dilemma while *Cheerful Wind* leaves the audiences with an open ending. Feng is one of the most important figures in the history of Taiwanese pop music. As a singer, she had a down-to-earth and friendly persona. She did not have many silver screen appearances and most of the films she made before *Cute Girl* were romantic tragedies. Hou brought her singer's charm onto the big screen, and successfully avoided the cliché of Taiwanese melodrama, which was completely detached from reality. After Feng, Hou continued to work with pop singers, in films such as *Green, Green Grass of Home* (1982) and *Daughter of the Nile* (1987).

The true muse in Hou's early works is Hsin Shu-fen, who was discovered by Hou in the street in Hsimenting [Ximending]. A non-professional actress, she was cast as the childhood sweetheart of the male protagonist in both *A Time to Live and a Time to Die* (1985) and *Dust in the Wind* (1986). Later, in *A City of Sadness* (1989), she became the author and the witness to both a personal and national history. Hsin undoubtedly embodies the qualities that Hou believes the "old world" possessed, including nostalgia, beauty, tranquility, modesty and strength.

In the 1990s, another female singer, Annie Shizuka Inoh, starred in *Good Men, Good Women* (1995) and *Goodbye South, Goodbye* (1996). However, this time, Hou challenged himself to turn the singer into an actress, rather than transferring a singer's charm to the big screen. In *Good Men, Good Women*, Inoh seems to have failed to enter the "old world," but she successfully conveyed the confusion of young people in the 1990s. This aspect of her performance was taken even further in *Goodbye South, Goodbye*. Therefore, it is not surprising that in *Flowers of Shanghai* – a film about power struggles, lust, and deception set in Qing dynasty China – Inoh was cast only as a minor character. The leading female roles were played by actresses from Hong Kong and Japan.

Shu Qi has become the most important actress in Hou's films made in the new millennium. Her performance in *Millennium Mambo* (2001) was well received by critics and audiences alike. Like a fairy, she leads the audience from the future back to the present. In contrast to the childishness and jealousy of her young lover (Tuan Chun-hao), the maturity and consideration of the older male lead (Jack Kao) once again demonstrates that, in Hou's world, only "the old" can offer us salvation.

All of this makes Yōko in *Café Lumière* even more important and unique. She is a woman who loves old things and feels utterly at ease with modernity; this is expressed in her relationships with different men and her decision to bring up her child on her own. Although it is set in Paris, the single mother played by Juliette Binoche in *Flight of the Red Balloon* (2007) is facing the difficulties (juggling work and family) that Yōko may encounter in the future. However, these difficulties do not undermine their confidence when they make important deci-sions. Hou has gradually eased his doubt about modernity. Through the choices his heroines make in their lives, Hou shows us his compassion.

Since it was a foreign-language film shot in a foreign country, I had once wondered whether *Café Lumière* would be an exception amongst Hou's works. I felt relieved and happy when I saw *La Belle Epoque*. Both Shu Qi and Hitoto Yō, the two unmarried women in Hou's recent films, are loved and respected.

Translated by Ethan Yeh (Tzu-chien)
and Isabella Ho

Abé Mark Nornes

Hou Hsiao-hsien and Narrative Space

The center [of film] is the movement, not movements but the logic of a consequent and temporally coherent action. The vision of the image is its narrative clarity and that clarity hangs on the conversion of space into place, the constant realization of a center in function of narrative purpose, narrative movement.

—Stephen Heath, "Narrative Space"[1]

In the epigraph above, Stephen Heath is writing about the narrative structures and operations of the Hollywood classical style, the coherence and seamlessness of which he pits against the art cinema of Jean-Luc Godard and Straub-Huillet. These filmmakers, for Heath, represent a more complex address with a "certain freedom of contradictions."[2] He is, of course, mounting an ideological attack on Hollywood to valorize the art cinema alternative. I will not rehearse the theories of suture here, but I *am* interested in the way Hou Hsiao-hsien converts space into place. On the face of it, Hou would seem to affiliate with the art filmmakers, as his films feel too oblique to think of as "centered around narrative purpose" and do seem to offer up the freedom to contemplate daily reality with all its contradictions, the qualities that Heath promotes. Indeed, what is so striking about Hou's cinema

is its odd combination of randomness – of narrative events, of *mise-en-scène*, of narrative space – with masterful control. That these two are brought into spectacular tension is our starting point here.

Hou's approach to cinema is singular. One knows it when one sees it. This is his real connection to the Japanese filmmaker Ozu Yasujirō, with whom he is often compared. They both developed such idiosyncratic approaches to narrative cinema that no one truly mimics them, either because their styles are too specific or simply too difficult to pull off. As for Hou, he has steadily loosened up what appeared to be a complex set of unwritten rules. They were at their most rigid and rigorous in *A City of Sadness* (1989): put simply, Hou liked to find a particular view on a given location and stubbornly stick to it. He set an axis of viewing through the set,

1) Stephen Heath, "Narrative Space," *Screen*, Volume 17, Number 3 (1976), 86

2) Ibid, 90

3) These qualities and more are explored in great depth in Abé Mark Nornes and Emilie Yueh-yu Yeh, *Staging Memories: Hou Hsiao-hsien's City of Sadness* (Ann Arbor, MI: University of Michigan Press, 2014).

4) I analyzed Edward Yang's construction of offscreen space shortly after encountering his first films in "Terrorizer," *Film Quarterly*, Volume 8, Number 2 (Spring 1989), 64–72.

A City of Sadness, 1989
The first scene following the title – in an Altmanesque cacophony
of action, six calligraphic scrolls adorn the walls in three rooms,
and women are hand-inspecting two more. A vase, which will soon
become the most prominent object in the film, sits on a table,
hardly noticeable in all the action and visual clutter. [Fig. 1]

moving his camera forward and backward with
only the occasional (and strategic) pan or track.
Close-ups were rare and the long take standard.
Shot-reverse shot figures are oddly staged, the
few times he uses them.[3]

This makes for a unique conversion of space
into place. One becomes hyperaware of offscreen space because of the lack of pans and reverse shots, a feature one finds in the work of
other Taiwanese directors, most notably Edward Yang.[4] Spaces remain slightly disorienting
and opaque – remain *space* at some level – until
the gradual repetition of views nurtures a fa-
miliarity with their nooks, crannies, pathways,
and the objects contained therein. This brings

me to the topic of this essay, the calligraphy in
Hou's films and its role in the construction of
this peculiar narrative space.

When it comes to Hou, the last thing one
thinks of is art direction. His sets – domestic or
public – are messy, littered with the objects of
daily life. The tightly controlled frame is full of
props, and their placement would *appear* to be
random at best (though it certainly is not). This
understated approach is in contrast to, say, the
splashy, more overtly designed films of someone like Tsai Ming-liang. This is a fount of
Hou's realism, as well as yet another difference
from Ozu, who was famous for obsessing endlessly over the placement of props to achieve

graphic matching and other effects (he would peer through the viewfinder and tell people to move some prop three centimeters. "closer to Tokyo").[5]

Among these props, works featuring calligraphy beckon to us. That is because calligraphy pops. Perhaps one factor is its high design; furthermore it is certainly the case that our attention naturally gravitates toward linguistic signs. This makes calligraphy a prop unlike any other. Unlike an oil painting, or a vase for that matter, it fulfills a wide array of functions. First, it is marked by a spectrum of legibility. Where stylistic flourish or linguistic archaisms render it incomprehensible, the calligraph serves as pretty ornament; at the same time, its mere presence can signify class and social status or period. Where it is legible, calligraphy proves itself a robust toolbox for inventive screenwriters and art directors. It delivers messages, letters, writs, and proclamations. It conjures spells and incantations. Adorning walls, it can comment on narrative action. In the hand, it can provide business for characters. The copulative possibilities of Chinese writing, through the montage of radicals, are provocative.[6] In all these cases, calligraphy sets itself apart from the props surrounding it, calling for attention by virtue of the ontological force of the brush-written word. This is to say nothing of its role in company logos, titles, credit sequences, intertitles, subtitles, and "the end" cards.

I have come to appreciate these many narrative functions – as well as the ubiquity of calligraphy in East Asian cinema – by working off a corpus. My research assistants and I have pulled frame grabs of calligraphy from DVDs in University of Michigan's Donald Hall Collection.[7] This corpus is 2,653 images and growing (there are over seventy images from Hou films alone). One of the astonishing discoveries in this body of work is a set of fascinating cultural tendencies across the region. For example, South Korean filmmakers, particularly those working in period films, often place calligraphic folding screens along the back walls of their sets. Their actors perform before a beautiful paperscape of calligraphic characters. By way of contrast, Japanese filmmakers use calligraphic props to

5) Satō Tadao, "The Art of Ozu Yasujirō," *The Study of the History of the Cinema*, Number 4 (1974), 96

6) I am referencing Sergei Eisenstein here, but the Soviet theorist actually had only the most superficial sense of the complexity of Chinese characters. Furthermore, he was deploying it as an analogue to cinematic montage, whereas I am pointing to filmmakers that actually play with linguistic signs in their diegeses.

7) This image archive was constructed with the help of student assistants Jini Kim, Sanako Fujioka and Emily Ho.

tip the balance of their compositions. They will place lanterns or scroll paintings at the edge of the frame, essentially creating a negative space within which the actors move (Figure 2).

As for the filmmakers of China, Hong Kong and Taiwan, they curiously default to *symmetry* when calligraphy enters narrative space. This seems to be quite unconscious. Chinese cinematography manuals only give conventional, classical definitions for symmetry: filmmakers use it to evoke the monumental. It is occasionally deployed for this effect, but generally the most mundane *mise-en-scène* snaps into symmetry when calligraphy is visible. Even filmmakers I have mentioned this to are surprised by this widespread and quite unconscious tendency, including Hou.

Now let us consider Hou's use of calligraphy. Arguably, the construction of narrative space begins with title cards, which instantly set a context for the photographic images to follow. Hou's early films all used a standard non-serifed typeface typical of Central Motion Picture Company productions of the era. After he went independent, the director captured the freedom to design title sequences for each film. He usually used typefaces, with the most notable calligraphic title gracing *Good Men, Good Women* (1995; Figure 3). Hou explains his

Calligraphy exerts a pressure on *mise-en-scène* in different ways for Chinese, Japanese and South Korean filmmakers. Chinese filmmakers use symmetry (top), Japanese filmmakers shuttle calligraphic props to the edges (middle), and South Korean filmmakers often drape the background in calligraphy (bottom). [Fig. 2]

157

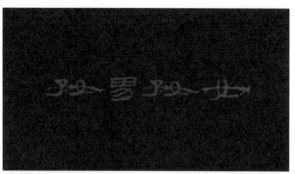

An unusual instance of symmetry in Hou's oeuvre,
from *A Summer at Grandpa's*, 1984 [Fig. 4]

This montage of characters is not atypical in the age of the digital remix. Surprisingly enough, designers in the Chinese-language cinemas are often scanning characters from different authors, styles and eras to construct their titles. That Hou did this back in 1995 is revealing. It belies his casual attitude about this art – something rather at odds with his persnickety approach to cinema.

It is perhaps in this casual mode that he sometimes follows convention and adjusts his seemingly random, unruly *mise-en-scène* to the symmetrical composition that Chinese seems to demand. *A Summer at Grandpa's* (1984; Figure 4) has the strongest example. This is probably because it features a complex combination of graphic and cultural elements that bore down on the cinematography. It is a formal wedding ceremony. There are couplets on the wall, with two candles before them. A priest stands precisely in the middle, his robe split by a symmetrical red trim and with his hands splayed out to either side. Above his head is a bold circle with the symmetrical character for double happiness. It shines in red neon no less. Moreover, not one but *two* couples bow before

choice: "I go by instinct. It ultimately depends on the content. In the case of *A City of Sadness*, the title contains the strong word 'sorrow' (*beiqing*). It describes an emotion and is pretty powerful. Because of this, I chose to use typography. In a way it expresses sadness better. In contrast, I chose calligraphy for *Good Men, Good Women* because the film itself called for it. I went through an art book filled with many examples of works by famous old calligraphers. When I found one I liked, I just cut out the three characters I needed and put them together."[8]

8) Hou Hsiao-hsien interview by author, August 15, 2011 (interpretation by Vivian Tsu-i Chiang)

The Puppetmaster, 1993. While most Chinese filmmakers snap to symmetrical composition whenever calligraphy enters the frame, Hou's approach is eclectic and unpredictable (left). An exception is the stage at the end of the film (right). [Fig. 5]

the priest, in synch. It is a scene that demands symmetry.

However, with few exceptions, Hou eschews symmetrical *mise-en-scène*, even for sets decorated with couplets. The mirrored structure of the couplet, gracing either walls or portals, exerts no pressure on Hou and his cinematographers. Other values guide their composition, notably the geometric complexities and possibilities of the built environment, particularly that of Chinese and Japanese architecture with its proliferation of frames – screens, sliding doors, windows and walls with the wooden framework exposed. This is not the off-kilter composition of Japanese cinema. At the same time, what appears to be ad hoc and random at first glance seems to have a certain tendency, if not a logic. Calligraphy, when it appears in Hou's films, gravitates toward the center, even if it is rarely centered. The axis of the camera is always nudged away, pushing the sign, painting, or couplet slightly to the side.

There is one curious exception to this rule, and that takes place late in *The Puppetmaster* (1993). Up to this point, all instances of calligraphy follow the tendency described above, where the placement of calligraphy would appear rather random. However, there is a moment of symmetry occurring late in the film, when the traveling puppet show has been thoroughly co-opted by the Japanese propaganda machine. In previous performances, the symmetrical placement of the small stage's calligraphy is offset by a slightly oblique camera placement. However, for the final performance celebrating Japanese exploits in the theater of war, the camera snaps to a frontal view, framed by two calligraphic banners across the bottom of the stage and the cinematic frame, reading: "The Taipei, Bunsan District Advance Guard for the Annihilation of America and Britain" (*Taipei Bunsangun Eibei gekimetsu suishintai*; Figure 5). Suddenly, the *mise-en-scène* departs from Hou's eclectic composition to follow conven-

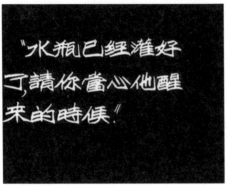

The Goddess, Wu Yonggang, 1934
A calligraphic intertitle from the silent era [Fig. 6]

tion – the frontality and symmetry lend the tiny puppet stage a monumentality that makes this stage, this play about Japanese militarism, seem so foreign to Hou's cinema – and perhaps foreign to Taiwan in a circuitous, formal manner.

Considering this seemingly clever exception to his own anti-symmetrical *mise-en-scène*, perhaps Hou's departures from, or deployment of, the conventional Chinese framing of calligraphy are less casual than they seem at first glance. In the pages that follow, I would like to explore these many aspects of the cinematic calligraph in Hou's most complex and powerful film to date, *A City of Sadness*.

What if we were to assume a rigorous placement of calligraphy, as opposed to indiscriminant or slapdash? After all, everything else about Hou's filmic form seems to be so calculated. While there is one scene in *A City of Sadness* that features calligraphy quite prominently, most viewers would probably ask, "What calligraphy?" This analysis will likely surprise such readers, jogging their memories by pointing to the ubiquity of the brushed word throughout this film, which is so full of

different kinds of writing. Indeed, it is the many forms of writing that help make *A City of Sadness* such a complex work of art. The writing that inevitably attracts the most attention is the intertitles. The photographer at the putative center of the story, Wen-ching, is a deaf-mute. To communicate, he and his silent interlocutors scribble in notebooks. Hou gives us access to these written conversations through silent cinema-style intertitles. However, it should be pointed out that, while Hou's intertitles are black cards with white typographic fonts, Chinese intertitles of the silent era were, in fact, brushed (Figure 6).[9]

Another major form of writing in the film – also handwritten with pen or pencil – is the diary of Wen-ching's lover Hinomi. Along with Wen-ching's intertitles, her writing establishes her as a second major enunciative position for the narrative. As Emilie Yueh-yu Yeh and I discuss in *Staging Memories: Hou Hsiao-hsien's City of Sadness*, these are the wellsprings of the storytelling. Significantly, both defy the pedagogical nation building of the newly arrived KMT [Kuomintang], with their loudspeaker and radio proclamations. That these writings are by a deaf-mute and a woman builds a rich

9) We analyze the intertitles at length in *Staging Memories*.

A City of Sadness
"You must live with dignity. Father is innocent." A message substituting cloth for paper, finger for brush, and blood for ink. This hints at the intimate connection between calligraphy and the human body. [Fig. 7]

irony into what could be a heavy-handed nationalist project in less skilled hands.

A final form of writing we should consider before turning to calligraphy is the message. The film is filled with the delivery of messages and letters. Almost invariably, they bear the worst of tidings. Many report the untimely demise of a loved one due to the political violence. The most unbearable of the messages hovers between crude handwriting and the calligraphic. Wen-ching visits the family of a friend he knew in prison. He hands the wife a message from her husband – "You must live with dignity. Father is innocent." – scrawled on cloth instead of paper, with the husband's finger instead of a brush, and not in ink but rather his own blood (Figure 7). It is this intimate connection to the (once moving, once living) human body that connects this scene with the calligraphic traditions of East Asia. The remarkably sensitive tools of writing – rice paper, ink and stone, brush – link any script to the absent act of writing and put the absent human being at the center of that moment in time.

This complex temporality of the calligraph is made palpably clear in the scene most prominently featuring calligraphy. It occurs twenty-five minutes into the film when a Japanese woman arrives at the hospital to bid farewell to Hinomi (Figure 8, upper left corner). She bears gifts: a kimono, a bamboo kendo sword, and a calligraphic scroll. The two sit, side-by-side in formal Japanese style on *tatami* (Figure 8, top-center). Shizuko, the Japanese woman, explains that the painting is for Hinoe's brother, who was present when her own brother wrote it. This sets the stage for a flashback which goes largely unmarked – a typical strategy employed by Hou that builds layers of ambiguity and undecidable temporalities into his narrative. Here, the jump in time is marked only by Shizuko's hair style and a subtle change in lighting. She plays "Red Dragonfly" ("Akatonbo"), a Japanese children's' song, for Hinoe's class of students (Figure 8, top-right). Her diegetic song slowly dissolves into a non-diegetic solo piano rendition and another undecidable ellipsis leading to an image of Shizuko wearing the kimono to arrange flowers (Figure 8, center-right).

The scene of writing arrives after yet an-

A City of Sadness
In this remarkable sequence, Hou has woven the tangled temporality of the calligraph – that visual trace of a long absent event of the human body in action – with the equally *and similarly* variegated time of cinema. The sequence starts at the upper-left and proceeds clockwise, ending with the center intertitle. [Fig. 8]

other ellipsis (Figure 8, bottom-right). Shizuko's brother carefully brushes a Japanese poem for the scroll while Hinoe observes, all the while grinding ink on an ink stone. The gifted painting, in fact, was created *collaboratively*. An intertitle displays not just the poem's Japanese-language text, but the calligraphic painting itself (see Figure 8, bottom-center):

> Fly away as you like
> I too will soon follow
> We all together.

A voiceover intones the poem in Japanese – the voice inflected with a Chinese accent. Upon finishing the reading, the intertitle gives way to a view of Hinoe, Hinomi and Wen-ching, as the sister delivers the presents to her brother; another ellipsis has taken place (Figure 8, bottom-left). The voice now diegetic, we retrospectively realize the flashback actually ended with the calligraphic intertitle – although the previous time's music continued – and the present of the film is flung forward to a Taiwan absent of Japanese. Incredibly, the complex layering of time continues. Hinoe begins telling a story about Japanese sentiments surrounding death and dying, as Wen-ching scrutinizes the painting in the background. Halfway through his narration, Hinoe's story is interrupted, disappearing with a cut, and Hinomi finishes the story off by writing in Wen-ching's notebook (Figure 8, center-left). Instead of intertitles, we hear Hinomi reading her writing in voiceover. The scene now ends with a silent soundtrack, the music having slowly faded to nothing, and a typographic silent-cinema-style intertitle that finally delivers a Chinese translation of the calligraphic painting (Figure 8, center). The next scene returns us to the hospital entranceway where the phenomenally complex sequence began. *Hou has woven the tangled temporality of the calligraph – that visual trace of a long absent event of the human body in action – with the equally and similarly variegated time of cinema.*

Calligraphy also plays a central role in the *space* of the film, or to be specific, in the conversion of space into place. The more straightforward and conventional of the contributions involves the establishment of setting. *A City of Sadness* depicts Taiwan's entry into a postcolonial world. One example comes from the powerful opening scene, when the eldest brother nervously awaits the birth of his child. The room is pitch black. In the background, two voices compete for the soundtrack. One is his wife, who screams in pain; the other is the Japanese emperor declaring an end to the Pacific War and Japan's colonization of Taiwan.

The brother fidgets with a light bulb, which spills light over a calligraphic charm pasted to a column. It reads "great happiness/felicity" (鴻禧, *hongxi*), and is brushed on a vertical strip of red paper with a gold border. The word and the paper, and the pasting of calligraphic charms or exhortations onto the architecture, are all cultural practices pre-dating and enduring the colonial occupation that is ending at this very moment. The scene introduces *A City of Sadness* as a (re-)birth of a nation that will be carrying many histories into the future.

There are some nineteen works of calligraphy in *A City of Sadness* (not including six rolled up scrolls sitting in vases), and not all make this kind of contribution to the establishment of setting or historical moment. Some appear only to grace the walls at happy moments like the opening of the restaurant or the wedding; others are partially obscured. At the same time, nearly all of them are bound by an unusual logic peculiar to Hou and the unique character of his narrative space.

The conventional, classical film typically turns space into place through the deployment of a set of normalized cinematic forms. Entering a space for the first time, "common sense" leads the director to introduce the setting, and simultaneously orient the audience to spatial relationships of people and objects, with a wide "establishing shot." The camera then moves closer to the action, using two-shots, point of view shots and most especially the shot-reverse shot figure. This last strategy is the volleying back and forth of camera views from face to face. It was this complex of formal choices and realist conventions – combined with the Quattrocento optics of the apparatus – that so deeply engages human subjectivity and, according to the screen theory of the late twentieth century, connects it to ideology.

Hou eschews this system for one of his own device, a major reason he richly deserves this book. He does not chop his scenes up with montage, favoring instead the long take. This is one reason close-ups are few and far between. He rarely uses point of view shots; the only example in *A City of Sadness* displays the bloody calligraphic message from late husband to traumatized wife. Hou does use the establishing shot, in a sense. That is because *most* of his shots look and feel like establishing shots. However, whereas most filmmakers introduce viewers to a new set through a wide view mapping the coordinates between objects in an attempt to achieve a cognitive mastery of space, we could say that Hou by contrast *establishes a view*. Instead of moving in and around the set, he

dwells on that view in long take to allow us to take it in, to settle in as it were, because every time the narrative revisits that space we more than likely see a variant of that same view.

At this point, I cannot resist indulging in an anecdote about this unique approach to narrative space. I was introduced to Hou Hsiao-hsien by Angelika Wong, his former assistant director. She revealed that whenever they worked on a set for the first time, the staff would actually place bets on where Hou would place the camera.[10] This story even surprised Hou himself, who had no idea this was going on behind his back. It suggests how crucial a decision that first placement is, as well as how deliberate a choice it is for the director, as everything in the film will happen there within the limits of that view. This unlikely dynamic between visual repetition and narrative novelty slowly but surely turns spaces into the most familiar kinds of places.

Attending to the calligraphic props helps us see how this works at the most basic level. Recall that red good luck charm from the opening scene. The room was so dark that the two character charm is one of the few recognizable ob-

10) This revelation took place at the interview with Hou referenced above.

jects. Much later in the film, Hou returns to the same view, now in the daytime. The ambient light from windows reveals a large work of calligraphy on the back wall. The small charm comes into view with a pan, jogging the viewer's memory – ah, this was the room where the oldest brother listened to the war's end as he awaited the birth of his son. The same dynamic of recognition holds true for the view on mute photographer Wen-ching's living room, where so much joy and sadness takes place. We immediately recognize the space at different times of day and with various configurations of furniture thanks to the calligraphic scroll painting in his *tokonoma*. It is in this patient, deliberate manner that Hou's narrative spaces encumber an overwhelming emotional resonance, where all the events that occur in a given view/place vibrate against each other.[11] This is quite unlike any cinematic experience I can think of.

At the very same time, a curious parallel process occurs in relation to offscreen spaces. These, too, become narrativized in a gradual process. Since Hou nearly always returns to the initial view on a space, each view slowly establishing it as narrative space, the viewer has only the vaguest sense of the local geography. Hou "activates" or "implements" adjacent spaces whenever a character walks into or out of the camera's view. In this way, he switches between familiar, established views, each with its energized offscreen spaces. *Then,* every once in a while, Hou will cut on a character walking off into offscreen space, and then into a previously established view in a new, temporally continuous shot; in other words, these are unusual matching shots in Hou's long take style and are designed to stitch contiguous or adjacent views together.

On other occasions, this kind of discovery is inspired by a simple, revelatory pan. One of the most important settings of the film is the Lin family restaurant, the "Little Shanghai." Somewhere in the house is the kitchen where the eldest son awaits the birth of a child in the precredit scene. After the opening title, we see our first view of the lobby. The shot is striking for its visual disorder (Figure 1). Many people mill through the space in an Altmanesque cacophony of action as they prepare for the opening of the restaurant. An interior wall of windows adds a profusion of lines; six calligraphic scrolls adorn the walls in three rooms, and women are hand-inspecting two more. A vase, which will

11) This aspect of Hou's work is also explored in *Staging Memories*.

A City of Sadness. Late in the film, two central settings are finally connected by an economical and quite unusual pan, scanning left to right. [Fig. 9]

soon become the most prominent object in the film, sits on a table, hardly noticeable in all the action and visual clutter. Hou cuts to another room somewhere in the house where the patriarch sits at a table; two scroll paintings grace either side of a shrine in the back room, obscured by plants and yet more windows. A third and final cut takes us to another space with the vase and a striking stained glass wall. Above it, calligraphy on a wood plank identifies the name of the establishment – the Little Shanghai – and another work of calligraphy is half-visible in a back room. The vase returns now, suggesting the camera has tracked back to the first space, but jumped a clean forty-five degrees to the right. However, even the most scrupulous viewer probably requires multiple viewings to make sense of this space. Not until the second half of the film, after Hou has introduced a number of other rooms to the house, does he stitch it all together. This is the scene where the eldest daughter-in-law marches past the restaurant table, and the camera pans to reveal the

second-brother brought into the shrine room (Figure 9).

It is only at this point – halfway through the film – that the narrative space of the Little Shanghai seems relatively complete. The connective tissue has been provided largely by the works of calligraphy ornamenting this initially bewildering space.

As the various spaces of the Little Shanghai gradually interconnect – mapping out the restaurant while acquiring emotional resonance – the semantics of the calligraphy transform and hold the potential for additional emotional amplification. The most striking piece of calligraphy in the film is in the shrine room. The shrine itself is dedicated to Guan Yu, a favored deity of Taiwanese merchants because he represents trustworthiness and personal loyalty. Adjacent to the shrine's calligraphic couplet and directly above the ancestors' tablet is a large *shou* (壽, "longevity") painted on red paper and framed. While not a typical practice, this could be a reference to the ancient *The Nine*

A City of Sadness. Hou shows only the edge of a calligraph with the character for "longevity" when we are introduced to the severity of the second brother's insanity (left); later he drapes it in darkness at a traumatic moment in Hinomi's life (right). [Fig. 10]

Songs, which refers to a Palace of Longevity.[12] Wang Yi (ca 89–158 CE), the first commentator on this anthology wrote: "The Palace of Longevity is the place where people make offerings to the spirits. To construct a shrine (a temple or altar) to worship the spirits and ancestors is nothing but for the purpose of obtaining longevity (for the worshipers). Thus it is named 'the Palace of Longevity.'"[13]

This painting next to the shrine makes its first appearance a third of the way into the film at an appropriately celebratory scene when Hinomi visits the house. At this point, it is perfectly lit, the red paper and size of the character calling for attention – although for no particularly evident reason.

Later in the film, we are introduced to the severity of the second brother's insanity when Hou cuts back to this space. The view is, once again, fractured by window panes, behind which the brother spastically walks (Figure 10; left). The "longevity" painting is still brightly lit, but now only its edge is visible. It is enough, just enough, to add a dark commentary on the brother's plight. In the last half of the film, the calligraphic painting floats in the background, obscured by architecture or only half lit. For example, one of the most moving moments of the film is when Hinomi sits alone at the table in the foreground, crying quietly (Figure 10; right). She is awaiting the return of photographer Wen-ching, and when he arrives it is clear they are in love and bound to be married; he then provides her an account of her brother's

12) David Hawkes uses "House of Life" in his translation: "He is going to rest in the House of Life/His brightness is like that of the sun and moon" (David Hawkes, *The Songs of the South: An Anthology of Ancient Chinese Poems by Qu Yuan and Other Poets,* New York: Penguin, 1985, 104). Hawkes also notes "the *House of Life* – literally 'Palace of Longevity' (Shougong) – a chapel specially constructed for the reception of spirits conjured up in shamanistic seances" (118).

13) Translation by Shuen-fu Lin. I am indebted to Professor Lin for helping me understand the culture and practices around this character. I would also like to thank Akiyama Tamako, who helped me puzzle through this and other scenes, not to mention a small but significant technological problem.

capture in the mountains. Appropriately enough, the "longevity" character is half-hidden by a dark shadow.

Only in Hou's cluttered narrative space, where singular views are repeated in long take, could a half-visible prop possess such a devastating effect. It is the combination of repetition and duration that enables viewers to master the clutter and recognize the smallest changes in setting and framing.

However, as I asserted above, calligraphy is a prop unlike any other. It calls for our attention. It emanates a kind of energy that filmmakers can tap into (or that others, like Itami Jūzō, avoid; he was known for ordering his staff to hide anything with text on it – and for this very reason).[14] Calligraphy, when it appears in cinema, must be accounted for. This is why filmmakers in South Korea drape backgrounds in swathes of brushed characters, why those in Japan shuttle calligraphic props to the edges of the frame, and why Chinese default to symmetry. The visual force of the calligraphy interacts with local aesthetic sensibilities, with architectural structures and styles, and cultural conventions.

As for Hou, it is likely that he feels a work of calligraphy is a prop *like* any other. Any object will suffice in the construction of his peculiar narrative space. Depending on the film, it might be a table, or a peculiarly shaped window, or merely some laundry hanging out to dry. Indeed, I had a chance to sit down with Hou to talk specifically about calligraphy. Our conversation ranged from fine art calligraphy to traditions of writing to his own filmmaking practice. Most of the things he had to say about calligraphy were a bit obvious, as if he were gamely playing along with the visiting scholar and his unexpected set of questions. His comments concerning calligraphy in his own films revealed that he never really thought about it that much. It was clear that he is an artist that mainly works by instinct. After over an hour of playing the scholar-filmmaker game, Hou stopped, leaned forward with a smile that was at once gracious and mischievous, and said, "You know, in all honesty, I have to admit that your research topic just doesn't interest me that much."

This research was conducted through the support of the 2011 Faculty Research Grant for Taiwan Studies, conducted by the Education Division, Taipei Economic & Cultural Office in Chicago.

14) Itami's aversion to signage was related to me by one of his art directors.

Kent Jones

In Time

In their now canonical book-length interview, Alfred Hitchcock and François Truffaut discuss the kissing scene between Cary Grant and Eva Marie Saint in the train compartment in *North by Northwest* (1959). "On the screen it's absolutely perfect," remarks Truffaut, "yet it must have seemed completely illogical during the shooting." Hitchcock responds by going into great detail about the difference between the way things appear on the set and the way they look on the screen. "Many directors are conscious of the overall atmosphere on the set, whereas they should be concerned only with what's going to come upon the screen."[1] He adds that certain directors "will place their actors in the decor and then they'll set the camera at a distance, which depends simply on whether the actor happens to be seated, standing, or lying down. That, to me, seems to be pretty woolly thinking. It's never precise and it certainly doesn't express anything...They think that everything on the screen will look just the way it looks on the set. It's ridiculous!"[2] In the scene in question, shot in handsome, glowing

VistaVision and Technicolor, Grant and Saint are performing a decorous enactment of passion in the cramped compartment. Saint is leaning against a wall. Hitchcock switches angles at one point and we look over Saint's shoulder at Grant, *through* the wall. As always in Hitchcock, the scene is broken into legible, elegant units combined to sustain emotion.

At a certain point in the early 1960s, Hitchcock wanted to go in a new direction. "I've often wondered whether I could do a suspense story within a looser form," he tells Truffaut late in the book, "in a form that's not so tight."[3] He was excited by Jean-Luc Godard's *Masculine Feminine* (1966) and by Michelangelo Antonioni's films, which led him to conceive of the aborted *Kaleidoscope* (also known as *Frenzy*, not to be confused with the 1972 film), for which he shot an hour of 16mm test footage in New York. Lew Wasserman and the executives at MCA/Universal were mortified by the project and officially rejected it in 1967.

In Hitchcock's last films, one can see traces of a living and evolving artist bursting out of the straightjacket in which he found himself, in individual scenes. The famous murder of the East German agent in *Torn Curtain* (1966) and the rape and strangulation of Barbara Leigh-Hunt's Brenda by Barry Foster's serial killer in *Frenzy*

1) François Truffaut, *Hitchcock* (New York: Simon and Schuster, 1967), 199

2) Ibid, 200–201

3) Ibid, 238

169

them on microfilm. Browne grabs a phony press card from Ebony Magazine and heads for the hotel. He and Stafford part ways across the street, where a crowd has amassed to gaze at the goings-on in the hotel. Hitchcock cuts back and forth between Stafford and Browne, and inadvertently creates the odd impression that he is cutting between two different movies. Stafford, coiffed and tailored within an inch of his life, is impeccably framed and lit in the high Hollywood manner; Browne, far more free-wheeling, as both an actor and a character, is shot from a great distance with a telephoto lens. We watch him crossing the crowded street, showing his credentials to the guard at the door, talking his way past the Cuban guard and then, by chance, finding the man he is looking for. The energy of the scene is new for Hitchcock. The shots are both immersive, imparting a sense of the street and its energies, and pointed. Browne's great resourcefulness as an actor and his languorous, confident manner (as if he had all the time in the world) become crucial. Our fascination with him guides us through the hotel, whose textures and surrounding energies become an object of fascination in turn. It is a quick but indelible stretch of a movie that otherwise observes the decorum and visual legibility we commonly associate with Hitchcock.

(1972) both come to mind: two scenes that are so uncomfortable as to be nearly unbearable. And near the beginning of the 1969 *Topaz,* Hitchcock explored a new approach to staging. Frederick Stafford's spy walks into a Harlem flower shop and instructs the owner, played by Roscoe Lee Browne, in reality a French spy, to talk his way into the Hotel Teresa (housing an official delegation from Cuba), find a potential Cuban turncoat, and persuade him to make secret documents available so that he can shoot

In this brief scene, character and environment are not just *equally* present, as in *I Confess* (1953) or *Vertigo* (1958), but joined together into one expressive whole.

In the years since *Topaz, the* major obsession in cinema has been the ever-increasing accommodation of reality within fiction. The elusive dream of merging the two into one uninterrupted stream haunts the cinema, or at the very least a majority of its more serious practitioners, like a specter. This endlessly repeated gesture of turning toward unpredictability and away from certainty was born in the late 1940s with Roberto Rossellini and Neorealism, spread throughout the world in the 1960s, and has since fully bloomed and hybridized in the digital/HD age.

One particularly powerful strain took hold in the years immediately after *Topaz* among the younger generation of American directors once known as the New Hollywood. I am thinking of the wedding scenes in *The Godfather* (Francis Ford Coppola, 1972) and *The Deer Hunter* (Michael Cimino, 1978), the planting and harvesting scenes in *Days of Heaven* (Terrence Malick, 1978), the bar scene in *The Color of Money* (Martin Scorsese, 1985), and the majority of Robert Altman's films between *M*A*S*H* (1970) and *Buffalo Bill and the Indians* (1976). One sees a shift away from both the high glamour of the star system and the meticulously pointed employment of space and distance exemplified by Hitchcock's cinema. A more immersive, environmentally based form of storytelling also started to appear in Europe and Asia in the late 1980s and early 1990s, in the work of Claire Denis and Olivier Assayas in France, Hou Hsiao-hsien and Tsai Ming-liang in Taiwan, Abbas Kiarostami and Jafar Panahi in Iran and, a little later, Jia Zhang-ke in mainland China and Apichatpong Weerasethakul in Thailand. One might say that this is now the predominant international style of low-budget art moviemaking.

I think that the Coppola film represents the beginning of a very particular strain in environmentally grounded cinema. The images of the parking lot or the bandstand in *The Godfather* – extremely specific details of a family wedding rendered in a manner that feels spontaneously generated, shot from a benign distance – feel like they have been summoned from memory. And this is where we approach Hou, who, unsurprisingly, is a particular fan of Coppola's film. Time and again in Hou's films, we are invited to linger within and scrutinize a space, a field of activity that contains an element of the story we are being told. Rarely do we have the sense of an individual shot as one legible unit in the tracking of human activity and emotion (an exception: Hou's contribution to the 2011 anthology film *10 + 10*, *La Belle Epoque*). Place frequently acquires a unique, resonating power in Hou's work, and it plays a role that is entirely different from the one it is given in, for instance, Malick's films, where the divide between the human and the inhuman is continually disclosed and restated; or Kiarostami's films, in which human adventures guide us through a series of environments (Tuscany, the road from Koker to Poshteh, the path up and down the hill in Siah Dareh) whose effects on the characters in question develop like photographs as the action unfolds. For Hou, who is finally as precise as Hitchcock, place has the intensely present but ghostly aspect of memory. The particular magic of Hou's work can be found in the extremely delicate balance between the ceaseless stream of lived experience and the instant of remembering. This sets it apart from Proustian enterprises like Assayas' *Cold Water* (1994) and *Something in the Air* (2012), Richard Linklater's *Dazed and Confused* (1993), or Federico Fellini's *Amarcord* (1973), which Hou named as his favorite film in the 1992 Sight and Sound poll (*The Godfather* was number ten). Certain Hou films (*A Time to Live and a Time to Die*, 1985; *A Summer

at Grandpa's*, 1984; the opening section of *Three Times*, 2005) are explicitly autobiographical; others, like *Dust in the Wind* (1986), are based on the experiences and memories of others (in the case of that film, the memories of the writer, Wu Nien-jen, who would later continue the story with his own *A Borrowed Life*, 1994).[4] Some are set in the past and some are set in the present. But all of Hou's films seem to take place in the interval of quickly passing clarity afforded by the flash of memory. I do not mean to imply that Hou sets everything in the past tense (although he has admitted to great problems whenever confronted with the task of filming the present). The question of tense in cinema is far more complicated than it has been made out to be, but in Hou's work the dividing line between films set in the past and those set in the present is borderline transparent: modern stories like *Goodbye South, Goodbye* (1996) or *Café Lumière* (2003) are as infused with the flavor of memory as *The Puppetmaster* (1993) and *Flowers of Shanghai* (1998). In Hou's work, the act of filmmaking itself, of capturing moments of time, is directly linked to the action of summoning, recalling.

The Electric Princess Picture House (2007), Hou's astonishing contribution to the anthology film *Chacun son cinéma* (comprised of thirty-four three minute films and commissioned by the Cannes International Film Festival to commemorate its sixtieth anniversary), seems to me emblematic. This small yet immense film begins with Hou's camera in motion, tilting down from old-fashioned painted movie ads above the eponymous movie theater to the action on the street below, framed from a slight angle. In a very typical Hou move, the camera pans left on the street and picks up a couple holding hands on frame right, buying food from a man with a cart and then walking into the theater as a pedicab crosses from the other direction. The object is to preserve the sense of random street life within a unified aesthetic form that imparts itself to us so gradually that we are hardly aware of its existence until after the film has finished. One essential component of that form is the careful direction of the viewer's attention through visual and sonic cues. On the level of production design, the appearance of ongoing

reality is achieved by means of the greatest artistry. The color scheme is more or less brown, beige, and white with deep pockets of shadow that tunnel into black (frequent in Hou's films), but lone figures in off-white, red, and electric green keep the crowd from devolving into an undifferentiated mass and ensure that our eyes remain alive and responsive to the scene.[5] The perfectly harmonic movements of the camera and the couple appear to be coincidental, but before we can even finish considering the question of which has prompted which, our attention is diverted by the pedicab crossing from the opposite direction at a greater rate of speed, the ding of its bell softly sounding amidst the street noise and the music emanating from the theater. The pedicab also attunes us to the existence of separate planes of action, thus introducing another Hou constant. David Bordwell has written brilliantly about Hou's staging, the wonders he works with dinner table scenes composed in "horizontal layers and flanking profiles" in *A City of Sadness* (1989) and, alternatively, in the mind-bending *Flowers of Shanghai*, with a "habitual play with perspective," a "momentary masking and revealing," and "tiny details blooming and vanishing in seconds" registered by a "side-winding camera."[6] In this film, like much of Hou's work composed with a min-

4) Editor's note: Hou acted as the executive producer for *A Borrowed Life*.

5) Editor's note: There are two versions of *The Electric Princess Picture House*. In one version (which has an extra cut and is approximately forty seconds shorter), the entire film is in black-and-white until the camera "enters" the theater.

6) David Bordwell, *Figures Traced in Light* (Berkeley, CA: University of California Press, 2005), 186; 237

imum of shots (three in all), our sense of dramatic space is continually redefined, as is our understanding of just what we are seeing: a portrait of a place slowly becomes a portrait of ways of being at an earlier moment in time, which in turn reveals itself as an eloquently rendered rhetorical gesture.

The strategy of criss-crossing motion is repeated. A black car enters from the right, from which an elegantly dressed man in a white suit emerges to open the door for two similarly elegant young women, as two bicyclists cross from the left. We linger with the women as they stand behind two children and consider buying some food from a street vendor, while the movement of a couple on a bicycle crossing from the left seems to gently urge the camera to drift to the right, in time to frame a military jeep entering and dropping off an officer and his family. It is only around the moment that Hou cuts to a closer angle, to follow the officer taking his wife and daughters into the theater, that we realize that the camera has all but imperceptibly borne its way *into* the scene on the street, by means of an extremely delicate combination of dolly-ins and barely perceptible zoom-ins that are gently broken up and deflected by seemingly "motivating" movements and brief resting points. Only when the family

walks through the billowing red curtain into the theater, at which point Hou dissolves to a tonally different image of the same red curtain and we enter the dilapidated interior of the theater as it exists today, do we understand that the layers of space we have slowly penetrated, almost without our noticing it, are also layers of time. Unlike, for instance, the camera movements in *Last Year at Marienbad* (Alain Resnais, 1961) or the slow zoom out the window and into the desert that prompts the flashback to the central story in *True Confessions* (Ulu Grosbard, 1981), Hou does not announce his rhetorical gesture but allows it – or rather, works very hard to create the *sense* of merely allowing it – to slowly come into focus. The entry into the theater as it is today carries a shock, like the sudden sound or movement that jolts a musing mind out of a reverie. The fact that, in each shot, we come at the action not frontally but on a diagonal further enhances the evocation of an individual consciousness drifting into memory, from a *sidelong* vantage point, as it were. When Hou finally enters the theater and settles on the sad vision of the busted chairs and the missing panels on the screen that open to the verdant daylight beyond, he doubles the shock by projecting the bumper car scene from *Mouchette* (Robert Bresson, 1967) – a passage of pure, ex-

The Electric Princess Picture House,
2007

Goodbye South, Goodbye, 1996   *Café Lumière*, 2003

hilarating motion caught and composed in a now distant past in sharp black and white, unspooling as if by phantom mechanics onto a rotting screen.

Once more, I would like to stress that Hou is not a primarily Proustian filmmaker. Rather, he has an extremely refined attunement to the interaction between the flowing present and the remembered past – each of his films seems to me to take place within the moment of their collision. Tony Leung lost in his thoughts

amidst drinking games and gossip (*Flowers of Shanghai*), Jack Kao riding up into the mountains on a motorbike with his cohorts (*Goodbye South, Goodbye*), girl and boy finally crossing paths within the complex circuitry of the Tokyo train system (*Café Lumière*) – each of them are poignant in a sense that can be said of very few characters in movies. They all carry the knowledge, unarticulated but *felt*, that the lived instant and the receding past are as close as teeth and lips.

Olivier Assayas

Hou Hsiao-hsien

In China and Elsewhere

I have often recounted my first meeting with Hou Hsiao-hsien in Taipei in 1984. It took me a moment to realize, incredulously, that it is now fourteen years since this meeting took place. Edward Yang was there, as well as his director of photography, Christopher Doyle, who a few years later would become Wong Kar-wai's favored collaborator and one of the great formal innovators of modern Asian cinema.

Did I feel then that these three figures would go on to radically transform Chinese cinema as we knew it? Frankly, I had no idea. What I do remember is how self-evident the affinities between us were; although we came from different cultural backgrounds, we spoke the same language and shared the same values. I was in Asia as a journalist, tasked with writing on Hong Kong cinema, but my strongest memory of this trip is of this meeting, and not in my role as a journalist, but as a future filmmaker.

The dialogue we initiated that evening in the improbable setting of a French restaurant in Taipei has been sustained in fits and starts ever since (depending on the necessities of the time); it has given me a sense of community that I had never felt before, neither in France nor anywhere else. This is the reason why, even though I do not have much tolerance for cinematic "families," I sometimes feel links with this one. Whether it was a family or an alliance of interests hardly matters, because none of them have spoken to each other for quite some time, each having chosen the solitude of a singular itinerary – and I can hardly reproach them for this, as I have done the same.

But I am describing all this in too simplistic a fashion. What I was immediately certain of was that Hou was an outsider – he was not part of the gang, he was not in on the conversation, or anything like that. There was simply the strength of a film (*The Boys from Fengkuei*, 1983) which had emerged and imposed itself for good reasons. In the cinema, such reasons are always metaphysical in nature.

In effect, Hou's style – at once intuitive, powerful and contemplative, at a remove from any attempts at seduction, and able to use sheer brute force to head towards the essential and nothing but the essential – boded extremely well for Chinese cinema. Starting from zero, he was able to bring about a veritable revolution in its manner of apprehending and regarding the world, and, overcoming the impasses of classicism and imported modernism, he defined the possibility of a new and original point of view on the contemporary world.

Nothing at the time existed in Chinese cinema that could approach the rough-hewn truth and autobiographical realism of Hou's early work, which, if we must find a reference point for it, evoked Maurice Pialat's films.

The sentiment it emitted was self-evident. First, Hou had found a contemporary style to express a contemporary sensibility. In so doing, he proved that China was able to – and from that point on would be able to – be in synch with modern cinema, and would find its own responses to the questions that modern cinema poses to us all. Is there any need to recall the context in which this took place?

Chinese cinema was absolutely invisible in the West, except for the occasional King Hu films, treated as curiosities, and a hyper-ghettoized parallel circuit of martial arts movies. Ann Hui, with two well-made, intelligent and effective films, had been given prizes at Cannes, but, like the other filmmakers of the ephemeral Hong Kong New Wave, she was already on the way to returning to the ranks of an old, tired and constrictive industry. Furthermore, no sign of renewal had yet come from mainland China, as neither Chen Kaige nor Zhang Yimou – whatever we may think of their work – had started to make films yet.

Hou, appearing on the scene like a miracle, was the great Chinese filmmaker that had always been lacking. I thought that one day,

perhaps, he would also be the most important Chinese filmmaker, which is manifestly what has happened.

In any case, it was a privilege to have had the opportunity to observe a truly great artist deploy his talents. The plenitude of his cinema was obvious from his first autobiographical masterpieces: *A Summer at Grandpa's* (1984), *A Time to Live and a Time to Die* (1985), and *Dust in the Wind* (1986).[1] His work has always given the sense of progressing in leaps and bounds, using the cinema as an instrument of individual revelation. Even if it may have briefly seemed – for the space of a year and a film (*Daughter of the Nile*, 1987, which will no doubt be re-evaluated one day) – that his work was fallible and human, it is probable that this gave him the impetus to transcend himself by opening up to collective history in his most ambitious, and most noteworthy, film: *A City of Sadness* (1989), which garnered him the Golden Lion at Venice.

Hou has not ceased to develop as a filmmaker, and this also means that I have seen him transform as an individual. Of course, the free, innocent quality of one's debuts, of one's first

1) Wu Nien-jen said that *A Time to Live and a Time to Die* is the most important film in the history of Taiwanese cinema and I am not too far off from agreeing with him.

Olivier Assayas and Hou Hsiao-hsien
(shooting *HHH: A Portrait of Hou Hsiao-hsien*,
Olivier Assayas, 1997)

HHH: A Portrait of Hou Hsiao-hsien

binlang (something like an herbal equivalent to speed).[3] But whereas before it was instinct alone that was crucial, now theory and philosophy have assumed an increasingly important dimension – not only in the sense of thinking about perception (which is usually the only type of thinking useful for filmmakers), but also about the classical Chinese tradition – with the serious intensity requisite of autodidacts. He also, perhaps, has an increasingly acute awareness of the historical import of his œuvre, of the importance of his responsibility towards it and towards the development of Taiwanese cinema.

It is as if each of his films, and the amplification of his themes, inscribed themselves in him, and it is as if the substance of the individual had ended up being contaminated and invaded by the substance of the œuvre.

There are several important articulations in his work, and in particular his trilogy on memory initiated with *A City of Sadness* (collective memory), continued with *The Puppetmaster* (1993, individual memory) and concluded – or rather interrogated once more – with *Good Men, Good Women* (1995). *Good Men, Good Women* is entirely constructed around the conflict between the former and the latter, between the memory which constitutes being, which is the very fiber of being, and the mem-

times, is always eternally lost and eternally renewed elsewhere, differently, with different people. The bars, nightclubs, and karaoke joints of Taipei, which we drifted through as part of our carefree lifestyle, became, last time I was there, settings for the shoot of a documentary I made about him.[2]

With time, Hou has become a more multilayered figure. His juvenile, playful qualities, his way of gliding from an abstract line of argument to a childlike laugh are, of course, intact, as is his way of circulating among intellectuals and petty gangsters with a look of studied uncertainty, shrouded in a fog of weed, alcohol and even ory of the nation, which can only be the object of an intellectual, voluntarist approach, ceaselessly subjected to approximation and doubt. This is political work, if you want, but it can only be envisaged if the question of personal memory, its intimate conflicts and wounds, is first resolved. That pretty much sums up the evolution of Hou's œuvre.

Today his work finds itself at another crucial juncture, because after the time of autobiography, and the time of memory, he has reached, since *Goodbye South, Goodbye* (1996), the present. There are no more scores to settle with his past, or with Taiwan's past, which has been kept hidden for so long, and which has, for this very reason, been the principal source of inspiration for the New Cinema of Taiwan.

In a certain manner, he is now face to face with himself, much as he was at the beginning. And now the cinema itself can barely support him, because in the meantime the local audience for Taiwanese films has dissolved, in favor, of course, of the cinema of technological distraction pumped out of Hollywood. His films have long been financed from abroad, and he is now confronted with the risk of being more seen, and better regarded, in Europe than in his home country. This would be the ultimate paradox for such an anchored, grounded filmmaker, whose identity is so linked to that of his country.

Nevertheless, there is ample evidence to suggest that the renewed interrogation of his surroundings, the belated reinvention of his approach to filmmaking, and the reformulation of the themes at work in his last two films, has brought him to the summit of his art. Between the youthful brilliance of his "second debut film" *Goodbye South, Goodbye* and the vertiginous success of *Flowers of Shanghai* (1998), where the essence of life itself swirls around among the opium vapors, and where he shows the ungraspable yet inexorable workings of time, Hou has become a universal filmmaker. He is one of the greatest filmmakers working today – in China or elsewhere. When it comes down to it, he was destined to be so from the beginning.

2) *HHH: A Portrait of Hou Hsiao-hsien* (Olivier Assayas, 1997)

3) Editor's note: Assayas is referring to betel leaves, which can be chewed like tobacco.

4) Editor's note: the first version of this essay was published in *Le Monde* on November 19, 1998. The version translated here was revised for inclusion in a volume of collected essays: Olivier Assayas, *Présences: Écrits sur le cinéma* (Paris: Gallimard, 2009), 349–355.

1998 [4]

Translated by Daniel Fairfax

Jia Zhang-ke

A Bard Singing the Remembrances of a Nation

The first time I saw one of Hou Hsiao-hsien's films was in 1995. At the time, I was still a student at the Beijing Film Academy. I was supposed to go to the World Cinema History class, but after learning that Hou's work was going to be shown in the small theater of our college at exactly the same time, I had no choice but to skip the class. It was *The Boys from Fengkuei* (1983) that was screened and I was very drowsy when I left the theater. The film felt close, but it was also very alien. I always have this question: why would a film about Taiwanese young adults across the Strait make me feel as if it is about friends in my hometown in Shanxi?

I was born in 1970, the period of the Cultural Revolution. During my childhood, in China, there were only the "Revolutionary Arts." "Legends" and "popular" were the key words of the Revolutionary Arts, because they made it more convenient to convey the political messages of Communism to the general public. In these legendary stories, neither quotidian life nor the writer's independent affections and judgment could be seen, because everything needed to contribute to the Party. *The White-Haired Girl*, the representative work of the Revolutionary Arts is about a girl who, persecuted by her landlord, hid herself in the mountains for eleven years, making her hair completely white. The

old society turned her from a human to a ghost, and eventually the Communist Party rescues her. The new society restores her humanity.

The Boys from Fengkuei is about several young adults traveling from their fishing village to the big city of Kaohsiung to have part-time jobs during Taiwan's economic transformation in the 1980s. In the 1990s, China experienced a similar transformation. Many peasants came to Beijing, Shanghai, and Guangzhou from the suburbs for part-time jobs, opportunities, and the possibility of involving themselves in modern society. Although the economic transformation happened in mainland China a decade after it happened in Taiwan, what the young adults experienced is similar. *The Boys from Fengkuei* offers a distinctly cinematic depiction of that social transformation, enabling us to experience the emotions of the people living through it. The film is above all an expression of shared human experience. That is why this film evoked feelings that echoed my own.

In *The Boys from Fengkuei*, I saw the youth from the fishing village run to the beach and start dancing, their back against the surging waves. I suddenly felt that I was so close to them. Those Taiwanese youth in front of Hou's camera were just like my brothers in the town in inland China. They carried their

The Boys from Fengkuei, 1983

suitcases and left home for Kaohsiung. Once they got to town, they were tricked into an unfinished building to watch a movie. There was actually neither a movie nor a romantic story. They looked at the city through a window as big as the screen. What the city presented to them was cruel reality.

The film actually made me think for a while and it made me understand one thing: in creating art, life experience plays a very important role and honest expression of it is fundamental. For a film, this requires not only the intertwining of popular legends, but also that the work itself come closer to writing, to the personal expression of experience. The writer should be informed by perspectives from history, society, and aesthetics, and then eventually express his own emotions and judgments.

The Boys from Fengkuei inspired me to start frantically reading Chinese literature written in the pre-1949 period – including novels by Shen Congwen and by Eileen Chang – because I realized that Hou's films inherited a kind of cultural tradition, and it is exactly that which was cut off in China due to the Cultural Revolution. I learned that Chinese cultural tradition all over again because of the inspiration from Taiwan's New Cinema, with Hou as the representative artist of the time.

For me, *A City of Sadness* (1989) carries a similarly profound meaning. If *The Boys from Fengkuei* provides us with the experience of social transformation, *A City of Sadness* leads us to the very essence of Taiwanese society, helping us to understand the complicated relationships linking politics, the family, and individuals. To Chinese people, every section in the film is like a fishbone stuck in our throat. At sunrise, a large family takes a picture before watching a son leave to serve in the military. In the rain, with the family in a funeral procession, several men in black watch as their brother is buried, with his mourning portrait in their arms. In an unknown train station, a couple with their child wait on a silent and empty platform. Nation, party, family, and individuals; birth, aging, illness, and death; weddings and funerals. The Japanese left and the KMT [Kuomintang] arrived. *A City of Sadness*, a film almost three hours long, sincerely depicts quotidian life and the memories shared by the whole nation.

History and memories are continuously passed in different ways over time, by Homer's hymns, ancient Chinese drama, etc. … Apparently, in our time, Hou Hsiao-hsien is the genius narrator passing down the memories of a nation through films.

Koreeda Hirokazu

Things I Learned from Hou

Maborosi, Koreeda Hirokazu, 1995

Films need people more than stories.

Landscapes also harbor emotions.
(Hou would often write on colored paper the characters that in Japanese
read "天地有情," which means "Heaven and Earth Have Feelings." These
words caution against viewing the world in an anthropocentric way.)

Life's details (for example, "eating") should be respected.

Music can blow like the wind through a scene.

Translated by Ryan Cook

Working within Limits

A Conversation with Hou Hsiao-hsien and Chu Tien-wen

RICHARD I. SUCHENSKI: I understand that you have been thinking about making *The Assassin* (2015) for quite some time. What motivated you to make a martial arts film in this stage of your career?

HOU HSIAO-HSIEN: I have been reading Chinese *wuxia* [martial arts] novels since I was 12 or 13. After I became accustomed to reading those, I started to read the literary sketches of the Tang dynasty and later periods, among which you can find the origins of the *wuxia* novels. These works have a long history, but they are difficult to adapt. Although I started shooting films many years ago, I still feel it is a challenge to really prepare a film of this kind because the movements of the characters and their kung fu are extremely hard to properly visualize. King Hu is a special case.

Then, I accidentally ran across a Tang dynasty story that I had read thirty years ago. The whole story is less than a thousand words and it is called "Nie Yinniang" [a ninth-century "Tang tale" or *chuanqi* by Pei Xing]. I liked the character very much, so I began working on an adaptation two years ago. Although it will be a *wuxia* film, I might not be able to switch out of the style I have been using since the beginning of my career. I do not know how the film will turn out since I haven't finished it

yet. It might be different from other *wuxia* films.

RIS: You just mentioned the Tang dynasty twice. Earlier period films like *Flowers of Shanghai* (1998) were set in eras that are less remote. What challenges did you face in making a film set in the Tang dynasty?

HHH: *Flowers of Shanghai* is set in the late Qing dynasty. At first, I didn't read the novel [by Han Bangqing]. Many readers have a hard time finishing it because it was originally written in the regional Wu dialect and only became accessible when Eileen Chang translated it into Mandarin Chinese. I once planned to shoot a film about Zheng Chenggong [Koxinga] in Hirado, Japan, where he was born.[1] Zhong Acheng [Ah Cheng] and I were responsible for the screenplay. Zheng Chenggong was taken back to China by his father Zheng Zhilong, and sent to the Imperial University in Nanjing. The intellectuals of the era loved to have drinks at places like that, especially around the Qinhuai River, so I needed some reference materials on these areas and I asked Chu Tien-wen if she knew of

1) Editor's note: Zheng Chenggong was a half-Japanese military leader of the Ming dynasty who resisted the Manchus and seized Taiwan from the Dutch East India Company in 1662, turning it into a haven for Ming loyalists.

any. She then recommended that I read Eileen Chang's translation of Han Bangqing's novel. The more I read it, the more it appealed to me, so I decided to adapt it.

The novel is astonishing. The author needed to devote a great deal of time to fully understand what took place in these "houses." He needed to take the imperial examination – one of the last times it was offered – but he did not pass. When he came back, he finished writing the novel and passed away shortly thereafter in his thirties. I had the feeling that he had truly experienced something, which is why I made *Flowers of Shanghai*. That period is much closer to me because Taiwan used to imitate Shanghai and we had similar brothel spaces here. We heard about them often from the older generations.

Getting inside the Tang dynasty is much more difficult. The novel used for *Flowers of Shanghai* was incredibly detailed, but there are only a thousand words in "Nie Yinniang" and the content is very simple. It is also written in Classical Chinese, so words carry more than one meaning. Although it is difficult to learn about the specifics of life in the era from it, there are many other "Tang tales" you can refer to and there are also many studies and archaeological objects. You could spend a great deal of time trying to understand life in the Tang dynasty, but it still would not be enough. It has been harder to shoot this film than *Flowers of Shanghai* because I like to use details from life. This time, it was not possible to fully grasp those.

RIS: That is actually one of the questions that I had. One of the things that strikes me most in your films is the depiction of the quotidian aspects of historical experience – the way people eat, speak, dress, etc. How did you approach those sorts of questions in *The Assassin*?

HHH: In my earliest films, we tried to shoot in real spaces – the places or houses where people really live, the vehicles they drive, the trains they take, etc. When you have to shoot in an actual house, you cannot simply ask an actor to dress well and say their lines. It seems wrong. You have to decide what the space is for. When you plan a shot, you have to decide when it will take place. Time is very important to me. Is it in the morning? Is it at breakfast or when you wake up? Is it at lunch or the time before lunch? Or is it at night? I would then try to determine the general customs of the household at that time and that would be the most important reference point.

I would arrange a shot so that you can tell when the wife is at home and when her husband returns. Why does he come back at this moment? Why is the child at home and not at school? These decisions are all very important to me. Once I have this information, I can then conceive of the whole situation and manage all the details in that particular space. This is how I work with my actors and crew and it is how I prepare shots (including the arrangement of the lighting). I tend to work with many non-actors and they would not know how to perform if you did not give this information to them. When they have it, they can easily get into their characters. That is what I learned from my earliest films.

RIS: Speaking of non-actors, how important are spontaneity and improvisation to your shooting process?

HHH: Since they are not trained to perform, they still have their true essence. When you cast non-actors, you get to learn something about their personalities. You have to arrange situations so that these personalities can manifest themselves. Usually, I will ask them not to think about how to act, but about why they are here at this moment, what their background is. We will discuss the motivation for everything – including the reason why this particular place was selected for shooting, its background, the character's relationship with it and with others

in the film – and the immediate context. For example, in *Flight of the Red Balloon* (2007), there is a female student living downstairs who happens to be the professor's student. What is her relationship with the professor and the character played by Juliette Binoche upstairs? I went over all of these details with the girl, because she had only ever acted in a very, very short film. Among the actors in *Flight of the Red Balloon*, she is the one who I talked to the most. I had to speak with her three times before she really understood. Finally, I asked her to go to the room downstairs. It had been abandoned for a long time and, even though it was cleaned, the kitchen was still a mess. Everything in the kitchen was very dirty and I asked her to clean it. This immediately gave her a feeling for the space. After that, we started to shoot. Although her time on screen was very short, the feeling was presented in the right way. She could convey it perfectly. This is my method. What I want is to find a way of expressing someone's true personality in an authentic way.

RIS: You can very clearly see these precise details and performances in your films. I want to go back to something you mentioned before about lighting and set design when we were speaking about *Flowers of Shanghai*. The lighting in that film, and in many of your films, is realistic insofar as the light sources are generally evident, but, at the same time, it is also very stylized and distinctive. How do you find that balance?

HHH: Electric lights were not common in the period depicted in *Flowers of Shanghai*. There might have been a few, but they were very rare. What people generally used instead were oil lamps or candles. Silk was commonly used in the traditional Chinese clothes of the Qing dynasty and the reflection of oil lamp or candle light on silk is very beautiful. It has a greasy quality that I like. This was the basis for the whole design of the film.

Presenting people's relationships and emotions in a confined space was not difficult for me once we had the right spatial details. That is why we went to Shanghai and shipped two containers worth of period bed frames, mattresses, tables, lighting equipment, and stoves over. I had initially wanted to shoot in a real Shanghai location, but it was impossible because the old *shikumen* houses (built by foreigners) were fully occupied. I came back to Taiwan, built one in a studio, and focused on creating and capturing the atmosphere there without any exterior shots. I told the cinematographer [Mark Lee] that you feel as if the author is actually present when reading the novel, and he was there because he had grown up in that environment. As a result, I treated the camera as the eyes of that man watching these people, watching them speak and act, very attentively. The overall form of the film – including the lighting and the mood that it creates, as well as the style of the cinematography – was based on the way I felt reading this novel.

RIS: How about in your other films? How do you conceive of the camera's point of view in relation to what you are shooting?

HHH: The choice of point of view in other films varies and there are many possibilities. Of course, the director is an objective narrator and, as such, you can shoot whatever you like. It is based on your imaginative conception, but it is also determined by the subjective point of view of the character. I used to be very old-fashioned in following the rules. After shooting many films, I realized that it is not actually necessary, because that is the freedom of the objective narrator – for example, the decision to simulate watching eyes in *Flowers of Shanghai*. The freedom in making a film lies in determining this viewpoint.

Aside from the need to establish clear characterizations, it does not really matter what kind of atmosphere you aim for or which details you emphasize in telling a story. At first, I was very scrupulous in the choice of point of view – either maintaining objectivity or adopting the view of a particular character. I was very focused on this. Later in my career, I became more free. I realized that a director can be either extremely objective or subjective since the film also reflects your point of view. When I want to express something or it adds energy, I will adopt a character's point of view and I will be very careful in doing so. Otherwise, I try to be as free as I can while shooting.

For my new film, *The Assassin*, I initially wanted to shoot entirely with a handheld camera. Instead of a large camera, I wanted to use a Bolex. The traditional Bolex can only shoot brief shots, less than thirty seconds and generally twenty seconds at most. You also have to wind it after every shot. The reason I wanted to use this method is, as you said before, that I want to try to change my approach to form.

Actually, what I look for is a limit. I want to use the restrictions of the Bolex, the fact that it can only shoot for twenty-something seconds, to catch things. Unlike digital cameras that can shoot without stopping – back in the day, a shot of 1,000 feet, or ten minutes, was very long – the Bolex can only catch things for a very short period of time. How can you use that to complete a feature film? It creates a limit that I enjoy playing with. Western films tend to use a

third-person point of view, which allows you to shoot whatever you like. However, when you are constrained, you become very attentive to what you are shooting. You can work more deeply within limits. The goal is still to hit the target, to capture the objects you want to shoot.

RIS: You mentioned digital technology, but I understand that *The Assassin* is still 35mm. All of your features have been shot on film. Do you plan to continue working that way or are you incorporating aspects of digital technology now?

HHH: It all depends on what you want to shoot, what sense of space you want to convey. I shot *Café Lumière* (2003) in Japan and *Flight of the Red Balloon* in France. If I could shoot them again now, I might choose to use digital cameras. Why? Because then I could have cameras hidden in the crowd, allowing me to capture the reality of the city. In both of those films, the time and space are real. The choice of which car a man will take to reach a certain place is based on reality. I would not have the man jump into a random car and then jump out somewhere. You can edit that in such a way that the audience will not notice, but it is unnecessary. I want real movement in real spaces. As long as you have a limit, you will be very fo-

Hou Hsiao-hsien at SPOT-Taipei Film House

cused on what you shoot. Now, nobody will pay attention to you if you shoot with digital cameras. You can hide yourself in a car and shoot, or do anything you like. Sometimes, you may be able to capture a situation that cannot be replicated.

RIS: *The Assassin* is largely shot on sets?

HHH: It is shot on sets, but there are some location shots as well. It was hard to do that, because of the Tang dynasty setting. Buildings in that era were mostly made of wood and the structure of the architecture was very different. I actually went to Japan to take some shots of this type of architecture. In Japan, many Tang-style buildings are preserved, especially the temple built by the monk Jianzhen [Tōshōdaiji in Nara]. Those buildings were actually built by the carpenters of the Tang dynasty. Other than that, I had no choice but to build sets because it was impossible to find real spaces we could shoot in. For some location shots, I went to distant areas in the mountains of China, in areas such as Inner Mongolia or Hubei. There, you can find buildings that still preserve their ancient structure. These buildings were for peasants and we took some shots there, but we had to add the tiled rooftops digitally. At the time, tiles were for aristocrats, so peasants seldom had tiles and we had to edit them in. Since we

have this sort of technology now, I shot many things knowing that we would adjust them later.

As for the main set, the story is about the *jiedushi* [regional commander] of a prefecture after the An Lushan Rebellion, so I needed a parliament building and a great palace hall. They had to be built at the studios of the Central Motion Pictures Corporation in Taiwan. I wanted to build sets that could be combined since all Tang buildings were designed that way. A large space could be created by adding columns to the preset base. The base could also be used to create smaller, less luxurious households. It would be like playing with building blocks, but the designers we consulted found this difficult. I had hoped that the buildings could still be used after the production. Since it was not possible to implement this, I constructed two buildings with real wood in an imitation Tang style.

RIS: Continuing in this vein, I wanted to ask about the idea of Chinese tradition, which you have mentioned on several occasions. Which elements or ideas have been most influential on your work?

HHH: Chinese traditions can seem really old-fashioned. For example, the fundamental structure of a family has something to do with phrases like "loyalty, filial obedience, benevolence, love, trust, justice, peace, and equality" or "let the king be a king, the minister a minister, the father a father, and the son a son." After reading many novels, it is quite easy to understand these relationships and there is a very clear standard you may yearn for. In my opinion, this happens around the world regardless of which country you are in.

I have read many *wuxia* stories, novels, and also some traditional Chinese plays (including puppet plays), and I have gradually found myself absorbed into this world. Concepts and values have changed and I started to realize that there is a fundamental question related to human existence in this world. Why do you exist? How do you deal with your surroundings, with details, with your friends, and with society? These things are all part of you. I don't want to elaborate, but I realize that my judgment, my instinct when faced with problems or with anything, has shown me to be a mature individual with a clear mind. Whenever I am handling public affairs, interacting with people, collaborating with my team, my friends, or my family, I always have a standard (as many others do).

I feel I am very clear about the question of how to be human and I don't find it necessary to define it in terms of Chinese culture. It is more like a universal value based on your own critical judgment as well as your respect for people, animals, and nature, which develops in its own way. I went to Inner Mongolia and noticed that there are many silver birch trees. They have a short life and when they wither, they become part of the dry humus, which slowly accumulates, causing the soil to darken. Trees can then grow better and live longer, finally forming the Black Forest [along the Tuul River]. The cycle of animal and plant life has its balance. In Chinese philosophy, the concept of balance has always been discussed, but I do not want to study in detail what was said before. I feel you always have to treat people and affairs with the same clear attitude. You can extend this and apply it to nature and even to society and the nation. This idea did not really develop through diligent study, by the influence of my Chinese background, or something outside. Chinese literature helped me see more clearly the reality that was already present.

RIS: Thank you for this very interesting answer. You mentioned reading novels and I wonder if you had a similar reaction to Chinese paintings?

HHH: No… To be honest, when I tried to appreciate Chinese paintings in childhood… well, you know how it is. They were too far from me. Now I am able to appreciate them because I realize they are based in realism. This became apparent after I started shooting films in China and discovered that these paintings depict landscapes that I actually experienced in person. The mountains, the highlands, the fogs, and the trees, for example, are very realistic, not impressionistic.

RIS: It is obvious that you are a keen cinephile with a broad understanding of international cinema. *The Boys from Fengkuei* (1983) includes a very memorable scene where the protagonist goes to see *Rocco and His Brothers* (Luchino Visconti, 1960) and one of your most recent shorts, *The Electric Princess Picture House* (2007), shows a local Taiwanese audience watching *Mouchette* (Robert Bresson, 1967). Some of what you said a few moments ago about shooting in the street with a camera reminded me of *Breathless* (Jean-Luc Godard, 1960). How has your own style developed in relationship to films from different parts of the world?

HHH: I watched *Rocco and His Brothers* very early, before I started my film career. In my youth, I saw many films, but most of them were fairly ordinary. *Rocco and His Brothers* is a film that I originally went to see because of Alain Delon, who was always great. As for *Mouchette*, I watched it once I was already mak-

ing films, when the Chinese Taipei Film Archive published a translation of Bresson's journals [*Notes on the Cinematographer*]. It was extremely impressive because it was so simple and at the same time extremely realistic. I really like the way Bresson presents things in a hidden way. It seems to represent surfaces, but it contains all the details of reality. This is very similar to many of my films.

Besides *Mouchette*, I also like his *Pickpocket* (1959). As I said, I like the furtiveness, which is something you experience in life as well. There is almost no dialogue in his films, but everything is still expressed so clearly, which is not easy to do. He talks about his hatred for theatricality in his book – about how theater practitioners took over when film transitioned to sound and the script took on a new importance. For him, it was all fake and he did not allow acting. This is indeed very similar to the approach I took in my earliest films. I especially like *Mouchette*, but later Bresson films are too stylized and, for me, harder to appreciate.

[Chu Tien-wen joins the conversation]

RIS: This is a question for both of you. The idea of realism has come up a number of times and I would be interested to know how that informs your writing process.

CHU TIEN-WEN: Hou and I have worked together

for eighteen films and he is definitely not a typical screenwriter. I once saw an interview with Ang Lee in which he said that he received countless scripts after receiving the Academy Award for Best Director and had to choose which one to shoot. This, for us, is completely incredible because we have never had the chance to read other people's scripts before deciding what to work on. From the very beginning up through the present, we have never experienced anything like this. That is the biggest difference between Hou and other directors.

In terms of the screenwriting process, Hou is the pitcher, the motivator, and I have to be the catcher. The flight of a bat depends on the projection of sonar to detect objects through their reflection. With this reflected information, the bat then knows how to fly. The role I play is pretty much equivalent to that of the bat. That is how we collaborate. Hou is actually a screenwriter himself; he began his career as a script supervisor and he has written countless scripts. In addition to being his echo – and it is not easy to be an echo since this only works if you share the same frequency – my contribution is to continue a long term discussion with him that takes place outside the production process. We discuss different genres of books and different things in life. It is a bit like the process of pottery making or alchemizing in that you have to keep throwing in materials to finally produce something valuable. Instead of a literary contribution, the composition of something, I keep throwing in things that might or might not be useful.

Hou records this discussion process in thin tattered notebooks, the kind his daughter always used in elementary school for homework. Since each of these is thin and easy to carry, he tends to keep them with him and writes everything down. For some films, he will have a dozen notebooks. The discussions can last for a couple of months or one or two years. For *The Assassin*, he gave me a dozen notebooks when he felt it was time to prepare a treatment. These notebooks are incomprehensible because his notes and sketches are fragments recorded over a long period of time. However, I can make sense of them because I was always involved in the discussions. I eventually use them to prepare a well-written treatment for everyone.

RIS: You just mentioned *The Assassin*, which, like *Flowers of Shanghai*, is a literary adaptation. Is the process you just described applicable in those cases?

CTW: *Flowers of Shanghai* and *The Assassin* stand at opposite poles of adaptation. The Chinese source for *Flowers of Shanghai* is in two volumes. You can imagine how thick it is and there might be more characters than in *Dream of the Red Chamber* [one of the Four Great Classical Novels]. There are also two strata in the novel and the lower stratum is made up of those who serve the courtesans like beggars. The novel is like *Gosford Park* (Robert Altman, 2001), with its two social tiers, or the labyrinth of a tropical forest, which contains enormous variety. How do you adapt all of these interwoven strands into a two hour film? How can you choose? That was the great challenge with *Flowers of Shanghai*.

The Assassin was very different. There are fewer than 1,000 words in the story, so you can not even truly consider it an adaptation. The experience was like finding the fossils of a dinosaur without knowing what they are. Among the fossils, there are some teeth, some claws, and some bones. How do you build a complete dinosaur without the other parts? That was what made *The Assassin* difficult.

RIS: One theme in many of these responses is the importance of limits, the idea of working within limits and using them to develop a form. Why is this so important to you?

HHH: Everything has its limit and you have to work within these to stay focused. Without a limit, you have no direction, so I find them necessary. There has to be something for you to respond to. Within these limits, you can then concentrate and follow a particular direction. I think it is impossible to work on anything unless you have the ability to focus on whatever it is that inspires you. It is normal to have limits.

Within limits, you are free. The reason why I wanted to work with a Bolex is because it creates a very significant limit. A shot can only last for twenty to thirty seconds and there are also sound issues that you need to deal with after shooting. The cinematographer working with this limit would have no time to position their camera and frame the shot, all they could do is try to capture what is happening at that moment. Each shot would be based on the cinematographer's instinct. This represents a huge limit, but freedom comes from the combination of instincts and limits. An experienced cinematographer would then be very attentive and could skillfully capture the actors' movements. There has to be a limit. It means freedom to me. Within the limit, you will not consider too much or greedily try to grasp everything.

CTW: While we were preparing *The Assassin*, Hou kept saying that he wanted to use a Bolex because his "one scene / one shot" method was taken to the extreme in *Flowers of Shanghai*, which is remarkable. It was also the extreme for the cinematographer, Mark Lee, who we call Ah-bin. Hou did not want to use the same method in *The Assassin*, which required a new limit for himself and Ah-bin. What would you do if you only have thirty seconds to capture something? He sets a difficult task for himself.

We have been working on literary writing and film production for so long that we have become skilled in all the relevant techniques. There is a Chinese proverb, "just coming out from the thatched cottage" (i.e., at the beginning of one's career). We have to return to where we started because when you are adept at things, you lose freshness and energy. Giving yourself a limit enables you to break through and make something different from what you are used to. Since people kept mentioning the "one scene / one shot" approach, Hou wanted to use a Bolex. I have the same problem in literary writing. Contemporary novels do not tell stories and I reached a "zero narrative" in my last work. What did I do next? I decided to tell a story about jet lag, which was a limit for me in the same way that the Bolex was for Hou.

RIS: How would you describe the local film-making situation?

HHH: Film industries are prosperous when local films reflect a localized point of view. This ap-plies to every country and it is something local people can truly feel. These films are super-ficially made, but they can still become block-busters and they establish trends that everyone follows. The result is that films are like TV shows. Images are like words. Although they can be seen directly, the meanings they express are indirect. The images used in these local films are comprehensible to everyone, but they are too blatant, too simple. This direction is chosen because of the promise of the box office.

RIS: You have spent a great deal of time sup-porting and mentoring younger filmmakers in Taiwan. Could you talk a bit about these activ-ities?

HHH: My greatest hope is that they will start to see, notice, and focus on the reality around them. It is very difficult because they grew up watching films and they unconsciously imitate them. They have not fully experienced reality in their own lives. That is what I have been try-ing to tell them through the Golden Horse Film Academy and conversations. They do not even think about following this path, they still want film stars, someone to write a script, etc. At the same time, the stories they come up with have already been told through film. I have been try-ing to communicate this for a long time and I

Flight of the
Red Balloon, 2007

always suggest that they try to experience their surroundings and the cities they live in.

I was not very familiar with either Tokyo or Paris when I shot *Café Lumière* and *Flight of the Red Balloon*. How did I find a way to express how I felt about the city? By observing it. I found places I responded to and decided to shoot there. After that, I ask questions like how far is it from the school? What school would this kid go to? How many routes home are there from school? What transportation methods could he use? These are all concrete questions based on reality. I choose real living situations in this way to give constraints to the characters and they can then explore within these constraints.

I often see people shooting in Taipei. When they need a shot on a street, they choose a street that is beautiful, not a street that a person might walk on in a particular way. They only care about the lights and the trees, and they prefer to have few people present so that it is easier to manage. The effect is totally removed from reality. If you are able to truly notice your environment, everything becomes worth shooting because each place is unique. Every coffee shop has its own customers and a train station looks different from each direction.

As I said, filmmakers need to learn how to recognize reality. It was difficult before because it was so expensive to shoot a film and also because they required stars and a crew. Now that digital technology is so developed, accessible, and convenient, why can't young filmmakers turn the camera towards the world around them? Reality provides a model and the more you understand it, the clearer your film will be.

Conversation conducted via videoconference
on July 11, 2013.
Translated by Dennis Li

Experiments with Realism

An Interview with Chen Huai-en

RICHARD I. SUCHENSKI: You were the cinematographer for four of Hou Hsiao-hsien's most important films – *Daughter of the Nile* (1987), *A City of Sadness* (1989), *Good Men, Good Women* (1995), and *Goodbye South, Goodbye* (1996). How did your collaboration develop?

CHEN HUAI-EN: My collaboration with him preceded my work as a cinematographer. I first worked with him as a script supervisor on *The Sandwich Man* (1983). Beginning with *Out of the Blue* (Chen Kun-hou, 1984), for which Hou was screenwriter and I was the assistant director, I also acted as the stills photographer. This continued for *Taipei Story* (Edward Yang, 1985) and *A Time to Live and a Time to Die* (1985). Hou asked me to work with him on cinematography after that, so I became Mark Lee's assistant on *Dust in the Wind* (1986).

The reason I mention all of this is because I became a cinematographer through an unusual process. My work as Hou's cinematographer developed out of my collaboration in other contexts and our many discussions about film.

RIS: How actively was he involved in the framing of the shots? The style is very distinctive.

CHE: Before I worked on *Daughter of the Nile*, I was not a professional cinematographer. I was just a guy who worked with many roles on films. The reason the framing in that film is dis-

tinctive is because I did not receive training as a cinematographer. My ideas and capabilities for framing came instead from my experience as a photographer. Photographers have to arrange the compositions by themselves, so we tend to conceive of shots in a different way. It is probably because Hou liked my approach that he decided to apply it to the film.

RIS: What sort of back and forth dialogue did you have about these compositions?

CHE: Hou's transformation started in *The Sandwich Man*. It was not as clear to me at the time because I had just started my film career and I wasn't sure what the "correct" way was. You can see this in the type of storyboarding used by the three different directors in *The Sandwich Man*. Tseng Chuang-hsiang and Wan Jen had studied film production abroad and their method inspired Hou, encouraging him to approach this film in a new way. He began using master shots. Since film stock was so expensive in Taiwan, this was generally not allowed on location.

Hou seemed to be intrigued by the idea of capturing a complete performance in a single shot. He hoped that his actors would be able to work this way without coverage and he would usually repeat a shot no more than three times. First, he would try to capture either the full

Good Men, Good Women, 1995

body or seventy percent of the body. Then, there would be a medium shot. When necessary, he would also add a close-up. He does not believe that an actor can repeat his performance precisely at three separate times for shots with different angles or scales, so he concentrated entirely on the long shots or the medium shots in editing.

Once he realized that actors could perform more realistically in a long shot, he stopped caring about closer shots. By contrast, Wan would take seven shots with seven different angles for each scene and Tseng would take three or four. Hou abandoned the method generally used in Taiwan, which entailed taking one shot after another based on storyboards. I think his ideas about shooting changed a great deal in this period. By the time we collaborated "officially" on *Daughter of the Nile*, we had a tacit understanding of each other and knew what to focus on. I had my perspective from photography and Hou had developed his own approach based on using master shots to arrange scenes. RIS: That is actually a good segue to my next question about *A City of Sadness*, which is one of the great achievements in cinematography anywhere. I am always struck by the number of deep focus images with multiple planes and also multiple zones of action in that film. They

simultaneously suggest a kind of realism and a very precise type of composition. What was your method in that film?
CHE: As I mentioned, I learned what Hou finds most important in an image from working with him for a number of years. The main thing is that he wants absolute realism and absolute spontaneity. Everything has to be both real and spontaneous – the performances, the cinematography, and even the art design. It is difficult to achieve this, especially because Hou hates meetings and has difficulty clarifying things. He tends not to communicate with his crew members. Whenever work on a new film began, we would spend a lot of time trying to understand the script and the design of the cinematography would be based on the story ideas. Scripts and stories were discussed in detail, but not cinematography.

There was a consensus that we would scout for locations based on instinct and feeling. There was actually no logic to it. How did we use the locations? We would find the angle from which the story could be told most easily and understood most comprehensively. For example, if you want to install a surveillance camera in your house, you will choose an angle that can help you see clearly what is happening when a thief breaks in. The most important thing in selecting locations was determining whether or not we could find a point from which we could witness the story and see the whole family vividly.

RIS: Is that why you shot in the area around Chiufen [Jiufen] in the Northern part of Taiwan, because of the way the preserved colonial architecture helped you clearly visualize the structure of the family?

CHE: During the Japanese colonial period, that area was important industrially, economically, and in terms of government. Chiufen had gold mines, which is why the Japanese were there and why it became prosperous. It had already declined by the time we shot there twenty years ago, but the buildings from the Japanese colonial period were still there, comparatively intact. To shoot a film about the past, you will definitely want to go to the places that are most relevant and it is easier to "return" to that era in Chiufen. We referred to historical documents about the area when we were preparing the film and it seemed possible to situate the story there.

As for what you mentioned about the buildings reflecting the structure of family life, Hou wanted to find an angle that could be used to present a family in a natural way. If the layout of a house would allow you only to show a narrow section of space, blocking a complete view, he would not use it. Such a house would not be able to convey the way of life of the people inside, which is what he wants most.

RIS: Let me ask you about the concept of landscape. One of the things that is most remarkable in *A City of Sadness* is the contrast between interiors that are very geometric, even architectonic, and exteriors which are often more evocative or poetic. This is something you can see in some of Hou's other films as well. Could you talk a bit about your approach to landscape?

CHE: Actually, this is the first time my work has been described as poetic [Laughs]. Chiufen has its own unique landscape and by staying there long enough to understand it, it was possible to create something special. Your comment is based on what is there in the film, but the results might not have been the same if we had gone with our original plan. We had a limited budget and it would have been difficult if we had chosen another location to build our period city. The Shanghainese brothels were actually located in cities like Keelung or Taipei – historically, this story should have taken place around Keelung Harbor – but there were not enough historical buildings there and our budget only allowed us to adjust sets, not to build them. All of our alterations were intended

Shooting *Daughter of the Nile*, 1987

to wipe out the smells of modernity. The digital technologies that would have made this possible in post-production were not available at that time, so our only option was to physically modify the sets.

That is why we focused on capturing the natural landscape in the exteriors and on family life in the interiors. The reason is not that we were trying to find poetic landscapes, but because we were unable to build a city and had to adjust. One of the reasons we selected Chiufen is because Hou liked the multiple layers of the streets there. If a street is flat on the horizon, you can see very far in the distance, which means you would need many people, many stores, etc. to evoke the image of the era. In that city in the mountains, all you need is a slope and the horizon disappears. We did not need to spend a lot of money creating everything.

RIS: You worked as the assistant director on *The Puppetmaster* (1993)?

CHE: We made *The Puppetmaster* because we wanted to make a documentary about Li Tien-lu. However, Hou is not a master of documentary and I think he made a feature film because he was better able to express his ideas about Li's creativity that way. The main setting was the metropolitan area of old Taipei and we had to scout locations in the Fujian province of China. I became the assistant director because I was more involved in coordinating the shoot in Quanzhou, Zhangzhou, and Fuzhou, which we used to present Li's tory in Taipei.

Filmmaking in Taiwan is somewhat different from other countries. My duties included preparing schedules, preparing for the shoot, and supervising its execution. Since Hou always changes content during filming, he is not always able to set clear requirements for the crew or to sort things out in order. I could help him coordinate all of these details because I was familiar with his method. The crew did not always understand his needs and that is because he is very unpredictable. Things always change. If we have 100 scenes, for example, we might start with scene twenty. If Hou gets what he wants from the scene, we might move on to scene nineteen, eighteen, or twenty-one. Otherwise, he might need to reconstruct other scenes to fit the new scene twenty. The reason I became his assistant director is because I understood this approach better than most.

RIS: Is it true that he does not use storyboards of any kind?

CHE: I don't think so. At the time I worked with him, he would usually talk to me about the structure of a scene the night before shooting it. There was no need for storyboards because he used so many long shots.

As a director, Hou insists on absolute realism. His approach is very special and it is different from what many people may think. His actors and crew do not even fully understand what it is he is looking for because he loves to anticipate the unknown. Instead of gathering the five or ten actors in a scene together and clearly explaining who should do what, he will speak with each actor individually. During these conversations, which might take place while putting on makeup or taking a rest, he simply describes the character's viewpoint on the scene, telling the actors what is relevant and irrelevant for that character. Everyone would learn what a given scene was about just before shooting, so crew members had to prepare for all possibilities in staging, lighting, and cinematographic design.

Shooting would begin without a formal declaration of "action" and we would wait for Hou to announce a cut. During the years I worked with him, there was no video monitor available, so we would check in with each other about the results based on our impressions during shooting. If he and the assistant director or cinematographer thought a shot came out fine, we would move on. Otherwise, we would shoot it again. Since he used very few insert shots, we did not reshoot scenes very often. There was always a good reason if we did. He would always stop shooting if the scene did not work after three takes. Sometimes he would try again another day, but other times he would try to work whatever it is he wanted to convey into another scene.

In my opinion, Hou's attitude and approach to managing his shots are products of his firm commitment to realism, including the realism of the shooting process. He would never expect someone to walk to such and such a place, to stand up, or to do something according to a prearranged timing. It was important for him that everyone be spiritually present in the situation, to feel as though they were actually experiencing it with a certain level of self-understanding, so that something could happen that would be a genuine surprise even to him. He would say "okay" when that happened.

Hou is a very interesting person. He is never satisfied if the results are as expected. Instead, he tries to anticipate situations with elements that he cannot fully predict. This is the most fundamental aspect of his work, and his aesthetics and thinking all develop out of it. It is the reason he has a unique style.

RIS: You became the cinematographer once again for *Good Men, Good Women. A City of Sadness* contains a number of shots with camera movement – there is, for example, a very memorable pan in the mountains. The camera is much more static in *The Puppetmaster*, although Mark Lee told me that there were some mobile shots that Hou cut out. In *Good Men, Good Women*, the camera is very active throughout. What motivated these changes?

CHE: To be honest, I have forgotten why we started to move the camera at that time. What I do remember is that Hou felt that when there are a small number of actors in an interior space, a fixed shot could make it difficult to fully understand the rhythms and emotions of a scene. In addition to panning, tracking was sometimes used to add more layers to a scene and to make the story development more precise. Hou did begin experimenting with this in *The Puppetmaster*. His approach in that film was very experimental, but he did not really believe these techniques would help him present his ideas. On the other hand, it is possible that this experience changed his critical perspective and inspired his approach in *Good Men, Good Women*. Annie Shizuka Inoh's storyline in the modern section is comparatively simple and the set was more metropolitan and narrow, which made camera movement necessary for the viewer to find a way into the story.

Hou did not want the audience to be distracted by the camera movement, but he did want their understanding to be guided by it. We all understood that the camera movement would need to be developed spontaneously in relation to the scene. Hou would never instruct an actor to walk from the sofa to the fridge and then from the fridge to the kitchen. He relies on the actors to develop their movements based on their understanding of the character and the needs of the scene. All of this meant that camera movement needed to be extremely slow. By using gradual pans and tracks, the story could be made richer and more layered. If a track is too fast, the audience will notice the movement and the camera might not end up where the actor ends up. Our job was to be more like an observer, which I was comfortable with due to my origins as a photographer. Capturing the essence of a scene is like taking a picture, you have to manage the timing and the rhythm when you frame. Hou's role was to find a way to link all the framings together, so our discussions focused on where the dolly should start and end and what the tempo should be.

There is one other thing I should mention. I was once asked a similar question about Hou's decision to start moving the camera and I made a joke, saying that it was because cinematographers would fall asleep if a fixed position was used for the entire scene, so he added dollies and tracks to keep us awake! This is just a joke. The real reason why we started to use tracking is that the method we used before only allowed us to understand a story from the surface. With camera movements, the images are able to reflect the inner life of the characters. It becomes possible to observe more.

RIS: This idea of multiple layers in *Good Men,* *Good Women* is very interesting because you have it with the time frames, with the cinematography, and also with the music. You are listed as one of the composers and I wonder if you could describe the work on the film's soundtrack.

CHE: Hou enjoys singing, but he does not listen to music. At the time, he had many friends in the music business who wanted to work on his films. They would send him demos and he would pass them on to me, because he knows I like listening to music. This is the reason I collaborated with Chen Ming-chang on the soundtrack for *Dust in the Wind*, which we were very satisfied with. I tried to do the same thing for *Good Men, Good Women*.

There is one frustrating thing about working with Hou. Since there is very little time left for post-production by the time the editing is finished, it is not possible to ask musicians to begin composing with the completed film. They would be under great time pressure. Since Hou has no time to speak with musicians during the editing stage, it was my responsibility to contact them. That is the main reason I became involved with the music of *Good Men, Good Women*.

Hou is of Hakka origin and we tried to work with Yen Chih-wen and Lin Shao-ying to incorporate Hakka culture into the music. We had scouted some Hakka villages in Guangzhou and when we realized that Hou shares that background (he was born in Meixian, Guangdong) and it was relevant to the content of the film, we decided to develop something around that.

Let me put it this way. The writer of *Song of the Covered Wagon*, which is performed in the theater in the modern section, is Lan Po-chou. Did you know that he is also of Hakka origin? Of course, Hou did not try to create something with the aim of presenting Hakka culture. He read Lan's work and we went to shoot the film in the *tulou* (large, enclosed, and fortified earthen buildings, most often with a rectangular or circular configuration) in the Hakka villages in Guangzhou where the story took place. We were there to shoot, to observe, and to understand what the culture is like. Since Hou is part of the Hakka people, he had an inner feeling for it. That is why we went in this direction. What I tried to do was to organize a collaboration with the musician Chiang Hsiaowen and to manage the overall tone. Yen Chih-wen, who is also of Hakka origin, wrote the Hakka song at the end.

RIS: Last question: *Goodbye South, Goodbye* seems like an experiment in many ways – the camera's point of view, the use of color filters, and also the massive amount of material shot for the film. What was your experience on that film like?

CHE: I only worked on part of the film due to family emergencies. It was the most experimental of all the Hou films I collaborated on. Hou almost completely rejected the idea of a script. We were only given a synopsis and we did not have any concrete ideas for the individual scenes. I was the cinematographer and my cameraman was Han Yun-chung. Since I was part of the directing team on *The Puppetmaster*, I had the ability to help manage the production, which meant that we could still progress even though Hou did not rely on the script. *Goodbye South, Goodbye* was much more difficult because we did not know what he would want to do next. Sometimes he would even jokingly ask us, "what should we shoot now?" At least, that is how things seemed at the start of the shoot.

As for the heavy use of color filters, I believe that was the contribution of Mark Lee, because he likes to use color filters. He actually did some research on the effects of color filters in that period.

From what I understand (since I was not present), things became clearer later on. Even on a very experimental film, the further along you get, the easier it is to finish the film. I only participated in the first third or half of the production and the challenge for me was not knowing where the film would go and how the material we shot would be used. I do not know why Hou decided to work entirely without a script to follow, but I think it is because his ideas about realism and spontaneity keep changing (even if the overall goal is the same). When he was shooting *Flowers of Shanghai*, I learned that the actors, who were generally not from Shanghai, needed to speak mainly in Shanghainese. I was curious about this and asked the crew, "Didn't these actors read a script? Didn't they have to rehearse their lines?" Yes, they did. Those actors could not speak Shanghainese at all, so they had to practice well before shooting. Hou wanted to respect the background and culture of the period, so he accepted that the actors would need more preparation for that film.

Hou always experiments with the language of cinema and he wants to make each film an adventure. At least with *Goodbye South, Goodbye*, I believe he wanted to make a breakthrough by experimenting with absolute realism. I heard that he and Yao Hung-i worked on a project after that – it must have been for *Millennium Mambo* (2001) – which went further in this direction. They did not even tell the actors when they were shooting. The actors were so shocked that they could not capture anything interesting and they gave up. Hou always has his own understanding of realism in his mind and it shapes his cinematic language.

That is why I found his films so interesting. Working with him was sometimes very confusing, but we followed his lead and we decided something must be right if he did not say it was bad. I still can't quite tell you what made it "right," though.

Interview conducted via videoconference
on August 14, 2013.
Translated by Dennis Li

Exploring Visual Ideas

An Interview with Mark Lee (Ping-bin)

RICHARD I. SUCHENSKI: *A Time to Live and a Time to Die* (1985) and *Dust in the Wind* (1986) both place a strong emphasis on naturalistic light and camera positions that are very different from the ones used in other Central Motion Picture Corporation films from the period. How did that style develop?

MARK LEE: The approach to style and color in my collaboration with Hou Hsiao-hsien was different in the early days. We began working together after he finished *A Summer at Grandpa's* (1984) and I realized when we were shooting *A Time to Live and a Time to Die* that he had not actively been involved in framing and lighting questions before that. *A Time to Live and a Time to Die* tells the story of a diasporic family and the experience of growing up in the midst of change. Hou and I had similar backgrounds – my father also died when I was a child and we even lived in the same town at one point.

The lighting arrangements that I developed for those films were intended to create visual contrasts while remaining realistic. I rejected the mainstream approach of the period and did not want to use delicate, full color and soft lighting. Hou was very supportive of my ideas and our goal was to create very strong images. We decided to apply black-and-white lighting techniques in color. During shooting, he would always tap me on the back and ask me to suddenly change the camera movement to capture something. This was very challenging for me at the time, but I learned to think about cinematography in a new way. Through our collaboration, I realized that the image can have a certain aura or flavor, which was very innovative at the time.

We continued our experiments with lighting on *Dust in the Wind*. I proposed even more daring visual ideas and he gave me room to explore. Sometimes he would suggest something that was beyond our technical capabilities and we would try to overcome these challenges.

RIS: You have been making films with Hou for almost thirty years. In what ways is your collaboration different from your work with directors like Wong Kar-wai, Tian Zhuangzhuang, Ann Hui, Jiang Wen, or Tran Anh Hung?

ML: As a cinematographer, I tend to approach every collaboration in a similar way. The methods differ because each director is different. As I mentioned, my work with Hou has been the most challenging since he does not use precise scripts or detailed storyboards. When we shot *A Time to Live and a Time to Die*, there would sometimes be a piece of paper with some ideas for the sequence written down as a reference, but he rarely broke the sequence down into shots. He prefers to keep checking and adjusting during shooting. Everyone is given space and I try to transform this space so that the camera is able to dance with the actors.

We have also been collaborating since we were young. Since we had similar family situations and experiences, as well as the thoughts and emotions shared by all human beings, images emerge by themselves in my mind and my heart when he discusses his stories with me. We have a special feeling for, and understanding of, each other because of this.

RIS: The color palette in *The Puppetmaster* (1993) is more vivid and many of the shots are very dark. Why did the style change?

ML: Our older method of collaboration continued until *The Puppetmaster*. Due to the content of that film, I suggested that it should be filled with rich colors. Hou rented a studio and asked the actors to participate in color experiments, after which he asked me to be fully responsible for determining the overall color palette for the film. Although he completely left that to me, he boldly requested that I use only natural light sources. This was probably because I had worked through all the challenges in our previous collaborations.

He kept asking for the lights to be more real-

istic and dimmer. Every time I turned off a light, he would ask me if I was still able to shoot. I always answered "no problem" as long as the camera could still sense the light that was present and he would reply by asking me to turn off another light. It frequently turned out to be the only light left, sometimes resulting in a total blackout. He would always ask why I was still able to shoot under these conditions, which were so dark that we could barely see anything with our own eyes. I would explain that I was able to find an exposure spot. He would wonder where that was and I would tell him that we would be unable to continue shooting if I revealed the spot, so he always left some lights on for me. After *The Puppetmaster*, the range of colors in Hou's films broadened.

When I was shooting the film, I would sometimes secretly put on soft focus lenses. Although they helped minimize optical aberrations, Hou still refused to accept them. I used a soft focus lens not to make the actors' skin look better, but to capture the unique qualities of the rugged wooden furniture. My assistants and I always used signals to signify the use of the soft focus. It was a white lie!

RIS: Could you talk a bit about the style of *Flowers of Shanghai* (1998)? What do you mean by the phrase "glamorous realism?"

Shooting
Flight of the Red Balloon, 2007

ML: Before *Flowers of Shanghai*, Hou's style relied on natural lights and performances. Realism was the basis of his images. Actually, at the beginning of the *Flowers of Shanghai* shoot, most of the crew members were very concerned and some even thought the film might be a disaster because there were so many challenges. It really was possible for the film to become a total disaster!

Hou spoke to me a year before we started shooting about the greasy light and silken textures that *Flowers of Shanghai* evoked in his mind. I kept looking for this, trying to figure out how to arrange the lights to meet Hou's needs while at the same time retaining the impression of realism. I designed some lights that would recreate the effect of oil lamps. After we started shooting, editor Liao Ching-sung, who was also Hou's producer at the time, decided that the footage was too bright and lacked a realistic atmosphere. He reminded Hou to be conscious of this and, one day, he turned off everything except the oil lamps, asking if this would represent the reality of the time.

The light from actual oil lamps is very dim and it creates drifting shadows, which suggests anxiety. I told Hou that, although I could work in this atmosphere, the results would be very different and it would be impossible to create the visual textures we had discussed for a year. Besides, I said, my lighting arrangements would only expand the range of the lights – they would still be very realistic – and I used the phrase "glamorous realism." Hou accepted my explanation and we continued to use this style for the remainder of the shoot.

RIS: Most of the recent films you have made with Hou have featured frequent camera movement, which is a marked shift from your earliest work together. How involved are you in determining the length and rhythm of these shots?

ML: I was already using some camera movement during the shooting of *The Puppetmaster*, but most of the shots in the final edit were still. Nevertheless, it was a start. There are also a number of mobile shots in *Goodbye South, Goodbye* (1996). As for *Flowers of Shanghai*, there were many tedious conversations in the script. Most of them were trivial and because of the language problem – most of the actors needed to speak Shanghainese – it would have been very difficult to shoot them in long takes. At an early stage, Hou asked if I would like to try filming them with a moving camera. I was, of course, very excited, so I started panning the camera slowly but aimlessly. Breaking with convention, I decided to follow those who are listening

Millennium Mambo, 2001
Three Times, 2005

rather than those that are talking, trying to capture their facial expressions. The reason for the slow panning was to keep the audience from being too distracted, to help them focus on the dramatic element of each scene. Hou left all decisions about what to capture to me and he asked me to move the camera based on what I felt was the rhythm. There was great pressure on me during filming, but innovating like that was also an adventure.

RIS: Contemporary films like *Millennium Mambo* (2001) and the last part of the *Three Times* (2005) make similarly evocative use of chiaroscuro, creating almost sculptural portraits of faces and bodies. What were your goals with those films?

ML: *Millennium Mambo* was filmed in 2000. Hou and I spoke at an early stage of the process and I explained that since the film represents a new century and a new generation, I wanted to convey that sort of excitement visually. With the colors, I wanted to suggest anticipation and acceptance of the new century. I attempted to suggest a digital sense of color and to combine digital color with film. It was a new experiment and a challenge. To manifest the anxiety and excitement that belongs to young adults, I included what are thought to be shooting errors. For example, using the moving scan lines of a television, using a 135mm long lens at night in a

bumping car to shoot actress Shu Qi in another car, or moving the camera myself during the shots on the overpass at the beginning of the film.

In *Three Times*, there are three periods of time that represent three different generations with three identical pairs of star-crossed lovers that are doomed to separate. It was difficult to unify these during filming, so I gave each generation a color shade that would not only appear strong but would fit the overall atmosphere.

In both films, the lighting strategies reflect my emotional connection to the atmosphere and the story.

RIS: A number of your recent films with Hou have been shot internationally (in France, Japan, China), and both *Café Lumière* (2003) and *Flight of the Red Balloon* (2007) were extraordi-

Hou Hsiao-hsien
and Mark Lee, 2001

narily sensitive to geographic and cultural specificity. How have you adapted your style to different locations?

ML: This is a difficult question. I would say that I try to respect the local culture while also inserting my own viewpoint through the choice of lighting, color, and camera angle.

RIS: You have spoken before about your interest in Chinese landscape painting and pottery. What relationship do you see between these art forms and your cinematography?

ML: Sometimes, artistic appreciation is a kind of spiritual balm.

When I was young, I trained myself to observe and to learn from all kinds of exhibitions, especially of color images. During that process, I fell in love with Chinese paintings and porcelain because of the culture they represent. What Chinese paintings try to do is to manifest poetry through images and vice versa. The poetic and the visual are unified in a very cinematic way. Chinese paintings are full of infinite imagination and melodious lyrics.

Porcelain is very similar. Each piece shows the craftsman's skill and his touch. I can feel the presence of the craftsman in the piece. Every time I get to appreciate works like this, my determination is renewed and I am inspired to continue my journey.

RIS: All of your films with Hou have been made using 35mm film. How do you feel about the transition to digital?

ML: Digitization seems to be progress, but actually it represents an aesthetic regression. The process has not ended and the results are still far from ideal. On the other hand, it cannot be denied that the era of digitization has arrived, even if we have yet to perfect everything.

Actually, I was already using some digital techniques to capture a sense of color in *Millennium Mambo*, which speaks to my expectations and concerns regarding digitization.

Interview conducted via email on July 29, 2013.
Translated by Dennis Li

Finding the Right Balance

An Interview with Liao Ching-sung

RICHARD I. SUCHENSKI: You have edited all of Hou's features. How did your creative partnership begin?

LIAO CHING-SUNG: Hou's first feature, *Cute Girl*, was shot in 1980. Before that, he worked as assistant director or screenwriter on films like *Spring in Autumn* (Chen Kun-hou, 1980) and *Love on the Wave* (Chen Kun-hou, 1978). Even though he was not the director, the shooting process on the set was still under his management because directors were behind the camera shooting. He was effectively the executive director. I had been working with him for more than five years when he made *Cute Girl*, beginning with his first documentary, *Small Leisure Activities in the Army* (1974). It was shot in the headquarters of the army located at that time in Longtan.

On the many films where Hou acted as executive director, he was also in charge of postproduction and I helped with the editing. I first became an apprentice at the Central Motion Picture Corporation (CMPC) in 1973 and I was officially hired in 1974, the same year I became acquainted with Hou (who began several months earlier than I did). We were introduced by Chen Kun-hou, who was the cinematographer of CMPC. Chen, Hou, Chang Hwa-kun, Hsu Shu-chen, and Tso Hung-yuan helped

shoot *Love on the Wave*. Chen was also charged with shooting commercials in the department of short film production established by CMPC's studio director Ming Chi. It was in this context that Hou was invited to shoot the department's first short film, *Small Leisure Activities in the Army*. At that time, CMPC produced two to three films a year, so I would see Hou every few months.

Before that, he was the script supervisor for one of Lee Hsing's films and he also learned from the directors Tsai Yang-ming and Lai Cheng-ying (Chen Kun-hou's uncle). Hou wrote the screenplay and served as assistant director for Lai's *Matchmaker* (1976). He made commercial films for nearly a decade and the training he received was comprehensive. Over the course of that, he changed a great deal. I used to be very self-contained and shy, living in a world of my own where I could focus on film editing. Hou would take the time to teach me things. We were sometimes like mentor and disciple, sometimes like friends, and sometimes we were competitors (like martial arts masters competing with our internal forces). It would be impossible to have that relationship with someone else. We stayed focused and we were very diligent. We were also secret rivals, which was fun.

Liao Ching-sung and
Hou Hsiao-hsien editing

What is more interesting is that it was possible for me to do film editing with him for decades. Our love-hate relationship is actually quite complicated. Every artist has their own ego to some degree and this relationship helped me cultivate my non-self. I cannot have my own ego, because if two big egos work together, they will just end up fighting. When Hou and I were young, we worked twelve hours a day and we would spend six or seven of them talking. The periods when we worked together were intense and when we met after a period of time, it was like having a battle. Hou often said to me, "I am not lying. If I lie, I will cut my head off for you to sit on as a chair." I probably have a warehouse packed with his heads already. Hou likes to think, but I rely on my instinct.

He also likes to be involved in all details. When I edit, for example, he likes to help me count the frames, telling me which one to join with which. When I am editing, I can't bother to care about those details, I simply rely on my instinct. One very positive thing in our collaboration is that he will take charge of the logical, rational side, so that I can concentrate on the sensitive, cinematic side. Things have been complicated throughout, but we continue to learn from each other. We collaborate and yet we compete. It is very hard to have a friend like him.

RIS: Could you describe the way you usually work together?

LCS: Actually, Hou is a meticulous perfectionist camouflaged by a quasi-casual attitude. He tends to say, "it doesn't matter," but it all matters. I am not a perfectionist and I would never say that something doesn't matter, but then continue working on it until the last possible moment. In this respect, we have very different working methods. I try to make a film as perfect as it can be based on my experience working with it. When someone works with me, for example, I try to observe talent, encourage it, and then recognize its fulfillment. Hou would instead ask you to be who he believes you are.

I respect objective judgment, while he tends to have a more subjective point of view. My view is that he finds absolute subjectivity in the most objective way. His films seem objective, but they are actually very subjective.

What's good about that is that he has his own Hou Hsiao-hsien style. The way I work with him is to maintain a mentor-disciple friendship. In the middle stage of our collaboration, he had become more of a life mentor, standing by me with a needle in hand. Whenever I would become more egoistic, he would stab me. In fact, I am very happy to have someone like him watching over me. Whenever I boast, he is the first one to deflate me with his needle. It is healthy to have someone who always has opposite opinions to you, so that you learn to realize that the world consists of different opinions. When I work with him, I want him to follow his own path, because there is no one else who can do that.

RIS: How did the evocative transitions used so effectively in Hou's films, especially since the late 1980s, develop?

LCS: I am pretty sure that this derives from the traditions of Chinese lyrical literature, which includes works of Du Fu, Li Bai, and Wang Wei. These traditions include broad depictions of landscape in the endings or the transitions. The sentiments within are merged with the representation of the landscape. Hou focuses not only on the emotions of the characters, but also on the landscape – the landscape is very noticeable in his shots – which adheres closely to Chinese poetic traditions. He talks about human sentiments, the development of their characteristics, and all kinds of mental states ranging from patriotism, to poeticism, to love relationships. This is all very poetic.

We naturally apply many techniques from this lyrical tradition – the Tang *shi*, Song *ci*, and Yuan *qu* forms of poetry.[1] In earlier eras, poets wrote about their affections for their nation, their family, and other people. They would project those emotions onto objects and the landscape. You can recognize these traits in the very poetic films of Hou. Since he tends to use amateur actors, he uses long shots to keep the camera away from them. One effect of that is that the focus is not on the expressions of the performers, but on the atmosphere created by objects and the landscape. There is an ambience to these that matches up with the tradition of Chinese poetry, particularly in the shifts from long shots to closer shots. The lyrical tra-

1) Editor's note: These forms emerged (respectively) in the Tang, Song, and Yuan dynasties.

dition creates the impression of a view from afar, which is why you will often see a man positioned this way in Chinese paintings.

We also have another tradition, a Taoist perspective that allows us to observe objects through objects, with everything treated equally. Man's viewpoint is that man is the paragon of animals and objects can only be observed by man. The concept of observing objects through objects presupposes their independent (yet relational) existence. Hou's cinematic language gives you a sense of objectivity, not of subjectively viewed objects. It suggests an attitude in which interpretation has been abandoned in order to fully perceive the natural existence of things. If this can be captured, then the audience's emotions will be spontaneous and striking.

I believe that Hou unconsciously moves his camera in and out of shots establishing relationships with the actors that are in accordance with the traditions of Chinese lyricism. This style is displayed most powerfully in *A City of Sadness* (1989). His camera started to move more after *The Puppetmaster* (1993) because, like Ozu [Yasujirō], he is self-aware. He would like to adopt an objective attitude stemming from the connections among people to observe their living conditions without criticism. Human problems

inevitably appear, but he will neither investigate nor attempt to solve them. That is his attitude and it is why I mentioned the Taoist perspective. He will keep everything at a certain distance and will never try to get closer or to move further way. His position is slightly closer than ours because it enables him to capture an atmosphere, making more details visible.

Both his style and the context he hopes to create can be described in terms of Chinese lyricism, the traditions of Chinese poetry. That Chinese poetic sensibility mingles with the Taoist sense of observing objects through objects. His philosophy is one of acceptance, which allows objects to exist on their own terms. As a result, the cuts away are very poetic, granting complete freedom to the audience while still creating contextual links with all the ideas to be addressed.

I have been very aware of this throughout our working process and I took classes at the Taipei National University of the Arts a couple of years ago to study these questions. The editing of *A City of Sadness* was all based on my instinct. Watching the images reminded me of Du Fu's poems. I felt as if I was possessed. It is as if I was working to master those techniques, like a martial arts practitioner, an intellectual, a poet, or a writer who is in training. You come to realize that life is all about training and nothing can ever be abandoned. Things work themselves out.

RIS: *A City of Sadness*, *The Puppetmaster*, and *Good Men, Good Women* (1995) each possess related but distinct editing styles. How did you approach the editing of these three films and what sorts of input did Hou give you?

LCS: *A City of Sadness* was based on the concepts of Tang *shi* and Song *ci*. *The Puppetmaster* then returns to pure Taoism, with one shot used to observe all things with objectivity and composure. There was a change there, a transition from the Chinese lyricism of *A City of Sadness* to the tradition of composed observation through objects.

In *Good Men, Good Women*, Hou started using more camera movement. One actress (Annie Shizuka Inoh) plays several characters in different spaces and different times. To some degree, I feel that I didn't do as well editing this film. I think Hou wanted to have three completely different characters played by one actress, but what I wanted was to show her as one character in different times and different spaces. This might have made more sense because you can't just have an actress play one character here and another there. It is as if the director was afraid that the audience would not realize that she is

actually playing different characters. What I hoped is that the audience would forget about the characters, about the different times and spaces, so that the character could show who she is. Finally, the audience would realize that these are all manifestations of different aspects of a single character. This is something I did not accomplish.

During editing, we discussed, negotiated, and compromised. I wanted to show the film in its most natural way. Hou instead wanted to connect the film to his subjectivity as closely as possible. He wants the film to have a certain look and, of course, the director is the main creator. I still respect him, so, no matter how I felt, I accepted his decisions on this film.

RIS: Which films have presented the greatest editing challenges?

LCS: There has been nothing that could be called a challenge, it is all about problem solving. For me, editing is like falling in love with someone. You have to try to understand the other person until you finally reach the point where you know them very well, which makes everything easier. A challenge would be presented only when you do not know the person well.

A film is just like a human being. It has a range of characteristics and it will present you with an image that you may like very much, only to then tell you that this is not the best it has to offer. There are still other perspectives, other secrets, to discover. It depends how you read it. Like a person, a film can lie to you. If you don't bother to communicate with it, it will give you a hard time, a really hard time. In my opinion, the only way to solve the problems presented by a film is to be more objective and to spend more time with it. If what you have produced deviates from your presumptions, then you have to accept this. If you are not willing to do so, but obstinately insist on dragging it back on track, you are asking for trouble. Would a very serious father be able to control his son? I can control neither my son nor a film. If you cannot really control him, why brother trying? All you can do is guide him in a way that he will fulfill your aspirations. For me, a film does have a life and a mystery. If you cannot understand that, you will be completely defeated.

RIS: Are the contemporary films different in this respect from the period films?

LCS: Costume dramas and modern dramas are the same. You have to understand the form, the content, the spirit of a film first. Only when you understand what is present can you change it. It is ridiculous to violate something without understanding it. Creativity comes from tackling a film on the basis of your understanding of its form, requirements, and sense of temporality. If you are not clear enough about this, editing is very risky.

RIS: How has your work as a producer complemented your work as an editor?

LCS: Working as a producer does affect my editing and it is like doing two things at the same time. When I am a producer, I pay more attention to details and to the overall atmosphere. When I am editing, I have to forget that I am also a producer, because the roles are diametrically opposed. The producer, the director, and the editor all conflict with and balance each other. In this sense, Hou and I are against each other. Working as the producer means I have to struggle with him on his shooting method and how he spends the budget. I also have to deal with questions such as, "should I support him or persuade him not to do certain things?" and "can his shooting requirements really be met?" I still struggle with him as the editor because he always aspires for certain things in editing, and there are things I can and cannot do.

My roles as producer and editor are against each other as well. There is trivia I have to deal with, but I have to stay focused. I also have to balance artistic and practical issues. What I am capable of doing is integrating things, approaching editing from a producer's perspective. Besides that, there is nothing beneficial. If the budget is spent before the post-production process begins, then I will have no room for editing.

I know Steven Spielberg's editor [Michael Kahn] can also work as the associate producer. There is one advantage to that arrangement. In that film industry, there are always pick-ups and only the person in the role of producer can actually ask the cinematographers to do that. I think it is quite reasonable for Spielberg to ask his editor to work as his associate producer because people will follow the associate producer's directions. There are several advantages, in terms of communication, to taking on both roles for an art film, but there is no obvious advantage in terms of editing.

RIS: Which aspects of Hou's aesthetic strike you the most?

LCS: I am still most moved by the long shots, which allow the actors to live on screen, and by their objective expression of the merger of emotion and landscape. This can move a person naturally, without any effort. The audience will accept what is presented and be moved when you shoot a film this way. For me, this is Hou presenting the non-self, the non-existence of himself. The audience cannot really notice his presence in the film, which is why they accept it.

RIS: Do you see any affinities with your own sensibility?

LCS: There are similarities. I love poetry, including Chinese classical poetry and the Taoist tradition, as well as Chinese aesthetics. Buddhist aesthetics are very spontaneous and this part of me totally matches Hou.

A cinematographer once asked me why I always use the first take. He said, "I haven't really got the lights set yet." I responded by saying that the shot is already amazing and everything feels right. That year, one of the judges at the Venice International Film Festival, Néstor Almendros, said, "People told me that the lighting is not good, but I feel everything is fine!" He has the same stance as me and I think he is very professional. He is not constrained by his professionalism and I am not constrained by my techniques. When I feel things are right, they are. As long as the audience does not notice any imperfections, they will accept the film. In a certain way, Hou and I are on the same page with this. In terms of atmosphere and emotion, the concept he aims to communicate and convey to the audience is the same as mine.

Interview conducted, with assistance from Chang Chuti, on September 12, 2013. Translated by Dennis Li

A New Era of Sound

An Interview with Tu Duu-chih

RICHARD I. SUCHENSKI: You worked on three of the films that launched Taiwan's New Cinema, all released in 1983 – *Growing Up* [Chen Kunhou], *That Day, on the Beach* [Edward Yang], and *The Boys from Fengkuei* [Hou Hsiao-hsien]. How did you become involved with the New Cinema?

TU DUU-CHIH: At the time, we were all working at the same studio [Central Motion Picture Corporation]. I had developed certain capabilities after years of training and the experience of *In Our Time* [a 1982 portmanteau film containing shorts by Tao Te-chen, Edward Yang, Ko I-cheng, and Chang Yi] inspired me to change my ideas about sound and try different things. This coincided perfectly with the ideas of the new directors who had just returned to Taiwan after studying abroad. We always had a good time when we met and shared our ideas about cinema. It was the best time ever for us.

RIS: You have been one of Hou's most consistent collaborators. What sorts of input does he give you before, during, and after shooting?

TDC: Hou once told me that actors perform with their lives and we will let them down if we are not prepared or if we let avoidable mistakes happen. His words still ring in my ears and in the ears of the sound engineers I have trained.

RIS: The relationship between sound and music in films like *Flowers of Shanghai* (1998) and *Millennium Mambo* (2001), for which you received an award at the Cannes International Film Festival, is extraordinarily nuanced. How actively are you in communication with Hou about the overall sound design of the films?

TDC: Actually, the biggest challenge with *Flowers of Shanghai* was that the main set was beneath the runway of an international airport. Airplanes flew by every five to ten minutes, so we had to switch our shooting schedule from day to night to solve the noise problem.

Hou does not like post-synchronization of the voices, because he prefers spontaneous performances. What he wants is a natural form of expression and he always manages the atmosphere to meet his needs. If he shoots a drinking scene, for example, he will select real dishes and alcohol and they must be delicious. Even the extras off-camera have to be real drinking buddies. There are always a few key points that need to be made in the conversation, but the actors need to go with the flow. Hou does not like rehearsals, repetitions of the same scene, or specifying the movements of the actors. He will manage all the actors, the props, and the technical details, but he creates an atmosphere that gives you the impression that something is really happening based on your own will.

His approach reached its peak in *Millennium Mambo*. There were very few scenes that needed to be shot more than once. If someone did not deliver their best performance or there was a technical failure, he would abandon the scene and shoot something similar another day somewhere. The crew has worked with him for many years and we are always quiet during shooting. There is no need to use the loudspeaker to direct us, we know what we have to do. Hou likes to film furtively. He doesn't like to tell the actors that we are going to officially begin filming because then they will "seriously" start to act.

RIS: *A City of Sadness* (1989) was the first Taiwanese feature film made with synchronized sound. Could you describe the context for that?

TDC: Before *A City of Sadness*, the soundtrack to Taiwanese films was dubbed in post-production. Even if the sounds we used in postproduction were very close to real sounds (for example, in Edward Yang's *The Terrorizers*, 1986), we still lost too much nuance in both the dialogue and the effects. There was a bottleneck and I felt stuck, so I was very excited when Hou told me that he would apply simultaneous sound recording techniques for *A City of Sad-*

A City of Sadness, 1989

ness. However, we did not have proper microphones or even a real boom. Nevertheless, I was too excited to sleep the night before we started the shoot.

We rented a soundproof camera from Hong Kong. I only had a monophonic recorder, a directional microphone, one other microphone borrowed from my friend, and a boom made from a drying rack. The experience was thrilling. After each day's shoot, I converted the recorded sound to 17.5mm tape and synchronized it to the film to see if anything needed to be improved. I used to struggle with the expressiveness of the dialogue and the sense of space created by the sound, but the new method meant that everything could be recorded perfectly. Even though we did not have enough equipment and the locations we used were sometimes very noisy, it was possible to manage everything.

We continued looking for a better approach throughout the shoot. After the film was finished, Hou thought that we should never again use equipment like this for recording. He asked me to give him a list of the equipment I would consider ideal. His only condition was that I had to continue training new recording personnel and to help other directors with limited budgets. We then bought the first comprehensive simultaneous recording equipment in Taiwan – including the noise reduction tools that are needed in post-production. The whole set was used for the first time on *A Brighter Summer's Day* (Edward Yang, 1991).

RIS: Hou began using stereo soundtracks in the 1990s. In what ways have recent advances in sound technology affected your work together?

TDC: The early films all used monophonic optical tracks. The technical conditions were not good and the equipment in theaters was not good either, which made it difficult to fully experience the sound during screenings. It was only possible to really see the results of our efforts at international film festivals. This is something we endeavored to overcome, but it was not possible at the time.

For *Dust of Angels* (Hsu Hsiao-ming, 1992), which Hou produced, we used Dolby stereo for the first time, which was also the first time the new technology had been used in Taiwan. We actually finished the mixing at the Nikkatsu

Studio in Japan and I was able to learn a great deal about sound design and sound technology as a result of this opportunity. Thanks to Hou's support, Taiwanese cinema was able to move into a new era of sound. After more than ten years of working with studios abroad, we finally have our own Dolby mixing studio, the 3H Sound Studio.

RIS: Which aspects of Hou's aesthetic strike you the most?

TDC: What I admire most is his relationship with actors. I have rarely seen him teach them how to perform. Instead, he spends most of his time managing the atmosphere at the shooting site. He is always able to mingle everything together, creating a situation in which the story will develop spontaneously, and he presents that in a very human way. The spontaneity of the characters and their behavior is always evident in his films. He always works to make the shoot seem as natural as possible, and he never tries to exaggerate the emotions contained within. As a result, the accumulated energy of his films is able to resonate with the audience.

Interview conducted via email on September 24, 2013.
Translated by Dennis Li

Conscious Engagement with Reality

An Interview with Chen Kuo-fu

RICHARD I. SUCHENSKI: You and Hou Hsiao-hsien have been friends for many years and you were involved in the New Cinema of the 1980s. How did that context affect your sense of his work?

CHEN KUO-FU: I did not choose which films to watch from the perspective of the "Taiwan New Cinema," but simply on the basis of my own preferences. Although my involvement in the cinema campaigns of the time was limited, I was very good friends with Hou and Edward Yang. My relationships with them were of a private nature and I rarely interacted with other Taiwanese filmmakers.

Hou had a huge impact on my personal life and my film career, but I am not sure if I can completely understand his films. Perhaps I will understand them more in the future. His intentions and the artistic quality of his creations were of a higher standard than was usual in Taiwan at that time, but I feel that he is still searching. Some of his works are astonishingly original and clearly display his worldview, while others reflect the ambiguities of his search.

RIS: How would you characterize the critical debates of that period?

CKF: The impost important thing was to "consciously engage with reality" and to look for the subjectivity of Taiwan.

RIS: Could you describe your involvement in ERA Films and the Film Cooperative [an organization that also included Hou, Yang, Chan Hung-chih, and Barbara Robinson, the future Managing Director of Columbia Pictures Film Production Asia]?[1]

CKF: When the Film Cooperative was established, there were two main projects – *A City of Sadness* (1989) and *A Brighter Summer's Day* (Edward Yang, 1991). In addition, I had my own project about the conflict between a mafia leader and his underling. The investor, Chiu Fu-sheng, wanted me to focus on the first two projects and that is why Hou's film and Yang's film came out before mine.

At that time, none of us had experience running a production company of this kind. Chan Hung-chih did not know where to start, although he wanted to help. I just ran errands for everyone on a regular basis. We hired, for example, the American Barbara Robinson to help us translate our film synopses. The office was in

1) Editor's note: The answers to the questions about the Film Cooperative and *A City of Sadness* include material excerpted from an interview conducted by Chang Jinn-pei that was provided to me by Chen Kuo-fu. Chang's interviews with many of the people involved in the production of *A City of Sadness* were published in the book *Looking Back at Hou Hsiao-hsien's* A City of Sadness, *Twenty Years After* (Taipei: Garden City Publishers, 2011).

Chen Kuo-fu and
Hou Hsiao-hsien in the 1980s

Taipei City and I cannot really say why the organization fell apart. It was probably because there was no real leadership.

The Film Cooperative consisted entirely of artists. Directors are only focused on their own films, so it is hard for them to organize a team. We thought that Chan might join and serve as General Manager, but he offered more spiritual support than practical assistance. Later, when I discussed this with Chiu, we both agreed that we really did need a production company like this. In practice, we were lacking in logistical structure!

RIS: What was the production of *A City of Sadness* like?

CKF: Hou was very focused on the preparations for *A City of Sadness* and he was always making progress. I vividly remember a meeting at Edward Yang's place. It was pretty similar to the previous meetings there. Many people showed up and we voted on titles for the film. Afterwards, we had a meal. In addition to *A City of Sadness*, there were titles such as *Night Rain in the Harbor City*. Everyone shared their opinion and I remember that I did not vote for *A City of Sadness* in the first round. People laughed and said, "Do you want to keep *A City of Sadness* as a title for one of your own future projects?"

The "meeting" was more like a gathering and we just spoke with each other. There was nothing concrete. That is Hou's approach to creation. The film has to go through stages from incubation to accumulation to full conceptualization.

As I recall, there were many different ideas for *A City of Sadness*. For example, Hou thought of inviting Chow Yun-fat and Yang Li-hua to play the leads. Why did he want to do this? Perhaps he was sensitive to the particular presence of the actors. He noticed Chow's onscreen image, which conveys enormous energy. On the other hand, Yang would have provided a cultural energy that was much more "Taiwanese." At the same time, they both strongly represent the lower class. We should not forget that Hou began his career making commercial films. He is very aware of the meanings and market implications of actors.

Hou tends to get inspired by his surroundings, for instance by the lives of miners or the impressions he got scouting in Chinkuashih [Jinguashi], Chiufen [Jiufen], and Juifang [Ruifang]. All of these details formed a unique world in his mind. He is also sensitive to the pathos of these histories.

My guess is that these things gradually developed over a long period of searching. During that process, we would just chat about random topics. I am more of a listener and there was no specific contribution from me.

RIS: Has Hou's work informed your own approach as a director?

CKF: He did not influence my approach, but my personal values, making me believe that I have to follow my own path.

RIS: Which aspects of his aesthetic strike you the most?

CKF: There is a Chinese term [*beimin*] for "sympathy." I do not how to translate it appropriately. It indicates something like pity and compassion and empathy, not in terms of person-to-person interaction or the position of an artist to his characters, but of God to humans. Whether they are successes or failures, Hou's works all embrace this attitude.

RIS: Do you see any affinities with your own sensibility?

CKF: I visited several of his shooting locations, but I did not observe carefully enough. What I noticed most was that his shooting rhythm was comparatively slow. He kept looking for inspiration and waiting for the actors to get into the right situation. I realized that he knows what he wants, but there is too much uncertainty on location and nothing can ever be fully under control. What you can do is patiently wait and adjust. I try to learn from this approach.

Interview conducted via email on August 12, 2013.
Translated by Dennis Li

Ichiyama Shōzō

Working with Hou Hsiao-hsien

In 1993, I was working at the Shochiku studio as a producer of ordinary Japanese films and never thought of working with foreign filmmakers. I was also working as the programmer for the Asian sidebar of the Tokyo International Film Festival at the time. Hou Hsiao-hsien and I first met when I showed *The Puppetmaster* (1993) as the opening film of this section that year. I admired his work, but I never imagined that I would produce his films.

The following year, Hou's assistant contacted me looking for Japanese investors for his next film. I do not believe Hou expected Shochiku to be an investor, and neither did I. Shochiku's studio regularly produced only commercial films, and Hou's work was classified in a different category. Without expecting a positive answer, I made a presentation to an executive at Shochiku. To my surprise, the executive immediately agreed to invest in *Good Men, Good Women* (1995). He then assigned me to the project.

Good Men, Good Women deals with the White Terror aimed at the suppression of Communism, which actually took place in the 1950s. To depict this, Hou adopted a more complex narrative structure than he had used in his previous films. I never asked why he used such a complex style. My impression is that Hou might have intended to change the stereotypical image of his films built up by audiences and film critics. I remember sensing a strong urge to change his style when I first read the script. This was what gave me the initiative to help realize this challenging project.

Although it was my first time working on an international co-production, the experience did not feel special or extraordinary. I thought of it as an extension of my duties as a Japanese film producer. Since the film was co-produced entirely by Shochiku and Hou's own company, the two of us were able to resolve almost all issues through a simple discussion. In most cases, Hou's decisions were very understandable. The only major problem we encountered was that the production fell behind schedule. I remember having to manipulate matters "behind the scenes" to avoid conflicts between Shochiku and Hou. This may have been the biggest contribution I made to his film.

His next film, *Goodbye South, Goodbye* (1996), was more challenging. The project began abruptly during the Cannes International Film Festival in May 1995, when Hou told me, "I would like to make a light comedy, getting back to the spirit in which I started." Although the project seemed very interesting, I did not think that I would be able to secure investment

Goodbye South, Goodbye, 1996

in a month. In June, Hou's assistant informed me that he was already preparing the shoot for the film, which he intended to premiere at the Venice International Film Festival in September. The assistant also pointed out that Hou expected Shochiku to invest again. I did think Shochiku would be interested in the new work, but I was missing two vital elements – time and the script. When I asked Hou to send me a complete script, he sent a kind of treatment and a message saying, "this is all I can write now." In order to make a presentation to the studio, I had no choice but to use this treatment to write my own script, in the name of Hou Hsiao-hsien.

The treatment depicted the daily lives of three youngsters living aimlessly in contemporary Taipei who take a short trip. Although the second half of the treatment was entirely changed, it was surely the prototype of *Goodbye South, Goodbye.* I again sensed Hou's desire for another stylistic challenge in this treatment, but I could not have imagined that the film would become such a masterpiece. Shochiku quickly agreed to invest and Hou started shooting in July. Once again, the production was dramatically delayed. He finished shooting at the end of August, but he was not satisfied with the result and he reshot almost the entire second half in October. The film was accepted for the

Cannes International Film Festival of 1996 while post-production was still under way. Hou eventually completed the film a few days after the festival had begun. Since I had business matters to attend to from the day Cannes opened, I first saw the completed work at its official screening at the Grand Théâtre Lumière. I vividly remember being so excited by the film that I almost forgot that I was the producer.

Flowers of Shanghai (1998) is the first and only film I was involved with from the beginning to the end. This time, Hou used star actors and actresses, but he kept the same filmmaking approach. I remember the shooting schedule

Hou Hsiao-hsien shooting *The Puppetmaster*, 1993

changing frequently. In one extreme case, the scene that was supposed to be shot was replaced with another during the one hour drive to the set in the suburbs of Taipei. Needless to say, some actors had to go straight back to the hotel. Unlike the other two films, where most of the dialogue was improvised by the performers, Hou and screenwriter Chu Tien-wen prepared a detailed script for *Flowers of Shanghai*. This is because most of the dialogue was in Shanghainese, which is totally different from standard Mandarin Chinese, and the actors had to memorize the accurate pronunciation. Only

the banquet scenes contained improvised speech. When I first read the script, I did not pay much attention to these scenes. After seeing the completed film, however, I realized their importance; they represent the atmosphere of that period in time.

If I had not had the chance to work with Hou, I would probably still be producing ordinary Japanese films and I would not have entered the field of international co-production. During the years I worked with him, I learned many things that I could not have experienced on a Japanese production. Moreover, I was very impressed by his courage in destroying his image and his struggle to create a new self. I am very pleased to see that he still continues to challenge himself, providing audiences with a handful of surprises whenever he makes a film. Now I am anxious to see his first martial arts film, *The Assassin* (2015), which must be one of the biggest challenges in his whole career.

Chung Mong-hong

What I Know about Hou Hsiao-hsien

In 1989, the news that *A City of Sadness* had won the Golden Lion arrived from Venice. Taiwan was in the midst of a politically transformative period. The Kuomintang (KMT) had exercised authoritative political power for decades and it was finally being transferred to a Taiwanese [Lee Teng-hui].[1] However, the new leader of the KMT was still constrained by the old conservative forces and the political landscape in Taiwan was very precarious. Dissidents ranged from victims of the White Terror to students.[2] *A City of Sadness* tackles a very sensitive subject in Taiwan: the outbreak of the "228 Incident" and the transfer of the KMT's political authority to Taiwan after the retreat from mainland China. The film does not focus on the history itself, but depicts the rise and fall of a family in a very detailed, serene way. Of course, the characters in the film do carry symbolic meanings to some degree. The mute played by Tony Leung, for example, represents the silent masses of Taiwan under that situation. What is

interesting is that because Tony Leung is from Hong Kong and could not speak Taiwanese, Hou Hsiao-hsien made him a mute to solve the language barrier. This is also a very deliberate arrangement, which creates more room for imagination.

A City of Sadness was widely discussed in Taiwan from the time it won the prize at Venice to the time it was released. The censorship bureau requested that the film be edited, but the cuts were minimized due to the strong support from the public. I was going through my military service (which all men were obliged to do for two or three years) and I had few chances for holidays. One night, shortly after the film had opened in theaters, I dreamt that I had attended the premiere ceremony of *A City of Sadness*. I was in the car for a long time and finally arrived at the screening venue somewhere in the suburbs of Taipei. The premiere in my dream took the form of an outdoor screening below the viaduct that hosted the night market. On the night of the premiere, the night market was still busy and the noise from the passing cars on the viaduct filled the space, which was completely packed. Without a clear sense of time, the film suddenly started to screen amidst the overwhelming tumult. I remember standing in a crowd, without any room to move,

1) Editor's note: Upon the death of Chiang Ching-kuo in 1988, Lee Teng-hui became the first President of the Republic of China who was born in Taiwan.

2) Editor's note: Taiwan was under Martial Law from 1949 to 1987 and oppression of political dissent was strongest in the early 1950s, the period of the White Terror explored in Hou's *Good Men, Good Women* (1995).

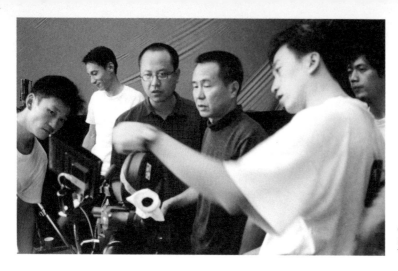

Chung Mong-hong and
Hou Hsiao-hsien shooting a
Toyota commercial in 2000

with everyone looking up to watch the film on the screen hung right under the viaduct. The cacophony overwhelmed me and I could barely hear the film. In my dream, I finished the film drowsily. When I woke up, I felt very exhausted as if I had just finished combat class.

Incredibly, the film was a blockbuster success, mainly because many Taiwanese witnessed and understood the Terror that had been hidden in our mind. In 1989, the Taiwan New Cinema reached its peak, but it also reached its end. Ironically, I did not see the film until the year 2000 when I borrowed a videotape from my friend.

For an entire generation, from the 1990s to 2008, the Taiwanese film business was very slow. During that period, documentary took on a surprisingly important role in Taiwan. Those young adults who decided to study cinema abroad in the 1980s and those who stayed in Taiwan dedicated to pursuing the dream of cinema encountered the same problem: Taiwan's cinema was dead. It was a complete void for two decades. Cinema is a career that can barely make a living. These aspiring filmmakers were mostly born in the 1960s and grew up watching the films of Hou and Edward Yang. However, they became the biggest victims of the Taiwan New Cinema and their dream for cinema died because of its demise. Those people, maintaining their dreams and working diligently, waiting for a chance, have finally been able to show themselves since 2008.

Hou's films realistically depict the diversity of Taiwanese society. People always say that his work lacks plot, but, for him, film should reflect the passing element of life – the wandering crowds, the trifles. I remember seeing *A Time to Live and a Time to Die* (1985). The very end moved me deeply, causing me to shed tears unconsciously. Most films coercively evoke your emotions and you feel as if you are being taken advantage of by a libertine when watching them. Hou's films communicate, in a very direct way, human helplessness in the face of the vicissitudes of life. He portrays fundamental human dilemmas while at the same time recalling the collective experiences shared by many Taiwanese.

There is another movie that also moves me deeply: Ozu Yasujirō's *Tokyo Story* (1953). Many people treat the films of Hou and Ozu as if they were in the same genre, but I cannot agree. Hou tends to set up a plot, or a situation, within which the actors are able to express themselves, and the camera tries to capture these moments. In Ozu's films, by contrast, every single detail is under his control, including the turning or lifting up of an actor's head and even the position of the camera and the props. Hou, of course, cares a great deal about the position of the camera and the sets, but his approach to actors is very different. He tries to anticipate incidents. A film full of emotions requires a simple narrative style, and Hou develops emotions and tensions in a natural way. The director's point of view is evident even in the early films, but so-called "cinematic" techniques are used sparingly.

I am one of the young adults who decided to study abroad after observing Taiwan's New Cinema. Since I did not have a job in the film industry when I returned to Taiwan, I began shooting commercials. After years of working as a production assistant, I became a director of commercials. I was amazed when I learned that I would be able to work with Hou. There was a car commercial and there were two perspectives within the advertising agency on how to pursue it. One figure wanted to work with me, while the other wanted Hou. After a series of arguments, they decided to put the two of us together; they ridiculously suggested that Hou should be the director and I should be the cinematographer. Oh boy! How do I know how to be a cinematographer, let alone Hou's cinematographer? That was the first time I met Hou and it was also my first time working as a cinematographer, which I had never considered doing before.

After two days of working, the producer came to tell me that Hou kept saying that he did not understand what the cinematographer was shooting, why the camera kept moving around, and why it would sometimes zoom in and out. There were many times that Hou came to me saying that he wanted to operate the camera himself. Of course, I then yielded my camera to him and he would pan it according to his usual aesthetic system. While we were doing the color grading together, he suddenly became excited. He was very interested in some rough images and some handheld close-up shots. In them, he saw something that was not purely his own style. He finally asked me to edit the commercial for him and he even did the voiceover. We shot dozens of commercial this way over the next few years. He was always credited as the director and I as the cinematographer. Most of his commercials were made in that period.

What strikes me most about Hou's shooting style is that he tends to look through the very essence of things, evoking emotions through the simplest means. Although I was never a cinematographer for his features (I had not even begun shooting my own films yet), I could always sense his serious regard for every single detail. I remember two things that impressed me very much. The first was his attitude. At the time, many Taiwanese film directors were expected to shoot commercials simply to make money. Hou would say, "Of course, you shoot commercials for money, but you have to make them perfect. No matter the format – feature film or commercial – as long as you are making it, you have to do the best work you are capable of." The other thing that struck me was his approach to the image, which he considers the most important aspect of film expression. He would say, "If the image is bad, you don't have to talk about other things." For him, the image encompasses the light, the composition, and the movement of people in a particular situation.

Hou is very laid-back. Instead of shouting "action," he would just say "start" in Taiwanese. The sound is like a gambler's cry when the banker is about to reveal his card.

It was a decade ago that I worked with him. Since then, I have often bumped into him at all kinds of film events. At the beginning of 2013, I even came across him on a plane, wearing his usual white sneakers and jerseys. He is a very humble man. To my surprise, he told me that Taiwan needs genre films since they are the only thing that will balance creativity and the box office in Taiwan's maket. Only within a genre can a director truly create on his own. He thinks that Taiwanese films are televisionized, that real film has already disappeared. He kept speaking from the moment the plane landed to the moment we claimed our luggage and I really wanted to ask him why he had never shot genre films. As a filmmaker of the younger generation, however, I could not ask him that.

I do not think Hou is going to shoot genre films, even though he has just finished the shooting of a martial arts movie. The reason he told me this is that he wants to find a way forward for Taiwanese films, with the hope of freeing them from the constraints of nationalism, nativism, and pseudo-televisionization.

If there was a survey among the Taiwanese filmmakers born in the 1960s about their favorite Tawanese films, most of them would name *A Time to Live and a Time to Die* or *Dust in the Wind* (1986). Some might even cite *The Boys from Fengkuei* (1983). These films were transformative for Hou. Before 1983, he made some very local, very commercial films. He then began discussing concepts from Western films with his friends in the New Cinema and he modified this cinematic language with his instinctive approach. Although they were unembellished, his 1980s films contained enormous energy. Later, once he was acknowledged internationally in the 1990s, his films became more remote for Taiwanese audiences. In my view, the Hou of the 1980s is like an unknown painter who became an artist with high self-awareness in the 1990s. He treated the elements from his earlier films more systematically and aesthetically and the narrative structure – in films like *Goodbye South, Goodbye* (1996) and *Flowers of Shanghai* (1998) – became more complicated.

Hou once explained the difference between his scripts and his films to me. He believes there has to be a complete script in which the relationship between the characters is very clear before shooting. However, the editing should focus more on the underlying emotions. That way, the audience will be able to sort out the story themselves, which is why the plot is not that important. Everything is oriented around a pure distillation of human experience. Shu Kuo-chih once said that watching Hou's films is much like standing on the street and observing people living their life genuinely through a window. That is the most perceptive description of Hou's films I have ever heard.

Filmmakers always ask where their audience is. What I find astonishing is that a film can strike someone you will never meet, regardless of whether they live in the Southern or the Northern Hemisphere. Hou's films are able to resonate this way. His work goes beyond the limits of Taiwan, but he is a very Taiwanese director (even though he was born in mainland China).

When we worked together, Taiwan was politically troubled, as if the whole island were about to sink. Many people started to emigrate. Hou said that if Taiwan was a ship that was really about to sink, with people jumping off to escape, he would stay and be the one who turns off the light. It was a joke, of course – when the ship sinks, there will not be any light to turn off – but it expressed his emotional attachment to this land.

Translated by Dennis Li

Acting without Boundaries

An Interview with Jack Kao (Chieh)

RICHARD I. SUCHENSKI: Could you describe your working method with Hou Hsiao-hsien?

JACK KAO: Working with Hou is very relaxing. There are no boundaries set for how to deliver lines and there is no fixed staging. He tries to use the personality of an actor as the basis for their performance and he allows total freedom with the use of our body. Sometimes, even uncoordinated movement might be revealing. What he wants is spontaneity.

RIS: What sorts of input does he give you before and during shooting?

JK: He rarely gives input during shooting, but he does remind me to go mountain climbing and to do exercises to train my breathing before a film starts. For him, an actor's breathing is crucial. He climbs mountains everyday and he has been doing that for decades. Before we shot *Millennium Mambo*, I was asked to help lead the actors on a joint mountain climbing excursion to train our breathing. There was no pressure to do so.

RIS: How has your collaboration developed since *Daughter of the Nile* (1987)?

JK: It was with *Daughter of the Nile* that I started to become acquainted with Hou. I originally participated in the production just for fun and I agreed to take part in *A City of Sadness* (1989) afterwards. Before we began that shoot, I went through four months of acting training. I was present when *A City of Sadness* won the Golden Lion at the Venice International Film Festival and I became part of his regular company. Whenever he needs me, I will be there.

RIS: How does Hou's approach differ from that of other directors you have worked with?

JK: He gives us, the actors, a great deal of room to develop our performances. There are no restrictions at all. I have never found another director with the same approach.

RIS: Do the long takes used in films like *Flowers of Shanghai* (1998) present particular challenges to you as an actor?

JK: The challenge in *Flowers of Shanghai* was the Shanghai dialect. There was a teacher there instructing us in the proper delivery of our lines.

RIS: You are listed as one of the writers for *Goodbye South, Goodbye* (1996). What was your experience on that film like?

JK: I contributed my life experience as a second generation Mainlander in Taiwan for the film. Chu Tien-wen was the screenwriter, I just provided stories. When the credits began to roll and I saw my name listed as a script contributor, I felt extremely honored. At that moment, I realized how much respect our big brother has for others.

Jack Kao (right) in *Goodbye South, Goodbye*, 1996

RIS: Which aspects of Hou's aesthetic strike you most?

JK: What strikes me most is that everything is so natural and spontaneous. Yes, both of us are very masculine and have the heroic spirit!

Interview conducted via email on July 11, 2013.
Translated by Dennis Li

Hwarng Wern-ying

Filmmaking is like Cooking

Hou Hsiao-hsien and I have collaborated for almost twenty years, since *Good Men, Good Women* (1995) and *Goodbye South, Goodbye* (1996).

Hou is a unique creator who is also very good at telling stories. He is not only the director, but also the screenwriter, and working with him requires me to follow his thoughts, to understand the images created in his mind, and to accompany him as his ideas develop. At work, Hou listens respectfully to professional advice. During the preparation of a film, he will have intense communications with the core team many times. The historical background of the story, the representation of the characters, and the details of the set design are all subjects for discussion. Hou has developed a customary working method. He always stops talking when he thinks he has covered the points he wants to make and he never gives unnecessary details. I always begin each of our collaborations by reading through the whole script, reviewing all the references, and scouting the locations. When designing costumes, I also talk with the actors about the characters' personalities and perspectives. During filming, I communicate with Hou to make sure that we are always on the same page for the production, which, I believe, is the key to our long-term partnership.

To complement Hou's creation, I will always adjust my approach to stimulate more aesthetic and technical possibilities. Hou is especially good at managing the production during shooting. He never draws storyboards in advance. Since I have no idea at all about the position of the camera beforehand, I have to think like a director and make comprehensive preparations when designing the sets. I have to arrange the whole space for all possible performances, but I also have to leave room for camera movement. It is also important to leave room for Hou to adjust the costumes. In order to work with Hou for such a long time, I have had to not only be professional, but also to build trust and share a tacit relationship with him, so that we can create opportunities to show our talents freely. If making a film was cooking, Hou would be the chef and I would be the prep cook. My duties consist of choosing the ingredients carefully, checking their quality, and meeting the chef's needs. That is the very first step in making a good dish.

As a result of our experience working together for years, Hou and I have built a relationship of trust and respect. I continue to be very gratified that our styles are so close to each other. Sometimes, I am very surprised by his ingenuity and aesthetic perseverance. Take the

The Assassin, 2015, scenic design (top) and costume design (bottom)

The Assassin, production still

Flowers of Shanghai, 1998,
scenic design and film still

Flowers of Shanghai,
costume designs

Flowers of Shanghai,
film still

Good Men, Good Women, 1995, film still

Three Times, 2005, film still

film we are working on, *The Assassin* (2015), as an example. There is a scene in which the heroine Nie Yinniang disguises herself as a concubine and pretends to have a deep sleep so that she can rescue the real concubine of her childhood beloved from being assassinated. Later, the assassin fails in his mission and runs away. Nie Yinniang gets up and leaves. There are no details for the performance in the script and I would have simply had Nie Yinniang put the sleeping gown above her assassin clothes and pretend to sleep. After the mission is done, she would resolutely take off the sleeping gown and walk away. I was not present when this scene was shot, so I asked my assistant to prepare the sleeping gown, along with some other possible choices for Hou to choose from. Later, I learned that Hou's decision about the costume was identical to mine. Incidents like that have made me more confident about our tacit understanding on matters of style.

In another scene from *The Assassin*, Nie Yinniang is assigned to assassinate a malicious governor, but she witnesses this governor playing with a young child and cannot bear to take action. For this scene, we cast suitable actors and prepared convincing costumes and sets. However, when Hou started to shoot the part about "the malicious governor gently patting the sleeping child," everything was suspended because we had to wait until the kid fell asleep. The staff then took him to the fitting room and lulled him to sleep. Once he was asleep, he was taken back. Since he woke up immediately, the shooting was once again suspended. The next day, we let the kid play on the sleeping pad on set until he really fell asleep and then we started to shoot. We were so afraid that we might wake him up and everyone was very careful. In the camera, we could see how vulnerable the kid really is in his sleep, which raised our sympathy. At that moment, I finally understood what sympathy is from the bottom of my heart. Through Hou's camera, we not only project our sympathy onto the story, we also look through that to see the most striking and mysterious part of our humanity.

Chu Tien-wen

Production Material for *Three Times*

BEST OF OUR TIME. **Background**

What is our best time?

It is not because it is the best that we are so sentimentally attached to it. A time becomes the best because it disappears forever and can only be reminisced.

Three periods of time are delineated in the film – Summer 1966, Spring 1911, and Winter 2005.

In 1966, the Cultural Revolution broke out in China. What happened in Taiwan, the Southern island far away from China?

Under the Cold War structure defined by the confrontation between the United States and the Soviet Union, Taiwan was included in the Pan-Pacific anti-Communist group. During the Vietnam War, Taiwan was even an intermediate destination for American troops. American films, television shows, pop music, and subcultures overwhelmed Taiwan and made as big an impact on Taiwanese culture as the fifty years of Japanese colonialism. The poolrooms and English songs in the film were part of the life of the Taiwanese teenagers of the period.

Of course, those teenagers knew nothing about revolution and war. They could only see girls and their dreams, a dream of love.

In 1911, with the Xinhai Revolution, the Great Qing Empire ended and the Republic of China was established. It had already been seventeen years since the Qing had ceded Taiwan to Japan.

The man in the film is the editor-in-chief of the Chinese department of a newspaper office. At the time, Chinese and Japanese were both used in newspapers. The man supports the New Thought with his writing. He even organized a poetry society, using the Chinese language to fight against the infiltration of Japanese colonialism. The poetry society was shaped by a national consciousness.

In March, Liang Qichao, the exile who was considered a traitor by the Qing, came to Taiwan from Japan. He greatly inspired the intellectuals in Taiwan for the one month that he was there. Liang thought that China would not be capable of rescuing Taiwan from Japanese rule for thirty years. He suggested that Taiwan should look to Ireland's strike against Great Britain as a model for impeding the misrule of the Governor-General's Office over Taiwan. This idea encouraged campaigns, which lasted more than a decade, for the establishment of a parliament consisting of gentry and intellectuals.

The gentry and intellectuals retained close relationships with courtesans, who were skilled at singing, playing music, and reading poetry.

最好的時光
Best of Our Times

Background :

什麼是最好的時光？

不是因為它最好所以我們眷念不已，而是倒過來，是因為它永遠失落了，我們只能用懷念召喚它，所以它才成為最好。

影片選擇了三個時間點來表達，1966年夏，1911年春，2005年冬。

1966年，這一年中國爆發了文化大革命，相對於中國的遙遠南方的海島，台灣呢？

在當時美蘇對峙的冷戰結構下，台灣是美國於太平洋地區反共體系裏的一環。越戰時期，台灣甚至成為美軍的中途站。美國電影、電視、流行歌曲、次文化等等，充斥於台灣，繼日本殖民台灣五十年後，深深地影響了台灣的文化風貌。影片中的撞球間，和美軍歌，都是當時台灣青少年生活的一部份。

當然，少年們不會知道革命與戰爭，他們只看見女孩，他們的夢，戀愛夢。

1911年，辛亥革命，大清帝國結束，民國成立。而大清把台灣割讓給日本，至今廿年。

影片中的男主是報佈漢文部筆，當時報紙，娛樂漢文並叙，那是對抗日本的新思潮。男主還組織了「詩士」，以使用漢文來根抗日殖民的侵蝕，詩社充滿濃厚的民族意識。

這年三月，被大清視為叛黨的流亡林梁啓超，從日本來到台灣，在台一個月，也認識了當時台灣的文人（letterman）們。梁認為，中國三十年內，絕無能力可以援救日本殖民下的台灣，建議台灣應效法愛爾蘭人的抗爭模式，即團結日本中央來牽制總督府對台灣的苛政。此想法，促成了一批仕紳和知識青年長達十數年的議會設置運動。

　　仕紳們靠與藝旦往來，藝旦能彈唱、吟詩。藝旦有自己的住處，或是出局到外面宴席獻唱陪酒。客人宴後若另邀幾位藝旦，事到藝旦住處捧場，以做「二次會」。遇有中意者，藝旦也與之結成情人關係。

　　影片中藝旦欲脫身妓人的不自由，男子志在遠方的追求自由，各自有夢，【自由夢】。

　　為了解決他們無法講台語和日語的問題，此段以默片形式出現。

　　【2005年】，台灣的當下（now and here）。

　　這個部分，由一位患有癲癇症的年輕女子舒淇飾。她在2010年三十歲的時候發病死亡。影片中的當下，短暫的生命，【青春夢】。

The courtesans had their own dwellings and they would travel to gatherings to sing songs or drink with clients. After the gathering, a client and his friends might visit the courtesan's dwelling, which was called "an after-party." If a courtesan met someone she liked, she might possibly become his lover.

In the film, the courtesan's lack of freedom – she wants to redeem herself and get married – is linked to the man's determined pursuit of freedom. They have their shared dream, a dream of freedom.

To solve the language problem of actors unable to speak archaic forms of Taiwanese and Japanese, this section is presented as a silent film.

In 2005, this is contemporary Taiwan (here and now).

The here and now will be presented through a young woman suffering from epilepsy. She will die in 2010 at the age of thirty. The here and now presented in the film suggests ephemerality, a dream of youth.

THREE TIMES. **Synopsis**

— SUMMER 1966, A DREAM OF LOVE —

A TIME FOR LOVE

A young man getting ready to serve in the military writes a letter to Haruko, the score lady at the poolroom, but she carelessly puts the letter into a drawer. Haruko leaves and May, who has taken over Haruko's job, sees the letter. The young man returns to look for Haruko and fails. He is very disappointed. May finds him interesting and she plays pool with him until very late on the night before he has to join the army. She soon receives a letter from the young man.

On his holiday, the young man takes a long trip back to the poolroom to see May, but she has already left. The new score lady says that May went to a poolroom in Chiayi [Jiayi]. The man takes the bus to Chiayi, but cannot find her.

The young man then takes a bus to Huwei to find May's home address as it was listed on the letter. May's mother tells him that she did write back and gives the letter to the young man.

Finally, the young man finds May at the poolroom in Hsinying [Xinying]. However, it is time for him to return to the army. After having noodles, May walks him to the bus at the terminal.

最好的時光
Three Times

柏住收
夏文 20×25＝500
2005.4.26.

本事 synopsis

1966年夏，戀愛夢 —— a time to love。

準備當兵的少年，寫信給撞球間的計分小姐春子，但春子隨便把信擱在柜子裏。春子走了，來接替工作的秀美，拾撿到這封信。少年來找春子沒遇見，很失望，看在秀美眼裏，感覺有趣。少年入伍前一天，與秀美撞球到很晚。不久，秀美收到少年從營區寄來的信。

放假時，少年坐遠遠的車回來，到撞球間找秀美，但秀美離開了，接替秀美的計分小姐說秀美去了左營，斗南，嘉義找他。少年坐車去嘉義找，沒有。

少年再坐車來到虎尾，按信封上的地址找到秀美的家，秀美的媽媽說秀美有寄信回來，取了信交給少年。

終於，少年在新營的撞球間找到了秀美。然而少年收假的時間也到了，吃碗麵，秀美送他去往南站坐車。

1911年春，自由夢 —— a time to free。

藝旦 迎接男子到來，這次東來以往五天，主要是為了歡送生從日本來，眾在藝旦芳家設宴款迎，歡送會請一小弟，彈唱歌勵。藝旦間就是戊戌年維新失敗，流亡日本的梁先生？男子五日後將陪梁先生南下台中。藝旦間陪男子家中敘流。

次日，秀美來子美說贖金事。

男子問起，才知婉妹妹懷有身孕，是藝旦小閘，想替妹妹贖身，願出兩百圓，但你要三百圓，談不成。另廂願意補足一百圓（便宜）。藝旦聞此，男子揮去起欠廉止納姜陌碧，如今何行價？男諒為木已成舟，只有成全。

交易談成，姓姓十分高興地坦姐。藝旦教導姓姓出家做人，你要知禮處息，卻不竟感傷自己身世。

男子從合生雨處勝，姓姓已歇虹妹，竟然在物色養女。原本是姓姓能夠接起藝旦間的生意後，藝旦即可贖身從人，但如今姓姓讓把藝旦再留些時日。

姓姓興茶莊中甥來家，討男子義助贖金。姓姓去後，藝旦終於問男子，她的婚事終身（草草如）何打算？而男子無言以對。

三個月後，藝旦接到男子來信，人在日本東京，已把籌款交給梁先生，將赴上海。男子此行曾過馬關春帆樓，想起了梁先生的詩云：

　　　　明知此是傷心地，亦到維舟首重回
　　　　十七年中多少事，春帆樓下晚濤哀。

詩通的是馬關條約，國事含恥辱，但也像男子對她的私情，藝旦偵下眼淚。

二○○五年冬，青春夢——a time to youth。

震與靖，激情起愛。

靖患早產兒，心臟有病，右眼幾盲只看得見色塊，而且要每天眼藥福藥。靖是創作歌手，和母親外婆住在一起。靖的女友Micky，還在念書，周末晚上到酒店上班，常常來靖家住，激烈的愛慕靖。

震「數碼服務中片沖洗店」店長，玩LOMO相機、樂友Blue同居。Blue發覺震愛慕靖，爆發了情怨。

　　四個人無解的糾葛，也許罷，只有死亡，讓一切歸於平靜……

— SPRING 1911, A DREAM OF FREEDOM —

A TIME FOR FREEDOM

A courtesan welcomes a man. He will be able to stay for five days this time, mainly due to Mr. Liang's visit to Taiwan from Japan. They gathered at the Tunghuifang [Donghuifang] restaurant to welcome him. Mr. Liang gave a talk for an hour and his speech struck everyone on the spot. The courtesan askes if this is the Mr. Liang who was exiled to Japan due to the failure of the Hundred Days' Reform. Mr. Liang plans to journey south to Taichung and the man will accompany him. The courtesan asks about the man's family.

The next day, the father and the son of the teahouse come to discuss the business of redemption.

The man learns that the courtesan's little sister is pregnant and the manager of the teahouse offers to make her his concubine for two hundred dollars. However, the madam wants three hundred, so the negotiations fail. The man is willing to cover the difference of one hundred dollars and the courtesan asks why he is willing to do this since he has always advocated the abolishment of concubinage in his writing. He replies by explaining that this is all he can do to offer support in this situation.

The deal is finalized and the courtesan's little sister is extremely grateful. The courtesan tells her little sister to be well-mannered and unsentimental about her background since she will now be someone's wife.

When the man comes back from Taichung, the little sister is already married and the madam is looking for another girl to adopt. The original plan was for the little sister to take over the business of the brothel and for the courtesan to redeem herself and get married. Now, the madam asks the courtesan to stay longer.

The courtesan's little sister and the manager of the teahouse come to express their gratitude to the man for the redemption money. After she leaves, the courtesan finally asks the man about his plans for her future. The man remains silent.

Three months later, the courtesan receives the man's letter. He had been in Tokyo, had given money to Mr. Liang, and is now preparing to travel to Shanghai. During his trip, the man visited the Shunpanrō hall in Shimonoseki and thought of Mr. Liang's poem:

Although this place has torn my heart,
It is wrenching to leave it.
Seventeen years have passed
And the sorrowful waves still break on its
shores.

The poem is about the shame of the "Treaty of Shimonoseki" [ending the First Sino-Japanese War], in which Taiwan was ceded to Japan. It also evokes the man's private love of the courtesan. Realizing this, she sheds a tear.

— WINTER 2005, A DREAM OF YOUTH –

A TIME FOR YOUTH

Zhen and Jing, the passionate devotion.[1]

Born prematurely, Jing has a hole in her heart. Her right eye is gradually going blind, and she can only see things in color blocks. She also needs to take medicine for epilepsy everyday. Jing is a songwriter and singer who lives together with her mother and maternal grandmother. Her girlfriend Micky still goes to school, but has to work at a club on weekend nights. She often comes to stay at Jing's place and is madly in love with her.

Zhen is the manger of the "Digital Film Development Store." He is addicted to the LOMO camera and lives with his girlfriend Blue.

It is probably only death that can make the unresolvable complications among these four disappear.

1) Editor's note: the switch to Hanyu Pinyin romanization for the names in the contemporary section of *Three Times* – they are listed this way in the film's pressbook – is related to the exploration of Taiwan's changing historical position.

THREE TIMES. **Script, Part One**

— PRELUDE

The poolroom is filled with the song "Smoke Gets in Your Eyes" broadcast from the radio. The young man is playing pool with friends. May, the score lady, is working.

Text: 1966

— SCENE 1

The young man rushes down the street on his bike.

— SCENE 2

He comes to the poolroom. There is no one here at noon. The young man sees Haruko and passes her a letter. Voiceover: "Miss Haruko, forgive me for writing to you like this. I am off to the army. My folks told me my call-up notice had arrived. The date of my enlistment is the second of next month, my family wants me to go back home as soon as possible. Time flies. I failed the university entrance exam twice, my mother has passed away, and I really have no idea what the future holds. The reason I am telling you this is because I want to say thank you. The days I have spent here in Chiho have been the best of my life. I am sincerely looking forward to hearing from you. Wish you the best. Anonymous. January 28th. P. S. The lyrics of 'Love Song' go like this: 'Missing you, missing you…'"

— SCENE 3

The young man is on the ferry headed for Kushan [Gushan]. On the oncoming ferry floating on the glimmering water is May with her suitcase. The two ferries pass each other at the Port of Kaohsiung.

— SCENE 4

May carries her suitcase, walking towards the poolroom at Chiho.

As they get ready for a meal, the madam tells Haruko that May is here to take over the job. May goes to the tiny compartmented room upstairs. Haruko has already packed.

— SCENE 5

As May cleans the small table in front of the scoreboard, she notices the letter. The madam tells her that this letter, written by the young man, is for Haruko.

— SCENE 6

In the afternoon, the young man shows up, and notices that Haruko has already left. He asks the madam, but she knows nothing. He is very depressed.

The madam senses his depression and tells him that the newcomer is called May, who reads the letter and is very touched.

May then asks him smilingly if she can keep the letter. The young man does not really answer.

— SCENE 7

The young man frantically plays pool with May. It is like Xue Dingshan encountering Fan Lihua on the battlefield in Chinese opera – they fight, but it seems like dancing. The young man and May play three times in a row.

— SCENE 8

The young man says goodbye. He is leaving for Taipei to visit his classmate who is now in college, and he will stay there until the day he goes to the railway station to meet other new recruits headed to the Military Police Training Center at Linkou.

Standing at the door of the poolroom, May sees the young man with his light baggage and says goodbye.

The ferry heads for Kushan at twilight.

— SCENE 9

May receives a letter from the young man. Voiceover: "Miss May, do you remember me? We played pool before I left for the army. Time flies. It is already March now. The spring rain drizzles. In our base, they keep playing the Beatles song 'Rain and Tears.' It sums up my feelings perfectly. I hope I can see you again. Stay beautiful!"

During the voiceover, May quits and says goodbye to the madam.

— SCENE 10

In the beginning of summer, at a port surrounded by shimmering water, the young man takes a ferry on vacation. He has become tan and burly.

The young man comes to the poolroom to see May.

May has gone and the man is told that she works at a poolroom in Chiayi. He asks for the address and leaves.

— SCENE 11

The young man is on the bus. On the provincial highway, he sees the subtropical trees of the South. The canopy blocks the sky and creates a green tunnel. Bus stops fly by –

Luchu, Tainan, Chiayi…[2]

— SCENE 12

The young man shows up at a poolroom. The score lady there says that May has already left, but she does not know where she is headed.

— SCENE 13

The setting sun falls in the Casuarina forest, looming like a piece of amber. The young man is on the bus. His face in the sunset is like that of an ancient warrior sculpted in gold.

The young man comes to May's home on Chienyeh Road in Hsinying. This is the address on the reply May sent. May's mother tells the young man that May is at a poolroom somewhere in Huwei. The young man notes the address carefully.

— SCENE 14

At night, the bus progresses from Hsinying to Huwei stop by stop.

When the young man finds the poolroom in Huwei, it is almost ten at night. May smiles like a blossoming lotus.

— SCENE 15

It is already eleven when May gets off work. The young man has to be at the base by nine in the morning, so he has to rush back.

May insists on treating him to a bowl of noodles. They have plain noodles and a dish of stewed food at the night market by the temple. They eat in silence and May simply smiles. It is very strange, May just smiles all night.

May walks the young man to the bus terminal. After saying goodbye, the young man boards the bus and leaves. The bus drives away and can no longer be seen. May still stands there. She is the blossoming lotus that no one notices.

Translated by Dennis Li

2) Editor's note: Luchu is replaced by Kangshan/Gangshan in the film.

最好的時光〈第一段〉

序場.

　　撞球間，瀰漫著從收音機傳出來的歌，〈Smoke Gets in Your Eyes〉，少年與友人在撞球，計分小姐夏荷在計分。

　　黑字幕：一九六六年。

1 場.

　　少年騎單車飛快僥過街行人。

2 場.

　　來到撞球間，中午靜悄悄一人。少年找到計分小姐春子，交給春子一封信。

　　信的 O.S.：「春子小姐，很冒昧寫這封信給你。我要當兵了，昨天接到我哥哥寄來的信，說收到我的兵役通知單，入伍日期是下個四月二日，家裏要我儘快回家。時光飛逝，想想這兩年大學沒考上，母親去世，未來的日子茫茫不可知。跟你說這些，是想謝謝你，這段在旗后的日子，每天能見到你是我最快樂的時刻。衷心的盼望能收到你的回音。p.s.，有一首〈戀歌〉，歌詞是這樣的，思戀你，思戀你啊……」　敬祝安康。知秋不謀，一月二十八日。

　　春子看了這封信。

3 場.

　　少年在渡輪上，往鼓山去，水波蕩漾著近面來的渡輪上，是提著行李的夏荷。兩艘渡輪交錯而過在高雄港埠。

4 場.

1.

夏奇提著行李往阿春家的撞球間。

春子跟阿奇他們正準備吃飯，頭家娘要夏奇是來接替春子的。春子幫夏奇上樓到房間，小小一個隔間，春子今日離職，行李都打包好了。

5場。

夏奇整理計分板前的小桌子時，發現了信，阿春說是少年寄給春子的。讀之，夏奇很感動，將信收起來。

6場。

午後，少年出現了，卻發現春子已經離職，問阿春什麼也不知道，非常沮喪。

阿春見狀，告訴少年新來的人叫夏奇，看了這封信很感動呢。

夏奇笑問，這封信她可不可以留著？少年不置可否。

7場。

少年與夏奇撞球。兩人拚殺起來，竟像是秦瓊和薛丁山，陣前過上了雙彩花，似鬥似舞，連打了三場。

8場。

少年告別了，他要先到台北找他唸大學的同學，待入伍日在台北車站與入伍新生們會合之後赴林口憲兵訓練中心。

撞球間悶熱的夏奇，瞪送少年拎著簡單行李來開。

暮色中，渡輪駛往鼓山。

9場。

夏奇收到少年寄自憲兵訓練中心的信。信的O.S.云：「夏奇小姐，還記得我嗎？

2.

入伍前教我修撞球的那個人。時間過得飛快，轉眼已經三月。春雨綿綿，此刻，營區正放著披頭四的歌，〈Rain and Tears〉，就像我的心情。期待能再見到你。祝福，永遠幸福。」

　　O.S.中，夏荷念完了，秀美與娘道別。

10場。

　　初夏，波光粼粼的嘉義的港口，渡輪上是放假回來的少年，曬黑了，臉膛峰峰。

　　少年來到撞球間找夏荷。

　　夏荷走了，接替的人叫秋月，頭家娘說夏荷去了嘉義某撞球場。少年留下蒐集地址，新兵。

11場。

　　少年搭上客運車。省公路上，南方茂盛的樹木，濃密得遮蔽天像走在綠色隧道裏。路牌飛快而過，「路竹」，「台南」，「嘉義」……

12場。

　　少年出現於某某撞球場，裏面的計分姐姐說夏荷已經都開了，不知去往何方。

13場。

　　落日埋在木麻黃林間像一塊琥珀，荒陰某現著。客運車上的少年，臉浸在夕暉裏好像金箔打貼的一張古代勇士的臉。

　　少年找到新營建業路夏荷家，這是夏荷曾經回給他的一封信上的地址。夏荷媽媽告訴少年，夏荷在虎尾某家撞球店，少年仍細記下地址。

14場。

3.

Three Times Script, Part One, page 3

20×25→500

　　夜晚，客運車車燈照亮裏必現的路標，從新營，一路往「箬尾」去。

　　少年找到虎尾撞球店時，已是晚上快十點了。吃驚又吃驚的夏荷，笑得像一枝盛開的荷花。

15場．

　　少年等到夏荷下班已經十一點，明天早上九點鐘收假，他必須往回趕路了。

　　夏荷一定要請他吃麵，兩人便在廟口吃了陽春麵和一碟滷菜。靜默無語時，夏荷只是笑。好奇怪我，訪問夜吃的夏荷，卻只是笑著。

　　之後夏荷陪少年走到客運總站，搭野雞車10台北。直到，少年登車離去。車子開走了，看不見了，夏荷仍站在那裏，夜中，他綻放的荷花。

　　　　　　　　無人知曉的

Appendix

Biographical Timeline

1947 Hou Hsiao-hsien is born to a Hakka family in Meixian, Guangdong province (Mei County, Kwantung province), China on April 8. In May, Hou's father is offered a position in Taichung (Taiwan). The "228 Incident," in which anti-government protests were violently suppressed in Taiwan takes place in February.

1948 Hou and his family immigrate to Taiwan, eventually settling in Fengshan due to his father's health.

1949 Martial Law begins in Taiwan in May. On October 1, the People's Republic of China is formally proclaimed. Approximately two million Nationalists move to Taiwan and Generalissimo Chiang Kai-shek declares Taipei the provisional capital of the Republic of China in December.

1950 In June, President Truman dispatches American naval forces to the Taiwan Strait, blocking a planned invasion of Taiwan by the People's Republic of China.

1951–52 The Treaty of Peace with Japan is signed in San Francisco by forty-nine nations on September 8, 1951 (effective April 28, 1952). Japan formally renounces its claims on Taiwan and the Penghu Islands (Formosa and the Pescadores), but the legal status of Taiwan remains ambiguous and neither the Republic of China nor the People's Republic of China is invited to the conference. On April 28, 1952, Japan and the Republic of China sign a separate peace treaty, officially ending the Second Sino-Japanese War.

1959 Hou's father dies.

1965 Hou's mother dies.

1966 Chairman Mao Zedong launches the Cultural Revolution.

1969 Hou completes his two years of military service and enters the Taiwan National Academy of the Arts, where he studies in the Department of Film and Theater.

1971 The Republic of China loses official representation at the United Nations to the People's Republic of China.

1972 Hou graduates and works as an electronic calculator salesman.

1973 Hou begins work at the Central Motion Picture Corporation and assists early mentor Lee Hsing with the continuity of *The Heart with a Million Knots*. He acquires apprentice experience on a number of productions and is soon promoted to assistant director and screenwriter.

1975 Chiang Kai-shek dies. *A Touch of Zen* (King Hu, 1971) wins a Technical Grand Prize at the Cannes International Film Festival.

1978 The Film Library, precursor to the Chinese Taipei Film Archive, is created.

1979 The United States establishes formal diplomatic relations with the People's Republic of China on January 1. President Carter signs the Taiwan Relations Act on April 10, permitting the continuation of unofficial relations with "the people on Taiwan." Pro-democracy demonstrations are held in Kaohsiung in December, leading to the arrest of many opposition leaders (the "Formosa Incident").

1980 *Cute Girl*, Hou's first film as director, is released.

1981 *Cheerful Wind*

1982 The Central Motion Picture Corporation announces a "newcomer policy" and produces the pioneering New Cinema portmanteau film *In Our Time* (containing segments directed by Tao Te-chen, Edward Yang, Ko I-cheng, and Chang Yi). The Government Information Office institutes screen quotas requiring theaters to allocate four weeks a year to domestic productions.

1983 *Growing Up* (Chen Kun-hou), Hou's first collaboration with writer Chu Tien-wen, is released, and he directs the important New Cinema films *Son's Big Doll* (part of *The Sandwich Man*) and *The Boys from Fengkuei*. Hou and Edward Yang become close during the period when *The Boys from Fengkuei* and *That Day, on the Beach* (Edward Yang) are edited simultaneously by Liao Ching-sung. Wide-ranging discussions at Yang's house are formative for the New Cinema and Hou's work.

1984 *The Boys from Fengkuei* wins the Golden Montgolfiere at the Festival of Three Continents in Nantes, generating international interest in Taiwan's New Cinema. *A Summer at Grandpa's* is released.

1985 *A Summer at Grandpa's* screens at the Festival of Three Continents and Hou wins the Golden Montgolfiere for the second consecutive year. *A Time to Live and a Time to Die* and *Taipei Story* (Edward Yang), co-written by and starring Hou, are released.

1986 *A Time to Live and a Time to Die* wins the International Film Critics Association (FIPRESCI) Award at the Berlin International Film Festival's Forum of New Cinema. *Dust in the Wind* is released.

Jack Kao, Annie Shizuka Inoh,
Hou Hsiao-hsien, and Lim Giong
at the Cannes International Film Festival
with *Good Men, Good Women*, 1995

1987 Martial Law in Taiwan is lifted on July 15, ending the ban on travel to mainland China. Supporters of Taiwan's New Cinema issue a public declaration requesting government support for noncommercial work. *Daughter of the Nile* is released.

1988 Upon the death of Chiang Ching-kuo, Lee Teng-hui becomes the first President of the Republic of China born in Taiwan.

1989 The People's Liberation Army suppresses student demonstrations in Tiananmen Square (Beijing) in June. *A City of Sadness* wins the Golden Lion at the Venice International Film Festival in September.

1991 *Raise the Red Lantern* (Zhang Yimou, 1991), for which Hou acted as executive producer, is released.

1993 *The Puppetmaster* wins the Jury Prize at the Cannes International Film Festival.

1995 *Good Men, Good Women*

1996 *Goodbye South, Goodbye* is released. Lee Teng-hui is re-elected as President of the Republic of China in Taiwan's first direct presidential election on March 23.

1998 *Flowers of Shanghai*

2000 Chen Shui-bian of the Democratic Progressive Party wins the presidential election in Taiwan, ending a half-century of continuous rule by the Nationalist (Kuomintang) Party.

2001 *Millennium Mambo* is released. Taiwan's remaining film quotas are abolished in preparation for admission into the World Trade Organization.

2002 Hou helps to found and manage the Taiwan Film and Culture Association and SPOT-Taipei Film House, an art cinema complex located in the former residence of the United States Ambassador to the Republic of China.

2003 To commemorate the centenary of Ozu Yasujirō, Hou directs *Café Lumiére*.

2004 Hou co-organizes the Alliance for Ethnic Equality, which advocates a nonpartisan perspective in the midst of a contentious presidential election (incumbent Chen Shui-bian is re-elected following an assassination attempt).

2005 *Three Times*

2007 *Flight of the Red Balloon*, Hou's first film shot outside of Asia, is released. He receives a lifetime achievement award from the Locarno International Film Festival. Edward Yang dies at the age of 59.

2008 Ma Ying-jeou of the Nationalist (Kuomintang) Party wins the presidential election.

2009 Hou founds the Golden Horse Film Academy to help train younger filmmakers.

2013 Hou receives the National Culture Award in Taiwan.

2015 *The Assassin*

Filmography

Features

CUTE GIRL (*Lovable You*, 就是溜溜的她, 1980)
DIRECTOR/SCREENWRITER Hou Hsiao-hsien **PRODUCERS** Yeh Chen-feng, Lu Ta-chuan **CINEMATOGRAPHER** Chen Kun-hou **EDITOR** Liao Ching-sung **SOUND** Wan Chung-fang **MUSIC** Tso Hung-yuan **CAST** Kenny Bee, Feng Fei-fei, Anthony Chan **PRODUCTION** Ta-yu Films
35MM, COLOR, ANAMORPHIC, 90 MINUTES

CHEERFUL WIND
(*Play While You Play*, 風兒踢踏踩, 1981)
DIRECTOR/SCREENWRITER Hou Hsiao-hsien **PRODUCERS** Yeh Chen-feng, Yao Pai-hsueh, Chang Hwa-kun **CINEMATOGRAPHER** Chen Kun-hou **EDITOR** Liao Ching-sung **SOUND** Hsin Chiang-sheng **MUSIC** Tso Hung-yuan **PRODUCTION DESIGNER** Chi Kai-ching **CAST** Kenny Bee, Feng Fei-fei, Anthony Chan **PRODUCTION** Ta-yu Films
35MM, COLOR, ANAMORPHIC, 90 MINUTES

THE GREEN, GREEN GRASS OF HOME
(在那河畔青草青, 1982)
DIRECTOR/SCREENWRITER Hou Hsiao-hsien **PRODUCERS** Chang Hwa-kun, Yao Pai-hsueh **CINEMATOGRAPHER/PRODUCER** Chen Kun-hou **EDITOR** Liao Ching-sung **SOUND** Hsin Chiang-sheng **MUSIC** Tso Hung-yuan **PRODUCTION DESIGNER** Chi Kai-ching **CAST** Kenny Bee, Chiang Ling, Chen Mei-feng **PRODUCTION** Tung-ta Films, Hsing-chiao Films
35MM, COLOR, ANAMORPHIC, 91 MINUTES

THE BOYS FROM FENGKUEI
(*All the Youthful Days*, 風櫃來的人, 1983)
DIRECTOR Hou Hsiao-hsien **PRODUCERS** Lin Jung-feng, Chang Hwa-kun **SCREENWRITER** Chu Tien-wen **CINEMATOGRAPHER/PRODUCER** Chen Kun-hou **EDITOR** Liao Ching-sung **SOUND** Hsin Chiang-sheng **MUSIC** Li Tsung-sheng, Bach, Vivaldi **PRODUCTION DESIGNER** Tsai Cheng-pin **CAST** Doze Niu (Cheng-tse), To Tsung-hua, Lin Hsiu-ling, Chang Shih, Yang Li-yin, Chang Shun-fang **PRODUCTION** Evergreen Film Company
35MM, COLOR, 99 MINUTES

A SUMMER AT GRANDPA'S (冬冬的假期, 1984)
DIRECTOR/SCREENWRITER Hou Hsiao-hsien **PRODUCERS** Chang Hwa-kun, Yu Chen-yen, Wu Wu-fu **SCREENWRITER** Chu Tien-wen **CINEMATOGRAPHER** Chen Kun-hou **EDITOR** Liao Ching-sung **SOUND** Hsin Chiang-sheng **MUSIC** Edward Yang, Tu Duu-chih **CAST** Wang Chi-kuang, Li Shu-chen, Ku Chun, Mei Fang, Yen Cheng-kuo, Chen Po-cheng, Lin Hsiu-ling **PRODUCTION** Marble Road Productions
35MM, COLOR, 98 MINUTES

A TIME TO LIVE AND A TIME TO DIE
(童年往事, 1985)
DIRECTOR/SCREENWRITER Hou Hsiao-hsien **PRODUCERS** Lin Teng-fei, Hsu Hsin-chih, Chang Hwa-kun **SCREENWRITER** Chu Tien-wen **CINEMATOGRAPHER** Mark Lee (Ping-bin) **EDITOR** Wang Chi-yang **SOUND** Hsin Chiang-sheng **PRODUCTION DESIGNER** Lin Chung-wen **MUSIC** Wu Chu-chu **CAST** Yu An-shun, Tien Feng, Mei Fang, Tang Ju-yun, Hsiao Ai, Hsin Shu-fen **PRODUCTION** Central Motion Picture Corporation
35MM, COLOR, 136 MINUTES

DUST IN THE WIND (戀戀風塵, 1986)
DIRECTOR Hou Hsiao-hsien **PRODUCERS** Lin Teng-fei, Hsu Hsin-chih, Chang Hwa-kun **SCREENWRITERS** Wu Nien-jen, Chu Tien-wen **CINEMATOGRAPHER** Mark Lee (Ping-bin) **EDITOR** Liao Ching-sung **SOUND** Hsin Chiang-sheng, Yang Ching-an **PRODUCTION DESIGNERS** Liu Chih-hua, Lin Chu **MUSIC** Chen Ming-chang **CAST** Wang Ching-wen, Hsin Shu-fen, Li Tien-lu, Chen Shu-fang, Lin Yang, Mei Fang, Lai Te-nan, Lin Yu-ping, Chang Fu-chih, Yang Li-yin, Shi Ming-yang, Hu Hsieng-ping **PRODUCTION** Central Motion Picture Corporation
35MM, COLOR, 110 MINUTES

DAUGHTER OF THE NILE (尼羅河的女兒, 1987)
DIRECTOR Hou Hsiao-hsien **PRODUCERS** Lu Wen-jen, Tsai Sung-lin, Wang Ying-chieh **SCREENWRITER** Chu Tien-wen **CINEMATOGRAPHER** Chen Huai-en **EDITOR** Liao Ching-sung **SOUND** Hsin Chiang-sheng, Tu Duu-chih **PRODUCTION DESIGNERS** Liu Chih-hua, Lin Chu **MUSIC** Chen Chih-yuan, Chang Hung-i **CAST** Yang Lin, Jack Kao (Chieh), Yang Fan, Li Tien-lu, Tsui Fu-sheng, Hsin Shu-fen, Chen Shu-fang, Wu Nien-jen **PRODUCTION** Hsueh-fu Films, Tsung Yi Productions
35MM, COLOR, 93 MINUTES

A CITY OF SADNESS (悲情城市, 1989)

DIRECTOR Hou Hsiao-hsien **PRODUCERS** Chiu Fu-sheng, H. T. Jan (Hung-tse), Michael Yang (Teng-kuei), Chang Hwa-kun **SCREENWRITERS** Wu Nien-jen, Chu Tien-wen **CINEMATOGRAPHER** Chen Huai-en **EDITOR** Liao Ching-sung **SOUND** Tu Duu-chih, Yang Ching-an **PRODUCTION DESIGNERS** Liu Chih-hua, Lin Chung-wen, **MUSIC** Tachikawa Naoki, Chang Hung-i **CAST** Li Tien-lu, Chen Sung-yung, Jack Kao (Chieh), Tony Leung (Chiu-wai), Hsin Shu-fen, Wu I-fang, Chen Shu-fang, Ko Su-yun, Lin Li-ching, Ho Ai-yun, Kenny Cheung, Yang Chang-chieng, Lin Yang, Liu Yiu-pin, Huang Chien-ju, Luo Cheng-ye, Nakamura Ikuyo, Nagatani Sentarō, Lin Chao-hsiung, Lin Chu, Chang Wen-chung, Lu Ching, Mei Fang, Lei Ming, Wen Shuai, Pi Li, Lai Te-nan, Li Chien-pin, Yeh Chih-chung, Ai Tsai-tu, Chen Yu-jung, Ah Pi-pe, H. T. Jan (Hung-tse), Wu Nien-jen **PRODUCTION** ERA International, 3H Productions

35MM, COLOR, 158 MINUTES

THE PUPPETMASTER (戲夢人生, 1993)

DIRECTOR Hou Hsiao-hsien **PRODUCERS** Chiu Fu-sheng, H. T. Jan (Hung-tse), Michael Yang (Teng-kuei), Chang Hwa-kun **SCREENWRITERS** Wu Nien-jen, Chu Tien-wen **CINEMATOGRAPHER** Mark Lee (Ping-bin) **EDITOR** Liao Ching-sung **SOUND** Tu Duu-chih, Meng Chi-lieng **PRODUCTION DESIGNERS** Chang Hung, Tsai Chao-i, Lu Ming-ching, Ho Hsien-ko **MUSIC** Chen Ming-chang, Chang Hung-ta **CAST** Li Tien-lu, Lim Giong, Chen Kuei-chung, Tsuo Chu-wei, Hung Liu, Vicky Wei (Hsiao-hui), Pai Ming-hua, Tsai Chen-nen, Kao Tung-hsiu, Yang Li-yin **PRODUCTION** ERA International, City Films

35MM, COLOR, 142 MINUTES

GOOD MEN, GOOD WOMEN (好男好女, 1995)

DIRECTOR Hou Hsiao-hsien **PRODUCERS** Ichiyama Shōzō, Mizuno Kastuhiro, Ben Hsieh, Hsi Hsiang, Okuyama Kazuyoshi, Michael Yang (Teng-kuei) **SCREENWRITER** Chu Tien-wen [Inspired by Lan Po-chou's *Song of the Covered Wagon*] **CINEMATOGRAPHER** Chen Huai-en **EDITOR** Liao Ching-sung **SOUND** Tu Duu-chih **PRODUCTION DESIGNERS** Hwarng Wern-ying, Lu Ming-ching, Ho Hsien-ko **MUSIC** Chen Huai-en, Chiang Hsiao-wen, Yen Chih-wen, Lin Shao-ying **CAST** Annie Shizuka Inoh, Lim Giong, Jack Kao (Chieh), Vicky Wei (Hsiao-hui), Hsi Hsiang, Tsai Chen-nen, Lan Po-chou, Lu Li-chin, Kao Ming **PRODUCTION** 3H Productions, Shochiku, Team Okuyama

35MM, COLOR, 108 MINUTES

GOODBYE SOUTH, GOODBYE (南國再見, 南國, 1996)

DIRECTOR Hou Hsiao-hsien **PRODUCERS** Ichiyama Shōzō, Mizuno Kastuhiro, Ben Hsieh, Hsi Hsiang, Huang Chung, Okuyama Kazuyoshi, Michael Yang (Teng-kuei) **SCREENWRITER** Chu Tien-wen [Story: Jack Kao (Chieh), Hsi Hsiang] **CINEMATOGRAPHER** Mark Lee (Ping-bin), Chen Huai-en **EDITOR** Liao Ching-sung **SOUND** Tu Duu-chih **PRODUCTION DESIGNER** Hwarng Wern-ying **MUSIC** Lim Giong **CAST** Jack Kao (Chieh), Hsu Kuei-ying, Lim Giong, Annie Shizuka Inoh, Hsi Hsiang, Kao Ming, Lien Pi-tung, Vicky Wei (Hsiao-hui), Lei Ming **PRODUCTION** 3H Productions, Shochiku, Team Okuyama

35MM, COLOR, 112 MINUTES

FLOWERS OF SHANGHAI (海上花, 1998)

DIRECTOR/PRODUCER Hou Hsiao-hsien **PRODUCERS** Ichiyama Shōzō, Michael Yang (Teng-kuei) **SCREENWRITER** Chu Tien-wen [Adapted from Eileen Chang's translation of Han Bangqing's novel] **CINEMATOGRAPHER** Mark Lee (Ping-bin) **EDITOR/PRODUCER** Liao Ching-sung **SOUND** Tu Duu-chih **PRODUCTION DESIGNER** Hwarng Wern-ying **MUSIC** Hanno Yoshihiro **CAST** Tony Leung (Chiu-wai), Hada Michiko, Carina Lau (Ka-ling), Jack Kao (Chieh), Michelle Reis, Rebecca Pan (Wan-ching), Vicky Wei (Hsiao-hui), Stephanie Fong Shuan, Annie Shizuka Inoh, Hsu Ming **PRODUCTION** 3H Productions, Shochiku

35MM, COLOR, 113 MINUTES

MILLENNIUM MAMBO (千禧曼波, 2001)

DIRECTOR/PRODUCER Hou Hsiao-hsien **PRODUCERS** Eric Heumann, Gilles Ciment **SCREENWRITER** Chu Tien-wen **CINEMATOGRAPHER** Mark Lee (Ping-bin) **EDITOR** Liao Ching-sung **SOUND** Tu Duu-chih, Kuo Li-chi **PRODUCTION DESIGNER/PRODUCER** Hwarng Wern-ying **MUSIC** Lim Giong, Hanno Yoshihiro, FISH **CAST** Shu Qi, Jack Kao (Chieh), Tuan Chun-hao, Chen I-hsuan, Takeuchi Jun, Takeuchi Kō, Doze Niu (Cheng-tse) **PRODUCTION** 3H Productions, Paradis Films, Orly Films, Sinomovie.com

35MM, COLOR, 119 MINUTES

CAFÉ LUMIÈRE (咖啡時光, 2003)

DIRECTOR/SCREENWRITER Hou Hsiao-hsien **PRODUCERS** Miyajima Hideshi, Yamamoto Ichirō, Osaka Fumiko **SCREENWRITER** Chu Tien-wen **CINEMATOGRAPHER** Mark Lee (Ping-bin) **EDITOR/PRODUCER** Liao Ching-sung **SOUND** Tu Duu-chih **PRODUCTION DESIGNER** Aida Toshiharu **MUSIC** Jiang Wen-ye, Inoue Yōsui **CAST** Hitoto Yō, Asano Tadanobu, Hagiwara Masato, Yo Kimiko, Kobayashi Nenji **PRODUCTION** Shochiku, Asahi Shimbun, Sumimoto, Eisei Gekijo, IMAGICA
35MM, COLOR, 103 MINUTES

THREE TIMES (最好的時光, 2005)

DIRECTOR Hou Hsiao-hsien **PRODUCER** Chang Hua-fu **SCREENWRITER** Chu Tien-wen **CINEMATOGRAPHER** Mark Lee (Ping-bin) **EDITOR/PRODUCER** Liao Ching-sung **SOUND** Tu Duu-chih **PRODUCTION DESIGNER/PRODUCER** Hwarng Wern-ying **MUSIC** Lim Giong, Li Kuo-yuan, The Platters, Aphrodite's Child **CAST** Shu Qi, Chang Chen, Mei Fang, Liao Shu-chen, Ti Mei, Chen Shih-shan, Li Pei-hsuan **PRODUCTION** Sinomovie.com, Paradis Films, Orly Films
35MM, COLOR, 130 MINUTES

FLIGHT OF THE RED BALLOON
(*Le Voyage du Ballon Rouge*, 2007)

DIRECTOR/SCREENWRITER Hou Hsiao-hsien **PRODUCER** François Margolin, Kristina Larsen **SCREENWRITER** François Margolin **CINEMATOGRAPHER** Mark Lee (Ping-bin) **EDITOR** Liao Ching-sung, Jean-Christophe Hym **SOUND** Tu Duu-chih **PRODUCTION DESIGNERS** Paul Fayard, Hwarng Wern-ying **MUSIC** Camille (Dalmais), Constance Lee **CAST** Juliette Binoche, Simon Iteanu, Song Fang, Hippolyte Girardot, Louis Margolin, Anna Sigalevtich, Charles-Édouard Renault **PRODUCTION** 3H Productions, Margo Films, Les Films du lendemain, Arte France Cinema, Le Musée d'Orsay
35MM, COLOR, 115 MINUTES

THE ASSASSIN (聶隱娘, 2015)*

DIRECTOR Hou Hsiao-hsien **SCREENWRITER** Chu Tien-wen **CINEMATOGRAPHER** Mark Lee (Ping-bin) **EDITOR** Liao Ching-sung **SOUND** Tu Duu-chih **PRODUCTION DESIGNER** Hwarng Wern-ying **CAST** Shu Qi, Chang Chen, Tsumabuki Satoshi, Ethan Juan (Ching-tien), Nikki Hsieh (Hsin-ying), Jiang Wen, Asano Tadanobu
35MM, COLOR

* At the time of this book's publication *The Assassin* was in post-production with a planned release in 2015.

Shorts

SON'S BIG DOLL / THE SANDWICH MAN
(兒子的大玩偶, 1983)*

DIRECTOR Hou Hsiao-hsien **PRODUCER** Ming Chi **SCREENWRITER** Wu Nien-jen [Adapted from a story by Huang Chun-ming] **CINEMATOGRAPHER** Chen Kun-hou **EDITOR** Liao Ching-sung **SOUND** Hsin Chiang-sheng **MUSIC** Wen Lung-chun **PRODUCTION DESIGNER** Li Fu-hsiung **CAST** Chen Po-cheng, Yang Li-yin **PRODUCTION** Central Motion Picture Corporation
35MM, COLOR, 33 MINUTES (HOU'S SECTION, 100 MINUTES FOR ENTIRE FILM)

* The onscreen title for *The Sandwich Man* uses the same Chinese characters as the title card for Hou's segment, but the English title printed below reads *Son's Big Doll* (the name of the story by Huang Chun-ming that inspired Hou's film). The other segments are titled *Vicki's Hat* (Wan Jen) and *The Taste of Apples* (Tseng Chuang-hsiang).

THE ELECTRIC PRINCESS PICTURE HOUSE
(電姬館, 2007), part of the anthology film
Chacun son cinéma (2007)*

DIRECTOR/SCREENWRITER Hou Hsiao-hsien **CINEMATOGRAPHER** Mark Lee (Ping-bin) **EDITOR** Liao Ching-sung **PRODUCTION DESIGNER** Hwarng Wern-ying **PRODUCTION** Cannes International Film Festival
35MM, COLOR AND BLACK-AND-WHITE, 4 MINUTES

* There are two versions of *The Electric Princess Picture House*. One version, which is just over four minutes long, contains three shots, and is entirely in color. Another version, which runs for approximately three minutes and thirty seconds, contains four shots and is in black-and-white until the camera "enters" the theater for the final shot.

LA BELLE EPOQUE
(黃金之弦, 2011), part of the anthology film *10+10* (2011)

DIRECTOR/SCREENWRITER/PRODUCER Hou Hsiao-hsien **PRODUCER** Wen Tien-hsiang **CINEMATOGRAPHER** Yao Hung-i **EDITOR** Liao Ching-sung **CAST** Shu Qi, Mei Fang **PRODUCTION** Taipei Golden Horse Film Festival
35MM, COLOR AND BLACK-AND-WHITE, 6 MINUTES

TAIPEI, LIFE, SMILE (台北, 生活, 微笑, 2010)
3D FILM MADE FOR 360-DEGREE EXHIBITION IN THE TAIPEI PAVILION AT EXPO 2010 SHANGHAI

In addition, Hou worked on short films for the Central Motion Picture Corporation (beginning with *Leisure Activities in the Army*, 陸軍小型康樂, 1974). He has also created a number of advertising and promotional films for (among others) Air France, Twinings, Kirin Beer, Suntory Whisky, Toyota, Mitsubishi, Nippon Shokubai, MIO GPS, Sanyo Whisbih, Lin Huai-min, the Taiwan Tourism Bureau, and the Taipei Golden Horse Film Festival.

Assistant Director

First Come, First Love (近水樓台, Li Jung-chih, 1974)
The Life God (雲深不知處, Hsu Chin-liang, 1975)
Revenge of Two Exorcists (桃花女鬥周公,
 Lai Cheng-ying, 1975)*
Matchmaker (月下老人, Lai Cheng-ying, 1976)*
Love in the Shadow (愛有明天, Lai Cheng-ying, 1977)
The Glory of the Sunset (煙水寒, Lai Cheng-ying, 1977)
Love on a Foggy River (煙波江上, Lai Cheng-ying, 1978)*
The Spring Lake (翠湖寒, Lai Cheng-ying, 1978)
The War of the Sexes (男孩女孩的戰爭,
 Lai Cheng-ying, 1978)
A Sorrowful Wedding (悲之秋, Lai Cheng-ying, 1979)
Love on the Wave (我踏浪而來, Chen Kun-hou, 1978)*
Spring in Autumn (天涼好個秋, Chen Kun-hou, 1979) *
The Misty Rain of Yesterday (昨日雨瀟瀟,
 Lai Cheng-ying, 1979)*
Spring in Autumn (天涼好個秋, Chen Kun-hou, 1980)
Bouncing Sweetheart (蹦蹦一串心, Chen Kun-hou, 1981)
Growing Up (小畢的故事, Chen Kun-hou, 1983)*
*Hou also served as a screenwriter (or co-screenwriter).

Screenwriter

Autumn Lotus (秋蓮, Lai Cheng-ying, 1979)
Good Morning, Taipei (早安台北, Lee Hsing, 1979)
Six is Company (俏如彩蝶飛飛飛, Chen Kun-hou, 1982)
Ah Fei (油麻菜籽, Wan Jen, 1983)
Out of the Blue (小爸爸的天空, Chen Kun-hou, 1984)
My Favorite Season (最想念的季節, Chen Kun-hou, 1985)
Taipei Story (青梅竹馬, Edward Yang, 1985)

Producer

Raise the Red Lantern (大紅燈籠高高掛, Zhang Yimou, 1991)
King of Chess (棋王, Yim Ho, 1991)
Dust of Angels (少年吔, 安啦, Hsu Hsiao-ming, 1992)
Treasure Island (只要為你活一天, Chen Kuo-fu, 1993)
A Borrowed Life (多桑, Wu Nien-jen, 1994)
Heartbreak Island (去年冬天, Hsu Hsiao-ming, 1995)
Why Don't We Sing? (我們為什麼不唱歌,
 Kuan Hsiao-jung, 1996) [Documentary]
Borderline (國境邊陲, Kuan Hsiao-jung, 1997)
 [Documentary]
Mirror Image (命帶追逐, Hsiao Ya-chuan, 2001)
Reflection (愛麗絲的鏡子, Yao Hung-i, 2007)
One Day (有一天, Hou Shi-jan, 2010)
Taipei Exchanges (第36個故事, Hsiao Ya-chuan, 2010)
Return Ticket (到阜陽六百里, Teng Yung-hsing, 2011)
Hometown Boy (金城小子, Yao Hung-i, 2011) [Documentary]
Beyond Beauty: Taiwan from Above (看見台灣,
 Chi Po-lin, 2013) [Documentary]

Performer

I Love Mary (我愛瑪莉, Ko I-cheng, 1984)
Taipei Story (青梅竹馬, Edward Yang, 1985)
Soul (老娘夠騷, Shu Kei, 1986)
God of Fortunes and Virtues (福德正神, Tao Te-chen, 1986)
Sunless Days (沒有太陽的日子, Shu Kei, 1990) [Himself]
Yang±Yin: Gender in Chinese Cinema
 (男生女相, Stanley Kwan, 1996) [Himself]
HHH: A Portrait of Hou Hsiao-hsien (Olivier Assayas, 1997)
 [Himself]
I Wish I Knew (海上傳奇, Jia Zhang-ke, 2010) [Himself]

Selected Bibliography

Books about Hou Hsiao-hsien

Peio Aldazabal and Nieves Amieva, eds., *Hou Hsiao-hsien* (San Sebastián: Filmoteca Vasca, 1995) [Spanish]

Jean-Michel Frodon, ed., *Hou Hsiao-hsien* (Paris: Éditions Cahiers du cinéma, 1999) [French, Second Edition in 2005]

Lin Wenchi, Shen Shiao-ying, and Jerome Chen-ya Li, eds., *Passionate Detachment: Critical Essays on Hou Hsiao-hsien* (Taipei: Rye Field Publishing Company, 2000) [Chinese]

Luisa Ceretto, Andrea Morini, Giancarlo Zappolo, *Il dolore del tempo: Il cinema di Hou Hsiao-hsien* (Torino: Edizioni Lindau, 2002) [Italian]

Roberto Chiesi, ed., *Hou Hsiao-hsien: Cinema della memorie nel corpo del tempo* (Recco, Genoa: Le Mani Editore, 2002) [Italian]

James Udden, *No Man an Island: The Cinema of Hou Hsiao-hsien* (Hong Kong: Hong Kong University Press, 2009)

Maeno Michiko, Hoshino Yukiyo, Nishimura Masao, and Setsu Kagen, eds., *Hou Hsiao-hsien's Prism of Poetics and Time* (Nagoya: Arumu Publishing Company, 2012) [Japanese]

Antony Fiant and David Vasse, eds., *Le Cinéma de Hou Hsiao-hsien: Espaces, temps, sons* (Rennes: Rennes University Press, 2013) [French]

Books about A City of Sadness

Bérénice Reynaud, *A City of Sadness* (London: British Film Institute Publishing, 2002)

Chang Jinn-pei, *Looking Back at Hou Hsiao-hsien's* A City of Sadness, *Twenty Years After* (Taipei: Garden City Publishers, 2011) [Chinese]

Abé Mark Nornes and Emilie Yueh-yu Yeh, *Staging Memories: Hou Hsiao-hsien's City of Sadness* (Ann Arbor, MI: University of Michigan Press, 2014)

Books about Taiwan and Taiwanese Cinema

Lai Tse-han, Ramon H. Myers, and Wei Wou, *A Tragic Beginning: The Taiwan Uprising of February 28, 1947* (Stanford: Stanford University Press, 1991)

Nick Browne, Paul G. Pickowicz, Vivian Sobchack, and Esther Yau, eds., *New Chinese Cinemas: Forms, Identities, Politics* (Cambridge: Cambridge University Press, 1994)

Tonglin Lu, *Confronting Modernity in the Cinemas of Taiwan and Mainland China* (Cambridge: Cambridge University Press, 2001)

Denny Roy, *Taiwan: A Political History* (Ithaca, NY: Cornell University Press, 2003)

June Yip, *Envisioning Taiwan: Fiction, Cinema, and the Nation in the Cultural Imaginary* (Durham, NC: Duke University Press, 2004)

Chris Berry and Feii Lu, eds., *Island on the Edge: Taiwan New Cinema and After* (Hong Kong: Hong Kong University Press, 2005)

Emilie Yueh-yu Yeh and Darrell William Davis, *Taiwan Film Directors: A Treasure Island* (New York: Columbia University Press, 2005)

Liao Ping-hui and David Der-wei Wang, eds., *Taiwan under Japanese Colonial Rule, 1895–1945: History, Culture, Memory* (New York: Columbia University Press, 2006)

Darrell William Davis and Ru-shou Robert Chen, eds., *Cinema Taiwan: Politics, Popularity, and State of the Arts* (New York: Routledge, 2007)

Sylvia Li-chun Lin, *Representing Atrocity in Taiwan: The 2/28 Incident and White Terror in Fiction and Film* (New York: Columbia University Press, 2007)

Guo-juin Hong, *Taiwan Cinema: A Contested Nation on Screen* (New York: Palgrave Macmillan, 2011)

Daw-ming Lee, *Historical Dictionary of Taiwan Cinema* (Lanham, MD: Scarecrow Press, 2012)

Interviews and Presentations

Peggy Chiao (Hsiung-ping), "Great Changes in a Vast Ocean: Neither Tragedy nor Joy," *Performing Arts Journal*, Volume 17, Numbers 2/3 (May–September 1995), 43–54

Hou Hsiao-hsien, et al, "My Challenge, My Asia," discussion upon receipt of the Grand Prize of the Fukuoka Asian Culture Prizes in 1999, available online at www.asianmonth.com/prize/english/lecture/pdf/10_01.pdf

Lee Ellickson, "Preparing to Live in the Present: An Interview with Hou Hsiao-hsien," *Cineaste*, Volume 27, Number 4 (Fall 2002), 13–19

Hou Hsiao-hsien, "In Search of New Genres and Directions for Asian Cinema," translated, edited, and introduced by Lin Wenchi, *Rouge*, Number 1 (2003)

Hou Hsiao-hsien, Chu Tien-hsin, Tang Nuo, Hsia Chu-joe, "Tensions in Taiwan," *New Left Review*, Number 28 (July–August 2004), 18–42

Michael Berry, *Speaking in Images: Interviews with Contemporary Chinese Filmmakers* (New York: Columbia University Press, 2005)

Cheuk Pak-tong, ed., *Hou Hsiao-hsien Master Class* (Hong Kong: Cosmos Books, 2009) [Chinese]

Special Journal Issues

Cinema Scope, Number 3 (Spring 2000)

Inter-Asia Cultural Studies, Volume 9, Number 2 (2008)

Reverse Shot, Number 23 (2009), available online at www.reverseshot.com/23/hhh

Articles and Book Chapters

Alan Stanbrook, "The Worlds of Hou Hsiao-hsien," *Sight and Sound*, Volume 59, Number 2 (Spring 1990), 120–124

Peggy Chiao (Hsiung-ping), "History's Subtle Shadows: Hou Hsiao-hsien's *The Puppetmaster*," *Cinemaya*, Number 21 (1993), 4–11

Geoffrey Cheshire, "Time Span: The Cinema of Hou Hsiao-hsien," *Film Comment*, Volume 29, Number 6 (November–December 1993), 56–63

Liao Ping-hui, "Rewriting Taiwanese National History: The February 28 Incident as Spectacle," *Public Culture*, Volume 5, Number 2 (1993), 281–296

Li Tuo, "Narratives of History in the Cinematography of Hou Xiaoxian," *Positions: East Asia Cultures Critique*, Volume 1, Number 3 (Winter 1993), 805–815

Robert Chi, "Getting It on Film: Representing and Understanding History in *A City of Sadness*," *Tamkang Review*, Volume 29, Number 4 (Summer 1999), 47–84

Kent Jones, "Cinema with a Roof over Its Head," *Film Comment*, Volume 35, Number 5 (September–October 1999), 46–51

Christopher Lupke, "The Muted Interstices of Testimony: *A City of Sadness* and the Predicament of Multiculturalism in Taiwan," *Asian Cinema*, Volume 15, Number 1 (Spring 2004), 5–36

Jerome Silbergeld, *Hitchcock with a Chinese Face: Cinematic Doubles, Oedipal Triangles, and China's Moral Voice* (Seattle, WA: University of Washington Press, 2004)

David Bordwell, *Figures Traced in Light: On Cinematic Staging* (Berkeley, CA: University of California Press, 2005)

Leo Chanjen Chen, "Cinema, Dream, Existence: The Films of Hou Hsiao-hsien," *New Left Review*, Number 39 (May–June 2006), 73–106

Samuel Y. Liang, "Ephemeral Households, Marvelous Things: Business, Gender, and Material Culture in *Flowers of Shanghai*," *Modern China*, Volume 33, Number 3 (July 2007), 377–418

Gary G. Xu, *Sinascape: Contemporary Chinese Cinema* (Lanham, MD: Rowman & Littlefield, 2007)

Jean Ma, *Melancholy Drift: Marking Time in Chinese Cinema* (Hong Kong: Hong Kong University Press, 2010)

Contributors

OLIVIER ASSAYAS is one of the foremost directors of his generation, whose films include *Desordre* (1986), *Cold Water* (1994), *Irma Vep* (1996), *Les Destinées sentimentales* (2000), *Summer Hours* (2008), and *Carlos* (2010). When he was working as an editor for *Cahiers du cinéma*, he urged the Festival of Three Continents in Nantes to include *The Boys from Fengkuei* (1983), bringing Hou's work to international attention.

CHEN HUAI-EN has worked with Hou in many capacities, most notably as a cinematographer (on *Daughter of the Nile*, 1987; *A City of Sadness*, 1989; *Good Men, Good Women*, 1995; and *Goodbye South, Goodbye*, 1996) and an assistant director (on *The Puppetmaster*, 1993).

CHEN KUO-FU is a Taiwanese director (of films such as *Treasure Island*, 1993; *The Personals*, 1998; and *Double Vision*, 2002), producer, and screenwriter. He began as a critic and became a close friend of both Hou and Edward Yang in the early 1980s.

PEGGY CHIAO (HSIUNG-PING) is Graduate Director of the Graduate Institute of Filmmaking at Taipei National University of the Arts. As a critic and producer, she played a key role in the recognition of Hou's work, and of Taiwan's New Cinema more generally, at international festivals.

CHU TIEN-WEN is a celebrated writer (including the collection *Fin de siècle Splendor*, 1990, and the novel *Notes of a Desolate Man*, 1994), who has been Hou's scriptwriting partner since the early 1980s.

CHUNG MONG-HONG is an acclaimed Taiwanese filmmaker, whose films include *The Fourth Portrait* (2010) and *Soul* (2013).

JEAN-MICHEL FRODON is a critic and historian, who was editor of the film section of *Le Monde* and the chief editor of *Cahiers du cinéma*. He edited the French-language book, *Hou Hsiao-hsien* (1999), and he currently teaches at Sciences-Po in Paris and the University of St. Andrews in Scotland.

HASUMI SHIGEHIKO is the most influential Japanese film critic of his generation and the Former President of the University of Tokyo. Several former students – including Kurosawa Kiyoshi, Aoyama Shinji, and Suo Masayuki – have become prominent filmmakers and his writings set the tone for critical debate about cinema in Japan during the 1980s. He is the author of dozens of books and articles on film directors such as Ozu Yasujirō, John Ford, and Howard Hawks as well as the literatures of France and Japan.

HWARNG WERN-YING is a production designer and producer, who began working with Hou on *Good Men, Good Women* (1995).

ICHIYAMA SHŌZŌ produced three of Hou's films (*Good Men, Good Women*, 1995; *Goodbye South, Goodbye*, 1996; and *Flowers of Shanghai*, 1998) during his time at Shochiku. Since joining Office Kitano, he has expanded his international reach, working frequently with Jia Zhang-ke and also producing films by Iranian directors Samira Makhmalbaf and Abolfazl Jalili.

JIA ZHANG-KE is the signature figure of China's Sixth Generation and the director of films such as *Xiao Wu* (1997), *Platform* (2000), *The World* (2004), *Still Life* (2006), and *A Touch of Sin* (2013).

KENT JONES is a critic and filmmaker as well as the Programming Director of the New York Film Festival. His books include *L'Argent* (1999), *Physical Evidence: Selected Film Criticism* (2007), and *Olivier Assayas* (2012). He co-wrote *Jimmy P.* (Arnaud Desplechin, 2013) and has directed films about Val Lewton (2007) and Elia Kazan (2010, co-directed with Martin Scorsese).

JACK KAO (CHIEH) is a Taiwanese actor who began working with Hou on *Daughter of the Nile* (1987).

KOREEDA HIROKAZU's feature films include *Maborosi* (1995), *After Life* (1998), *Nobody Knows* (2004), *Still Walking* (2008), and *Like Father, Like Son* (2013). One of his documentaries is about Hou's work.

MARK LEE (PING-BIN) is an internationally renowned cinematographer. In addition to his many collaborations with Hou, he has also worked with Wong Kar-wai (*In the Mood for Love*, 2000), Tran Anh Hung (*Vertical Ray of the Sun*, 2000), Tian Zhuangzhuang (*Springtime in a Small Town*, 2002), Jiang Wen (*The Sun Also Rises*, 2007), and Koreeda Hirokazu (*Air Doll*, 2009).

LIAO CHING-SUNG is an editor, cinematographer, and producer, who has been working closely with Hou since he made his first documentary short in 1974.

LUNG YING-TAI is a Taiwanese author and essayist who became the first Minister of Culture of the Republic of China in 2012.

JEAN MA is Associate Professor of Art and Art History at Stanford University. Her books include *Still Moving: Between Cinema and Photography* (2008) and *Melancholy Drift: Marking Time in Chinese Cinema* (2010).

NI ZHEN is a Professor at the Beijing Film Academy, where he helped to mentor many of the Fifth Generation directors in China. He has also written the screenplays for a number of films, including Zhang Yimou's *Raise the Red Lantern* (1991), for which Hou acted as the executive producer. His *Memoirs from the Beijing Film Academy: The Genesis of China's Fifth Generation* was translated into English in 2003.

ABÉ MARK NORNES is Chair of the Department of Screen Arts and Cultures and Professor of Asian Cinema at the University of Michigan. His books include *Japanese Documentary Film: From the Meiji Era to Hiroshima* (2003), *Forest of Pressure: Ogawa Shinsuke and Postwar Japanese Documentary* (2007), *Cinema Babel: Translating Global Cinema* (2007), and *A Research Guide to Japanese Cinema Studies* (2009).

JAMES QUANDT is Senior Programmer at Toronto International Film Festival Cinematheque, where he has organized internationally touring retrospectives of the films of Robert Bresson (twice), Imamura Shōhei, Ichikawa Kon, Mizoguchi Kenji, Ōshima Nagisa, Naruse Mikio, Aleksandr Sokurov, and Nicholas Ray. He is the editor of critical compendiums on the work of Bresson, Ichikawa, Imamura, and Apichatpong Weerasethakul, and is a regular critic for *Artforum International*.

RICHARD I. SUCHENSKI is the Founder and Director of the Center for Moving Image Arts and Assistant Professor of Film and Electronic Arts at Bard College. His academic work focuses on the development of cinematic modernism internationally and on the relationship between film and the other arts. He has curated and organized retrospectives and traveling programs focusing on filmmakers, film movements, and particular moments from the silent era to the present at a number of venues (including "Also like Life: the Films of Hou Hsiao-hsien," the series organized in conjunction with this book).

TU DUU-CHIH is the foremost sound specialist in Taiwan. He began working with Hou, Edward Yang, and other New Cinema directors in the early 1980s and he won the Technical Grand Prize at the Cannes International Film Festival in 2001 for his work on *Millennium Mambo* (Hou Hsiao-hsien, 2001) and *What Time is it There?* (Tsai Ming-liang, 2001).

JAMES UDDEN is Associate Professor of Interdisciplinary Studies at Gettysburg College and the author of numerous works on Hou, including *No Man an Island: The Cinema of Hou Hsiao-hsien* (2009).

WEN TIEN-HSIANG is a film critic and the CEO of the Taipei Golden Horse Film Festival.

A Note on Names and Romanization

Since this book includes texts originating in several different languages from authors in the United States, Canada, France, Japan, Taiwan, and China, the question of romanization has been both pressing and challenging. The Wade-Giles system that was widely used in the period depicted in many Hou Hsiao-hsien films is no longer the international norm. Hanyu Pinyin, the system developed in the People's Republic of China during the 1950s has, until recently, not been in official use in Taiwan, where, in addition to Wade-Giles, there are at least three other systems (Gwoyeu Romatzyh, MPS II, and Tongyong Pinyin). The manifold issues this can create have been compounded by the particularities of Taiwanese culture (including the use of Taiwanese Hokkien and Hakka) and significant, sometimes politically charged, variations in convention and practice.

Every attempt has been made to achieve consistency while recognizing regional differences and the styles of individual authors. The names of all individuals from Taiwan have been romanized using Wade-Giles without apostrophes except in cases where clear preferences have been expressed or there is an alternative international standard (e.g. Hwarng Wern-ying or Shu Qi). Hyphens are generally included for the names of people from Taiwan or Hong Kong and excluded for figures from mainland China unless individual or historical practice suggests otherwise (e.g. Jia Zhang-ke or Lin Wenchi). Place names in Taiwan have generally been romanized in Wade-Giles without apostrophes or hyphens. Individuals, periods, places, and concepts associated primarily with mainland China have instead been rendered in Hanyu Pinyin (e.g. Song dynasty). In ambiguous cases or situations where names may be more familiar according to a different system, the main alternatives are listed in brackets (e.g. Guo Xi/Kuo Hsi) or addressed in footnotes. Where appropriate (e.g. Confucius, Taoism, or Keelung), the established English versions of words or names have been used.

To respect the complex history of linguistic and cultural encounters in East Asia as well as the varying responses to Westernization – issues treated with subtlety and nuance in many of Hou's films – the following rules have been used for name order. As is customary, Chinese, Japanese, and Korean names are presented with family name (Hou) followed by given name (Hsiao-hsien) except in the case of overseas figures working with a Western name order (e.g. Wen Fong). Adopted Western names are used in place of Chinese equivalents when they exist (e.g. Peggy Chiao instead of Chiao Hsiung-ping or Mark Lee instead of Lee Ping-bin).

Chinese and Japanese characters appear only when specifically referenced in texts.

The Retrospective: List of Venues

ALSO LIKE LIFE:
THE FILMS OF HOU HSIAO-HSIEN
International retrospective organized by Richard I. Suchenski (Director, Center for Moving Image Arts at Bard College) in collaboration with Amber Wu (Taipei Cultural Center, NY) and the Ministry of Culture of the Republic of China (Taiwan)

AUSTRIAN FILM MUSEUM (Vienna)
CENTER FOR MOVING IMAGE ARTS, BARD COLLEGE
   (Annandale-on-Hudson, New York)
MUSEUM OF THE MOVING IMAGE (Astoria, New York)
HARVARD FILM ARCHIVE (Cambridge, Massachusetts)

PACIFIC FILM ARCHIVE (Berkeley, California)
GEORGE EASTMAN HOUSE (Rochester, New York)
FREER AND SACKLER GALLERIES, SMITHSONIAN INSTITUTION
   (Washington D. C.)
PACIFIC CINEMATHEQUE (Vancouver)
TORONTO INTERNATIONAL FILM FESTIVAL CINEMATHEQUE
MUSEUM OF FINE ARTS, HOUSTON AND THE CHAO CENTER FOR
   ASIAN STUDIES AT RICE UNIVERSITY (Houston)
GENE SISKEL FILM CENTER (Chicago)
CLEVELAND CINEMATHEQUE
NATIONAL MUSEUM OF SINGAPORE
BRITISH FILM INSTITUTE (London)
SÃO PAULO INTERNATIONAL FILM FESTIVAL

Acknowledgments

This book – published through a collaboration between the Austrian Film Museum, Columbia University Press, and the Center for Moving Image Arts at Bard College (CMIA) – has been a genuinely international enterprise. I would first like to thank Alexander Horwath, Regina Schlagnitweit, Andrea Glawogger, Gabi Adébisi-Schuster, and everyone else at the Austrian Film Museum. This project could not have been completed without the generous support of the indefatigable Amber Wu, Minister of Culture Lung Ying-tai, Susan Yu, Tony Ong, Brian Su, Benjamin Chi, Leanne Kao, Peter Yuan, and Benny Yang. Hou Hsiao-hsien, his collaborators, and his office (especially Chang Chuti) have been gracious and helpful throughout. Very special thanks are due to Haden Guest, a longtime enthusiast of Hou's work. Thanks are also due to Michèle Dominy, Norton Batkin, Jake Perlin, and Michael Blum for their support of CMIA and this initiative. Translators Dennis Li, Ryan Cook, and Daniel Fairfax worked above and beyond the call of duty to meet tight timetables.

The contribution by Olivier Assayas was published in French, as "Hou Hsiao-hsien: en Chine et ailleurs," in his book *Présences: Écrits sur le cinéma* (Gallimard, 349–355) © Éditions GALLIMARD, 2009.

The comprehensive retrospective connected to this book is traveling to major venues on four continents. David Rodriguez, CMIA's intrepid and devoted Manager/Archivist, has made the inordinately complex logistical arrangements manageable. Invaluable assistance of various kinds has also been provided by Teresa Huang, Chang Jinn-pei, Lin Wenchi, and the Chinese Taipei Film Archive; Chiaki Omori and Shochiku Company, Ltd.; Enga Chang and the Central Motion Picture Corporation; Chang Hwa-kun, Elodie Sobczak, Cindy Banach, Justin DiPietro, Margot Rossi, Dennis Doros, Amy Heller, and Livia Bloom.

I would like to dedicate this book to Mary and Jim Ottaway. Their passionate commitment to education and insatiable curiosity has been a true inspiration.   *R. I. S.*

Image Credit List

3H Productions – Cover, 183, 191
Olivier Assayas – 179, 180 (bottom)
The Austrian Film Museum – 41, 49, 59, 61, 83, 84, 107, 131, 136, 203, 223
Chen Kuo-fu – 226
Chu Tien-wen – 243–244, 246–247, 252–255
Chung Mong-hong – 232
Fortissimo – 213 (top)
Hwarng Wern-ying – 239–240
Jack Kao (Chieh) – 230, 259
Mark Lee (Ping-bin) – 211, 214
Liao Ching-sung – 216
The Collection of the National Palace Museum – 24, 32
Stadtkino – Back Cover, 6, 198
Tamasa – 78, 119, 213 (bottom)
trigon-film – 13, 27, 89, 95, 180 (top), 185, 200, 229 (bottom), 237
Wen Tien-hsiang – 145

FilmmuseumSynemaPublikationen

All FilmmuseumSynema Publications
are distributed internationally by
Columbia University Press (**cup.columbia.edu**).
In the German-language area please also see
www.filmmuseum.at.

English Language Titles

Volume 19
JOE DANTE
Edited by Nil Baskar and Gabe Klinger
Vienna 2013, 256 pages
ISBN 978-3-901644-52-8
In the often dreary landscape of
Hollywood's blockbuster era, the
cinema of Joe Dante has always
stood out as a rare beacon of fearless originality. Blending
humor with terror and trenchant political satire with
sincere tributes to "B" movies, the "Dante touch" is best
described as a mischievous free-for-all of American pop
culture and film history. This first English language book on
Dante comprehensively examines the filmmaker's universe
of piranhas, gremlins, explorers, small soldiers, and many
other creatures. It includes a career-encompassing interview, new essays by Michael Almereyda, J. Hoberman,
Christoph Huber, Gabe Klinger, Violeta Kovacsics,
Bill Krohn, Howard Prouty, Dušan Rebolj, Jim Robison,
John Sayles, and Mark Cotta Vaz, as well as a treasure
trove of never-before-seen documents and illustrations.

Volume 17
A POST-MAY ADOLESCENCE.
LETTER TO ALICE DEBORD
By Olivier Assayas
Vienna 2012, 104 pages
ISBN 978-3-901644-44-3
Olivier Assayas is best known as a
filmmaker, but cinema makes only a
late appearance in *A Post-May Adolescence*. This is an account of a personal formation, an initiation into an individual vision of the world; it is, equally, a record of youthful
struggle. Assayas' reflective memoir takes us from the massive cultural upheaval that was May 1968 in France to the
mid-1990s when he made his first autobiographical film
about his teenage years, *L'Eau froide*. The book also includes two essays by Assayas on the aesthetic and political
legacy of Guy Debord, who played a decisive role in shap-
ing the author's understanding of the world and his path
towards an extremely personal way of making films.

Volume 16
OLIVIER ASSAYAS
Edited by Kent Jones
Vienna 2012, 256 pages
ISBN 978-3-901644-43-6
Over the past few decades, French
filmmaker Olivier Assayas has become a powerful force in contempo-
rary cinema. Between his first feature *Désordre* (1986) and
such major works as *Irma Vep*, *Les Destinées sentimentales*,
and, most recently, *Summer Hours* and *Carlos*, he has
charted an exciting path, strongly embracing narrative and
character and simultaneously dealing with the 'fragmentary
reality' of life in a global economy. He also brought a fresh
perspective to the problem of politics after '68, a subject
that he revisits in his memoir *A Post-May Adolescence* and
in his film *Après-Mai*. This first English-language monograph
on Assayas includes a major essay by Kent Jones, based on
his two decades of correspondence with the filmmaker, as
well as contributions from Assayas and his most important
collaborators. The richly illustrated book also contains
16 individual essays on each of the filmmaker's works.

Volume 15
SCREEN DYNAMICS
MAPPING THE BORDERS OF CINEMA
*Edited by Gertrud Koch, Volker
Pantenburg, and Simon Rothöhler*
Vienna 2012, 184 pages
ISBN 978-3-901644-39-9
This volume attempts to reconsider
the limits and specifics of film and the traditional movie
theater. It analyzes notions of spectatorship, the relation-
ship between cinema and the "uncinematic", the contested
place of installation art in the history of experimental cin-
ema, and the characteristics of the high definition image.
Contributors include Raymond Bellour, Victor Burgin,
Vinzenz Hediger, Tom Gunning, Ute Holl, Ekkehard Knörer,
Thomas Morsch, Jonathan Rosenbaum and the editors.

Volume 12
APICHATPONG WEERASETHAKUL
Edited by James Quandt
Vienna 2009, 256 pages
ISBN 978-3-901644-31-3
Apichatpong Weerasethakul is widely
praised as one of the central figures in
contemporary cinema. This first Eng-
lish-language volume on the Thai filmmaker looks at his
works from a variety of angles and is extensively illustrated.

With contributions by James Quandt, Benedict Anderson, Mark Cousins, Karen Newman, Tony Rayns, Kong Rithdee, and Tilda Swinton. With two interviews and personal essays the filmmaker's own voice is also a strong presence in the book.

Volume 11
GUSTAV DEUTSCH
Edited by
Wilbirg Brainin-Donnenberg
and Michael Loebenstein
Vienna 2009, 252 pages
ISBN 978-3-901644-30-6
According to Viennese filmmaker Gustav Deutsch, "film is more than film." His own career proves that point. In addition to being an internationally acclaimed creator of found footage films, he is also a visual artist, an architect, a researcher, an educator, an archaeologist, and a traveler. This volume traces the way in which the cinema of Gustav Deutsch transcends our common notion of film. Essays by Nico de Klerk, Stefan Grissemann, Tom Gunning, Beate Hofstadler, Alexander Horwath, Wolfgang Kos, Scott MacDonald, Burkhard Stangl, and the editors.

Volume 9
FILM CURATORSHIP. ARCHIVES, MUSEUMS, AND THE DIGITAL MARKETPLACE
By Paolo Cherchi Usai,
David Francis, Alexander Horwath,
and Michael Loebenstein
Vienna 2008, 240 pages
ISBN 978-3-901644-24-5
This volume deals with the rarely-discussed discipline of film curatorship and with the major issues and challenges that film museums and cinémathèques are bound to face in the Digital Age. *Film Curatorship* is an experiment: a collective text, a montage of dialogues, conversations, and exchanges among four professionals representing three generations of film archivists and curators.

Volume 6
JAMES BENNING
Edited by Barbara Pichler
and Claudia Slanar
Vienna 2007, 264 pages
ISBN 978-3-901644-23-8
James Benning's films are among the most fascinating works in American cinema. He explores the relationship between image, text and sound while paying expansive attention to the "vernac-

ular landscapes" of American life. This volume traces Benning's artistic career as well as his biographical journey through the United States. With contributions by James Benning, Sharon Lockhart, Allan Sekula, Dick Hebdige, Scott MacDonald, Volker Pantenburg, Nils Plath, Michael Pisaro, Amanda Yates, Sadie Benning, Julie Ault, Claudia Slanar and Barbara Pichler.

Volume 5
JOSEF VON STERNBERG
THE CASE OF LENA SMITH
Edited by Alexander Horwath
and Michael Omasta
Vienna 2007, 304 pages
ISBN 978-3-901644-22-1
The Case of Lena Smith, directed by Josef von Sternberg, is one of the legendary lost masterpieces of the American cinema. Assembling 150 original stills and set designs, numerous script and production documents as well as essays by eminent film historians, the book reconstructs Sternberg's dramatic film about a young woman fighting the oppressive class system of Imperial Vienna. The book includes essays by Janet Bergstrom, Gero Gandert, Franz Grafl, Alexander Horwath, Hiroshi Komatsu and Michael Omasta, a preface by Meri von Sternberg, as well as contemporary reviews and excerpts from Viennese literature of the era.

Volume 4
DZIGA VERTOV
DIE VERTOV-SAMMLUNG IM ÖSTERREICHISCHEN FILMMUSEUM
THE VERTOV COLLECTION AT THE AUSTRIAN FILM MUSEUM
Edited by the Austrian Film Museum,
Thomas Tode, and Barbara Wurm
Vienna 2006, 288 pages, ISBN 3-901644-19-9
For the Russian filmmaker and film theorist Dziga Vertov KINO was both a bold aesthetic experiment and a document of contemporary life. This book presents the Austrian Film Museum's comprehensive Vertov Collection: films, photographs, posters, letters as well as a large number of previously unpublished sketches, drawings and writings by Vertov including his extensive autobiographical "Calling Card" from 1947.